# THE GOOD […] GUIDE

Edited by

Chris Barrett
and
Jeremy Longley

© GMG Publishing

*The Good Menu Guide* is published by:

GMG Publishing
PO BOX 78
Evesham
Worcestershire
WR11 5ZB

© 1998 GMG Publishing

ISBN: 1-901681-02-5

Front Cover photographs reproduced by kind permission of:
*(clockwise from top left)*
Gravetye Manor, East Grinstead; Langshott Manor, Horley;
Angel Hotel, Midhurst; Castle Inn, Chiddingstone.

Back Cover photograph reproduced by kind permission of:
Amberley Castle, Amberley.

Page 1 photographs reproduced by kind permission of:
La Barbe, Reigate

Contents Page photograph reproduced by kind permission of:
Erik Michel of Michels', Ripley.

All the other photographs in this book are reproduced
by the kind permission of the participating restaurants.

All rights reserved. No part of this publication may be
reproduced, stored in a retrieval system, or transmitted,
in any form or by any means, electronically or mechanically,
including photocopying, or recording, without the express
prior permission in writing from the copyright owners.

Printed and bound in Great Britain.

Although every effort has been made to ensure that the information
contained in this book is correct, the publishers, GMG Publishing,
accept no responsibility whatsoever for any errors or omissions.
The restaurants featured in this book reserve the right to change
their menus and prices without prior notice.

Also published in this series:
**The Good Menu Guide - *The Cotswolds* (ISBN 1-901681-00-9)**
**The Good Menu Guide - *The Midlands* (ISBN 1-901681-01-7)**

# Contents

| | |
|---|---|
| 5 | Introduction<br>How to Use the Guide |
| 6 - 219 | Guide Entries |
| 220 | Alphabetical Index of Main Entries |
| 222 | Map of the Area |
| 224 | Other Books in this Series |

# ALSO AVAILABLE IN THIS SERIES

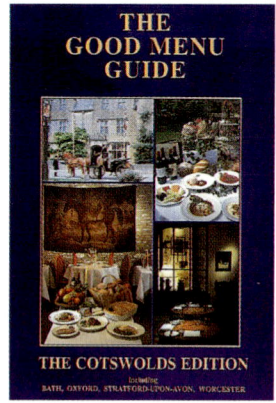

The Cotswolds Edition
ISBN 1-901681-00-9

The Midlands Edition
ISBN 1-901681-01-7

AVAILABLE THROUGH ALL GOOD BOOKSHOPS

or

DIRECT FROM THE PUBLISHERS

Please make your cheques
(for £9.99 per copy)
payable to:

GMG Publishing
The Coach House
Swynnerton
Stone
Staffordshire
ST15 0QE

Tel: (01782) 796281

# Welcome to the first South East edition of *The Good Menu Guide*.

# How to use *The Good Menu Guide* and other useful information

The aim of this book is to introduce you to our selection of the very best places to eat in The South East. Entries range from the top hotel restaurants to period country pubs and intimate bistros, with the criteria for selection being placed very firmly on the high quality food which they all serve.

It must be stressed that **no-one pays, directly or otherwise, to be in this guide** and we personally recommend them all.

Because our taste in style of food and type of restaurant may well differ from your own, we have tried not to let on which are our own particular favourites. We simply want to encourage you to go out for a meal and discover some of the many wonderful establishments that are featured in the following pages.

So we let the menus that accompany every entry tell their own story.

Please bear in mind that restaurant menus change frequently, some seasonally, some daily. All the menus and prices were correct at the time of going to press and, when ultimately they change, should still be indicative of the style and value for money of that particular restaurant.

We would also like to say that we welcome your comments and criticisms. So if you have had a great meal (or a bad meal) or you think we have missed somewhere worthy of inclusion, then please let us know!

In the meantime, let our recommendations whet your appetite, then indulge yourself. You will not be disappointed.

The main entries featured on pages 6 to 219 are all displayed in the same easy-to-use format - menus appear on the left and colour photographs, a brief description of the establishment and the style of food, directions and useful information are shown opposite. They are in alphabetical order by the name of their nearest town or village. These names appear at the top of each page, together with the page number.

At the back of the book you will find an alphabetical index and a map of the area to help you locate a particular establishment featured in the guide.

Abbreviations for charge cards used in this book:
V=Visa, MC=Mastercard, S=Switch, D=Delta, AE=American Express, DC=Diners Club

The majority of establishments featured in this edition welcome disabled customers. However, due to the age of many of the buildings, the facilities are not always ideal for those in wheelchairs and may occasionally involve being helped down a stair or to the toilets. We strongly advise you to check when making your reservation, in order to avoid any potential inconvenience or discomfort that may later affect your enjoyment.

**Please mention *The Good Menu Guide* when making a reservation.**

# MOONRAKERS

Tel: (01323) 870472

High Street, Alfriston, East Sussex, BN26 5TD

### STARTERS

Cream of Lemon and Leek Soup with Herby Croutons £3.50
Avocado and Mushrooms Melton Mowbray - Ripe Avocado
and Mushrooms combined with Melted Stilton £3.95
Parfait Chicken Livers with Tarragon £3.95
Prawn, Apple and Celery Salad with Aioli Dressing £3.95
Warm Salad of Roasted Wood Pigeon Breast drizzled
with Balsamic Dressing £4.50
Terrine of Smoked Trout on a Rocket Leaf Salad
with Oranges and Toasted Pine Nuts £4.50
Seared King Scallops with Leeks and Fresh Ginger, served
on a bed of Aromatic Rice £5.50

### MAIN COURSES

Pancake Cannelloni with Ricotta, Parmesan,
Mozzarella and Gorgonzola Cheeses £8.50
Breast of Corn-fed Chicken stuffed with Brie, coated in Breadcrumbs,
Pan-fried and served with Apricot Chutney £8.95
Croustade of Sole, Salmon and Prawns in a Creamy White
Wine and Dill Sauce £9.95
Cassoulet of Venison, Rabbit & Hare with Red Wine & Tarragon £9.95
Sea Bream Sauté on a Pool of Sweet Carrot Coriander Sauce £10.95
Poached Delice of Halibut with a Lobster Butter Glaze £12.50
Pan-fried Supreme of Barbary Duck served sliced on
a Fruity Plum Sauce £12.50
Breast of Guinea Fowl stuffed with Bacon and served with
a Sauce of Light Marsala £10.95
Saddle of English Lamb studded with Rosemary and served with
a Sauce of Redcurrants and Horseradish £12.50
Chargrilled Prime Scotch Fillet Steak, with or without a
Piquant Green Peppercorn Sauce £14.95

The above served with a selection of vegetables

Previously two cottages and at one time a wig maker's, this beautiful 14th century timbered building is now home to a quite delightful restaurant. Moonrakers is one of those places that is so nice that you almost want to keep it a secret.

The ambiance is intimate, yet unpretentious, and so is the food. A casual mix of English and French cuisine pervades an à la carte menu which changes about eight times a year. During the week various dishes are drawn from the à la carte and presented as table d'hôte menus (there are usually two 3 course options at £12.95 and £15.95).

The dessert menu may include Blackberry Crème Brûlée, Orange Segments in a Cointreau Syrup, Coffee & Walnut Pudding with a Mocha Sauce, or Rhubarb Compôte with Ginger Ice Cream.

Directions: Alfriston is a few miles south of the A27 between Lewes and Eastbourne. Moonrakers is easily found in the village high street.

### USEFUL INFORMATION

**SERVING TIMES:**
Dinner 7pm-10pm (Mon-Sat)
and by reservation only on Sunday
**CLOSED:** for lunch every day except Sunday
**SEATING CAPACITY:** 44
**C/C:** V, MC, S, D, AE
**OUTDOOR EATING:** no

**NUMBER OF WINES:** 100
**HOUSE WINE:** £8.95
**NO SMOKING** area available
**RESERVATIONS:** advisable, but compulsory at weekends
**OFF-STREET PARKING:** no
**CHILDREN:** over 8 years old are welcome

# AMBERLEY CASTLE
Tel: (01798) 831992
Amberley, near Arundel, West Sussex, BN18 9ND

### A Selection from the A La Carte

#### STARTERS

Flan of Langoustine and Mussels with Scallops, Coriander and Cucumber
£11.95

Warm Salad of Foie Gras, White Beans and Parsley with
Tomato Chilli Vinaigrette
£13.75

Coulibiac of Chicken, Herbs and Asparagus, Spiced Fig Chutney
£10.85

#### MAIN COURSES

Grilled Fillet of Salmon, Fondant Potato stuffed Courgette
Flowers and Basil Veloute
£18.95

Stuffed Cutlets of Lamb, Celeriac Mint Rosti,
Carrot Mousse and Lamb Jus
£21.75

Pot Roasted Guinea Fowl with Potato, Ham and Chive Muffin
Butter Beans and Shallot Tarragon Dressing
£17.95

Roast Lobster, Sautéed Salsify, Wild Morels and Cepes, Spinach and Sabayon
£29.95

Grilled Veal Chop, Risotto of Globe Artichoke, Spring Vegetables
and Sage Tomato Butter
£23.50

Goats Cheese Spinach Torte with Basil Jus and Ragoût of Baby Vegetables
£15.95

*All Main Courses are accompanied by their appropriate vegetables*

A south-facing elevation of high stone walls, mighty battlements and a massive gate-house provide a breathtaking welcome to Amberley Castle. Dating back to the 12th century, it was transformed in 1988 by Joy and Martin Cummings into a remarkable hotel and restaurant.

The elegant Queen's Room Restaurant, with a pretty barrel-vaulted ceiling and lancet windows, enjoys an excellent reputation for the quality of its cuisine. The à la carte, a small selection from which is shown opposite, changes regularly to accommodate seasonal specialities. Desserts (£8.75 each) may include Bitter Chocolate & Coffee Mousse with Cognac, Prunes and Praline Sauce, or Glazed Pineapple and Ginger Crisp with Curacao Bavarois and Ginger Soup.

A daily Chef's Menu (3 courses £29.50) presents a choice of three dishes with each course, and the renowned Castle Cuisine (5 courses £45) is a set gourmet dinner.

Directions: The hotel is signposted off the B2139 just outside the village of Amberley which is found about 5 miles north of Arundel.

## USEFUL INFORMATION

**SERVING TIMES:**
Lunch 12pm-2pm (every day)
Dinner 7pm-9.30pm (every day)
**SEATING CAPACITY:** 34
**C/C:** V, MC, S, D, AE, DC
**CHILDREN:** over 10 years
**DRESS CODE:** jacket & tie
**OUTDOOR EATING:** yes
**NO WHEELCHAIR ACCESS**

**NUMBER OF WINES:** 350
**HOUSE WINE:** £13.50
**OFF-STREET PARKING:** yes
**NO SMOKING** in the restaurant
**RESERVATIONS:** advisable, but essential at weekends
**ACCOMMODATION:** 15 rooms (B&B £140 to £300 per night, but special offers are available)

# EASTWELL MANOR
### Tel: (01233) 219955
Eastwell Park, Boughton Lees, Ashford, Kent, TN25 4HR

### MENU

#### First Courses

A Summer Salad of Whole Hythe Bay Lobster with Basil Sauce £20.00
Croustade of Marinaded Salmon with Sorrel Coulis £9.50
Roast Scallops, Apple & Ginger Purée, Beetroot Jus £10.50
Warm Quail & Boudin Blanc with Leeks in a Black Truffle Vinaigrette £10.50
Shredded Crab & Salt Cod with Caviar, Avocado & Curry Oil £10.50

\* \* \* \* \*

#### Main Courses

Saddle & Braised Leg of Rabbit with Asparagus
& a Risotto of Leeks & Pancetta £18.50
Roast Sea Bass with "Niçoise" Vegetables & Crushed Jersey Royals £18.50
Rump of Lamb with Rosemary, Confit Garlic & Ratatouille £19.50
Fillet of Beef "Bordelaise" with Wild Mushrooms & Button Mushrooms £20.50
Napoleon of Asparagus & Spring Vegetables, Sweetcorn & Basil Broth £16.50

\* \* \* \* \*

A Selection of Cheese served with Walnut & Raisin Bread £7.00

\* \* \* \* \*

#### Desserts

Chilled Pineapple Soup with "Hot" Coconut Ice cream £6.50
Iced Chocolate Truffles with a "Box" of Orange Compôte £6.50
Warm Tart of Raspberries with a Lime Sabayon £6.50
Apricot Parfait with Warm Poached Apricots & Almonds £6.50
"Millefeuille" of Strawberries, Mascarpone, Vanilla & Kirsch £6.50

\* \* \* \* \*

Coffee & Petits Fours £3.00

Eastwell Manor is an independent, family-owned, country house hotel situated in sixty-two acres of private grounds in the midst of a three thousand acre estate. From the moment you turn into the long tree-lined drive and catch your first glimpse of the creeper-clad, grey stone mansion with its turrets, tall chimneys and arched, leaded glass windows you can feel the history of almost a thousand years past.

As you would expect from this luxurious hotel, their kitchens have a reputation for creative and innovative cuisine. The *carte* opposite is supplemented by set price menus at lunch (£12.50 for two courses, £16.50 for three courses) and dinner (£28.50 for three courses).

Directions: Eastwell Manor is situated approximately 3 miles to the north of Ashford on the main A251 Ashford to Faversham road.

### USEFUL INFORMATION

**SERVING TIMES:**
Lunch 12.30pm-2pm (every day)
Dinner 7.30pm-9.30pm (Sun-Thur)
7.30pm-10pm (Fri & Sat)
**SEATING CAPACITY:** 46
**C/C:** V, MC, S, D, AE, DC
**NO SMOKING** in the restaurant
**OUTDOOR EATING:** no
**OFF-STREET PARKING:** yes

**NUMBER OF WINES:** 200
**HOUSE WINE:** £15.50
**RESERVATIONS:** advisable, but essential at weekends
**DRESS CODE:** gentlemen prefer to wear a jacket and tie for dinner
**CHILDREN:** welcome
**ACCOMMODATION:** 23 rooms (B&B fr £160 per room per night)

# THE ANCHOR INN
### Tel: (01273) 400414
Barcombe, near Lewes, Sussex, BN8 5BS

*A selection from the restaurant A La Carte*

### STARTERS

French onion soup with croûtons and grated cheese £3.50

Hot oysters wrapped in spinach and glazed with a champagne sauce £6.95

Roasted goats cheese on tartines accompanied by a fresh herb and rocket salad with raspberry vinaigrette £5.50

A terrine of salmon and cod with a lemon balm sauce £4.75

Braised lambs kidneys in a rich port and brandy sauce £4.95

### MAIN COURSES

Grass-fed Aberdeen Angus fillet steak accompanied by a pink peppercorn sauce £14.95

Pan-fried fillet of lamb served with a Madeira and thyme sauce £12.75

Breast of Barbary duck oven baked in honey then served with a port and sage sauce £13.25

Fillet of sole Dieppoise - lemon sole with prawns, mussels, and mushrooms in a creamy sauce £12.95

Chicken breast stuffed with crab and cream cheese served with a lemon butter sauce £11.75

A trio of tartlets filled with creamed mushrooms and leeks, spicy ratatouille and stilton and avocado £9.25

### DESSERTS

Orange and Grand Marnier Crème Brûlée £3.75  Tarte Tatin £3.75
Chocolate and Amaretto Mousse £3.75
Pagoda pudding - a dark moist sponge with a hint of nutmeg and ginger, sticky toffee sauce and fresh cream £3.75

Don't turn up at this idyllic 18th century country pub in a snazzy new Japanese sports car and expect anyone to be impressed. They're all Jaguar fanatics here, they're all very quick and they've got E-type lap records at Silverstone and pictures all over the walls to prove it!

Fast cars maybe, but certainly not fast food, because The Anchor Inn has a well-deserved reputation for its wonderful home-made meals. The large garden on the banks of the Ouse is very popular in the summer, and the cosy bars and restaurant are friendly and inviting. In the Pagoda Room a weekly à la carte is offered and an example is shown opposite. The seasonal bar menu includes all the traditional pub snacks like sandwiches and jacket potatoes, and this is supplemented by a range of excellent daily specials and vegetarian options. Perhaps Smoked Salmon Parcels filled with Cream Cheese, Prawns & Fresh Herbs (£5.25) to start, with Baked Red Mullet with a Basil & Anise Sauce (£7.25) to follow.

Directions: Barcombe is found between the A26 and the A275 about 3 miles north of Lewes. From the village take the road towards Piltdown and Newick. Take the first right at Boast Lane leading to Anchor Lane (marked with a No Through Road sign) then first left by the Post Box.

## USEFUL INFORMATION

**SERVING TIMES:**
Lunch in the bar 12pm-3pm (every day) & in the restaurant 12pm-3pm (Sunday)
Dinner in the bar 6pm-9pm (every day) in the restaurant 7pm-9.30pm (Thur-Sat)
**CLOSED:** in the restaurant for dinner Sunday to Wednesday
**SEATING CAPACITY:** 30 in the restaurant, 30 in the bar
**C/C:** V, MC, S, D, AE, DC

**NUMBER OF WINES:** 40
**HOUSE WINE:** £8.25
**NO SMOKING** in the restaurant
**OFF-STREET PARKING:** yes
**CHILDREN:** welcome
**OUTDOOR EATING:** yes
**RESERVATIONS:** advisable, but compulsory in the restaurant
**ACCOMMODATION:** 2 rooms (B&B single £30, double £52)

# THE ORANGERY at POWDER MILLS
### Tel: (01424) 775511
Powdermill Lane, Battle, East Sussex, TN33 0SP

Two Courses £21.50   **DINNER MENU**   Three Courses £24.50

*Carrot, Orange and Coriander Soup*

*Rillettes of Pork with Black Plum Chutney*

*Crostini of Wood Pigeon with Mediterranean Salad*

*Game Terrine with a Tangy Cumberland Sauce*

*Carpaccio of Tuna with Tomato Concasse and Parmesan*

*Duck Liver Parfait with a Haricot Vert and Hazelnut Salad*

\* \* \* \* \*

*Seared Pigeon Breasts with Smoked Bacon, Bubble and Squeak*

*Grilled Calves Liver with Red Onion Marmalade and Creamed Olive Oil Potato and Prosciutto*

*Grilled Fillets of Red Mullet and Sea Bass with Mussel and Saffron Sauce*

*Roast Rack of Lamb with a Mixed Bean Panaché, Basil and Tomato Jus*

*Aged Fillet of Scotch Beef with Balsamic Cooked Mushrooms and Parmesan (£2.00 Supplement)*

*Roast Breast and Confit of Duckling with Aromatic Sauce and Chinese Stir-fry*

*Baked Fillet of Salmon with a Horseradish Crust*

\* \* \* \* \*

*Iced Lime and Yoghurt Terrine with Summer Berry Compôte*

*Trio of Fresh Fruit Sorbets and Almond Wafer*

*Selection of British Cheeses*

*Apricot Mousse with Honey Wafers and Apricot Coulis*

A sweeping drive between lakes and landscaped gardens anticipates the graceful elegance of PowderMills, a beautiful listed country house hotel which dates back to the 18th century.

The acclaimed Orangery Restaurant presents delicious modern English cuisine. A daily table d'hôte is offered at luncheon (3 courses £14.95). This includes a good selection of dishes with each course, perhaps featuring Butterfly Sardines with Parmesan and Thai Dressing to start, Ballantine of Guinea Fowl with Savoy Cabbage to follow, and Raspberry Crème Brûlée to finish. The Library menu offers lighter dishes such as Grilled Goats' Cheese and Bramley Salad with Smoked Bacon (£4.95), and Chinese Style Chicken on Crispy Noodles (£6.95).

In the evening a fixed price à la carte is available. This changes daily and an example is shown opposite.

Directions: Heading towards Hastings from Battle on the A2100, take the first right into Powdermill Lane. Continue for 1 mile and the hotel is on your right.

### USEFUL INFORMATION

**SERVING TIMES:**
Lunch 12pm-2pm (every day)
Dinner 7pm-9pm (Mon-Sat)
　　　 7pm-8.30pm (Sunday)
**SEATING CAPACITY:** 100
**C/C:** V, MC, S, D, AE, DC
**CHILDREN:** welcome at lunch, but only if aged 10+ in the evening

**NUMBER OF WINES:** 70
**HOUSE WINE:** £9.95
**OFF-STREET PARKING:** yes
**DRESS CODE:** smart casual
**OUTDOOR EATING:** yes
**RESERVATIONS:** compulsory
**ACCOMMODATION:** 35 rooms
(B&B single £70, double £95)

# THE GABLES RESTAURANT
### Tel: (01403) 782571
Pulborough Road, Parbrook, Billingshurst, Sussex, RH14 9EU

### STARTERS

*Orkney Crab Cocktail ~ Fresh Orkney White Crab Meat,
Melon Parisienne and Prawns bound in a light Garlic Mayonnaise*

*Mediterranean Style Fish Soup infused with Mussels and garnished
with Fresh Home-made Crab and Prawn Dumplings*

*Italy's finest Parma Ham Curls served with fanned Galia Melon
and shavings of Vintage Parmesan (supplement £1.50)*

*Salad of Home-smoked Chicken and Puy Lentils bound in
spiced Mayonnaise and finished with a sprinkling of French Parsley*

### MAIN COURSES

*Half a Roast Norfolk Duck served with Sage and Onion Stuffing
and presented on a Red Wine Gravy*

*Roast Rack of Lamb served with Creamy Polenta that has been infused
with Olive Oil and served with a Basil and Redcurrant Sauce*

*Fresh Dived Scallops served with Saffron, baked Fennel and presented
on a light Grain Mustard Sauce*

*Fresh Tuna Steak served with a Creamy Wild Mushroom and Shallot Sauce*

*Spinach and Mushrooms bound in a Satay Sauce wrapped in
Filo Pastry served with a Chive Cream Sauce*

*Served with a selection of Vegetables and Potatoes, or a mixed salad*

### DESSERTS

*Jaffa Cake Pudding - a Sponge Base with Home-made Orange Jelly
and covered in a Chocolate topping*

*Home-made Fresh Fruit Pavlova served on a Pool of Red Fruit Coulis*

*Trio of Home-made Sorbets or Ice Creams*

Supposedly the finest example of a timber framed building in Sussex, The Gables dates back to 1480 and has all the necessary ingredients for a successful restaurant in this part of England. Intimate, relaxed, romantic and owned by a member of the Illes family!

Nick Illes has been the proprietor here for five years and enjoys an enviable reputation for the quality of his Modern British cuisine. Weekly trips to the premier London markets ensure that only the very best of fresh produce is used. An extensive set menu is offered in the evening (2 or 3 courses including coffee £19 and £23 respectively) and this changes every six weeks. A small selection from it is shown on the facing page. The Sunday luncheon menu (3 courses £17.50) is different every week but will always feature at least one traditional roast dish.

Also worthy of a special mention is the wine list. It is well-researched and offers an interesting range of predominantly French and South African vintages.

Directions: Leaving the centre of Billingshurst on the A29 towards Bognor Regis, the restaurant is easily found on the left.

### USEFUL INFORMATION

**SERVING TIMES:**
Lunch 12.15pm-1.45pm (Sunday)
Dinner 7.15pm-9pm (Tues-Thur + Sun)
　　　 7.15pm-9.30pm (Fri-Sat)
**CLOSED:** all day Monday, and for lunch every day except Sunday
**SEATING CAPACITY:** 50
**C/C:** V, MC, AE
**NO SMOKING** of pipes and cigars

**NUMBER OF WINES:** 120
**HOUSE WINE:** £10
**OFF-STREET PARKING:** yes
**RESERVATIONS:** advisable, but compulsory at weekends
**CHILDREN:** welcome during the week and for Sunday lunch
**OUTDOOR EATING:** no

# THE CHESTNUT TREE

Tel: (01323) 833651

Boreham Street, Herstmonceux, East Sussex, BN27 4SF

### *A Selection from the Dinner Menu*

### Starters

A terrine of smoked salmon, trout, mackerel and haddock served with seasonal salad

King vol-au-vent filled with mushrooms and chicken livers sautéed in garlic

Fillet of sardines, shallow fried in a crisp coating and accompanied by a cucumber and red pepper salad

Moules marinières - fresh mussels steamed in white wine, onions and garlic with fresh cream

A warm salad of smoked chicken breast and pine nuts on a bed of seasonal salad leaves

Cushions of smoked salmon filled with scrambled egg

Home-made duck liver pâté served with cranberry sauce and fingers of toast

### Main Courses

Fillet of beef topped with home-made chicken liver pâté, baked in puff pastry with a demi-glaze sauce

Roast rack of lamb coated with fine herbs and mustard

Chestnut Tree steak, Guinness and oyster pie

Sirloin steak cooked to your liking. Classic black pepper, spicy cajun or mushroom and brandy

Crisp roast duck served with black cherry and kirsch sauce

Seabass steak poached with fresh lime and lemon, white wine and butter

Vegetarian stroganoff with turmeric rice

All main dishes come with a selection of fresh vegetables

Fanny Craddock's collection of menus from all over the world adorn the walls in The Chestnut Tree's elegant lounge area, and I am sure that she would be pleased with the home that they have found. Although dating back to 1463, the dining area is now found in a tasteful extension which enjoys exceptional views across the Sussex Weald.

The seasonal dinner menu, a selection from which is shown on the facing page, consists of crudités, choice starters, sorbet, main course, pudding and home-made bread (£21.95). As one may expect, everything here is home-made, with Phil's delicious ice cream being worth a special mention! There is always a good selection of puddings, which may include Gooseberry Pie with Custard, Spotted Dick with Custard, or Apricot Charlotte and Cream.

The Sunday lunch menu (2 courses £13.95) offers a choice of about six starters and seven mains, with the emphasis being placed very firmly on the traditional. It is very popular so please book early.

Directions: The Chestnut Tree is located in Boreham Street on the A271 between Hailsham and Bexhill.

### USEFUL INFORMATION

**SERVING TIMES:**
Lunch 12pm-2.30pm (Sunday) and parties of 8+ by reservation (Mon-Sat)
Dinner 6.30pm-9.15pm (Tues-Sat)
**CLOSED:** all day Monday, for lunch in the week, and Sunday evening
**SEATING CAPACITY:** 42
**C/C:** V, MC, S, D

**NUMBER OF WINES:** 36
**HOUSE WINE:** £10
**OFF-STREET PARKING:** yes
**OUTDOOR EATING:** no
**RESERVATIONS:** advisable, but compulsory at weekends
**DRESS CODE:** smart casual
**NO SMOKING** pipes and cigars

# TANYARD HOTEL
Tel: (01622) 744705
Wierton Hill, Boughton Monchelsea, near Maidstone, Kent ME17 4JT

## MENU £27.50

Twice Baked Cheese Soufflé

Local Asparagus Soup

Marinated Mediterranean Prawns with Red and Yellow Peppers

Beef Tomatoes stuffed with Herbs and Gruyère

\*\*\*\*\*\*\*\*\*\*

Breast of Duck with a Bitter Orange Sauce

Darne of Salmon with Hollandaise Sauce

Suprême of Chicken with Sesame Seeds
with a Lime, Cream and Mango Sauce

Fillet of Scottish Beef with a Green Peppercorn Sauce

\*\*\*\*\*\*\*\*\*\*

Sticky Toffee Pudding with a Pecan Sauce

Vanilla Cream with a Summer Fruit Coulis

Chocolate and Ginger Cheesecake

Local Strawberry Shortcake

\*\*\*\*\*\*\*\*\*\*

A Selection of British Cheeses

\*\*\*\*\*\*\*\*\*\*

Cafetière Coffee and Chocolates

# BOUGHTON MONCHELSEA 21

The Tanyard is a small medieval country house hotel situated in the heart of rural Kent with far-reaching views across the Weald. The building is thought to date from circa 1350, with the restaurant being the oldest part of the house.

The westerly wing, that is the hall and lounge, was rebuilt after a possible fire in 1475 and is slightly grander than the eastern wing, with higher ceilings, moulded beams and carved stonework.

The kitchen produces food that is imaginative, using the best local produce, and which is modern but unpretentious in style. The fixed price à la carte changes every month or so and is priced at £22.50 for the three-course lunch and £27.50 for the four-course dinner (both include coffee).

Directions: From the B2163 (about 4 miles south of Maidstone) turn right at a pub called The Cock and drive along Park Lane. Take the first right down Wierton Road and bear right down Wierton Hill. The Tanyard Hotel is at the bottom of the hill on the left. And good luck!

## USEFUL INFORMATION

**SERVING TIMES:**
Lunch 12.30pm-1.45pm (Wed-Fri, Sun)
Dinner 7pm-9pm (every day)
**CLOSED:** Mon, Tues & Sat lunch
**SEATING CAPACITY:** 28
**C/C:** V, MC, S, D, AE, DC
**NO SMOKING** in the restaurant

**NUMBER OF WINES:** 40
**HOUSE WINE:** £9.50
**RESERVATIONS:** essential
**OUTDOOR EATING:** no
**OFF-STREET PARKING:** yes
**ACCOMMODATION:** 6 rooms
(B&B sgl from £65, dbl from £100)

# ONE PASTON PLACE
### Tel: (01273) 606933
1 Paston Place, Brighton, East Sussex, BN2 1HA

## MENU

Carpaccio of Beef, Parmesan Tuile £6.00
Monkfish Beignet Salad with Squid, Chinese Vinaigrette £7.50
Light Crab Soup with Sorrel, Crab Tortellini £5.00
Wood Pigeon Salad, Artichoke Crisps, Walnut Dressing £6.50
Foie Gras and Sweetbread Millefeuille with Girolles £8.00
Green Beans Topped with Red Mullet, Pink Grapefruit Vinaigrette £6.50

---

Pavé of Ostrich, Venison-style, Lemon and Coriander Pasta £16.50
Canon of Lamb, Sauce Mistral, Roasted Garlic Mash £16.00
Barbary Duck, Fig Sauce, Pearl Barley Risotto £14.50
Pot Roast Saddle of Rabbit, Summer Vegetables, Pommes Rissolées £15.00
Grilled Fillet of Seabass "à l'Arlesienne", Saffron Potatoes £17.50
Roast Cod, Shellfish Jus, Pommes Boulangères £14.00

---

Assiette Gourmande £6.50
Trio of Chocolates £5.50
Raspberry Soufflé £5.50
Iced Banana Parfait, Bitter Chocolate Sorbet £5.00
Spiced Peach Sablé, Spiced Peach Sorbet £5.00

---

*10% service will be added to your bill*

One Paston Place, very much a London restaurant that has decided to take a long vacation on the South Coast, is the domain of Mark and Nicole Emmerson. Mark excels in the kitchen inspiring fine modern European cuisine, while Nicole takes charge front of house with service that is formal yet relaxed.

No butter or cream is used in the preparation of the food. A quotation from Mark's book "A Feast of Oils", which he co-wrote with Jeannette Ewin, tells the story: "My goal in cooking is to prepare food that is enjoyable to look at and taste, but is also nutritious". I promised to plug the book and, to return the favour, Nicole hinted that she might put a copy or two of this guide in their toilets. Seems fair!

One Paston Place has over the years become extremely successful, but manages to avoid the pretentiousness that often accompanies such popularity. Perhaps the sea air helps.

Directions: One Paston Place is easily found in the Kemp Town area of Brighton, approximately one mile east of the town centre. Follow Marine Parade eastwards and look out for the turning into Paston Place on your left.

### USEFUL INFORMATION

**SERVING TIMES:**
Lunch 12.30pm-2pm (Tues-Sat)
Dinner 7.30pm-10pm (Tues-Sat)
**CLOSED:** all day Sun & Mon
**SEATING CAPACITY:** 48
**C/C:** V, MC, S, D, AE, DC

**NUMBER OF WINES:** 36
**HOUSE WINE:** £9.40
**RESERVATIONS:** essential
**OFF-STREET PARKING:** no
**OUTDOOR EATING:** no

# GEORGE AND DRAGON
Tel: (01903) 883131
Burpham, near Arundel, West Sussex, BN18 9RR

## A LA CARTE RESTAURANT MENU

Two Courses £16.50  Three Courses £19.50

**Salad of Salmon and Strawberry**
Warm Strips of Salmon, Guacamole Quenelles and Strawberry Dressing
**Asparagus and Brie Pithiviers**
Light Puff Pastry Parcels Surrounded by a Tangy Lime Sauce
**Gingered Crab Cakes**
Served Golden on a Red Pepper Coulis
**Consommé of Game and Braised Vegetables**
Accompanied by a Pan-fried Breast of Wood Pigeon
**Tagliatelle Verde**
Tossed in a Basil and Cream Sauce, Topped with Toasted Pinenuts
**Chicken and Parma Platter**
Fillets of Chicken Wrapped in Parma Ham,
Served on a Pool of Seasoned Passata

\* \* \* \* \*

**Medallions of Scotch Fillet**
Presented on a Sweet Potato Rosti on a Drambuie Sauce
**Platter of Smoked Fish**
Four Varieties of Smoked Fish Served with a Lemon Crème Fraîche
on an Orange and Watercress Salad
**A Brace of Boneless Quail**
Filled with Pork, Sage and Apricot Stuffing Arranged on a Crisp Potato Galette
Surrounded by a Brandy, Cream and Mint Sauce
**Seared Fillet of Salmon**
Served on a bed of Drunken Cabbage and a Light Pernod Glaze
**Millefeuille of Aubergine and Goats' Cheese**
Served Warm with a Walnut and Balsamic Dressing
**Fillet of Marinated Southdown Lamb**
Oven-roasted Pink, Garnished with a Field Mushroom Parcel
on a Pool of Lavender-scented Verjus Sauce
**Breast of Magret Duck**
Grilled Pink, Accompanied by a Lemon and Onion Compôte

\* \* \* \* \*

**A Selection of Freshly Prepared Desserts**

\* \* \* \* \*

**Fresh Coffee and Mints**
(included in the price)

The George and Dragon is a traditional 18th century country pub set in a picturesque hill village with magnificent views down to Arundel Castle and the river. In order to avoid disappointment, it really is essential to book a table in advance (for both the restaurant and the bar) as this popular dining pub fills up very quickly. You would need to arrive at about 7am to see it looking as deserted as in the photograph below.

The simple wooden furniture, exposed beams and inglenook fireplace provide a friendly atmosphere and, although a certain degree of organised chaos reigns during busy periods (i.e. all the time), the food is well worth the wait. The restaurant menu featured opposite is seasonal and the specials written up on the blackboards in the bar change daily. These might include Perch Supreme in a Cream & Tarragon Sauce (£7.95), Pork Chop & Apricot Casserole (£5.90) or Beef & Cranberry Pie (£5.70).

Directions: The George and Dragon is easily found at the top end of the village of Burpham, which lies approximately 3 miles to the north-east of Arundel and is signposted from the main A27 Chichester to Worthing road.

## USEFUL INFORMATION
(R = restaurant, B = bar)

**SERVING TIMES:**
(R) Lunch 12.15pm-2pm (Sun only)
(B) Lunch 12pm-2pm (every day)
(R) Dinner 7.15pm-9.45pm (Mon-Sat)
(B) Dinner 7pm-9.45pm (Mon-Sat)
   7pm-9pm (Sun, summer)
**SEATING CAPACITY:** 36 in the restaurant, 40 in the bar

**NUMBER OF WINES:** 43
**HOUSE WINE:** £9.95
**RESERVATIONS:** essential for both the restaurant and the bar
**OUTDOOR EATING:** yes
**C/C:** V, MC, S, D, AE
**OFF-STREET PARKING:** yes

# TUO E MIO
Tel: (01227) 761471
16 The Borough, Canterbury, Kent, CT1 2DR

## A SMALL SELECTION FROM OUR MENU

### ANTIPASTI - HORS D'OEUVRE
INSALATA DI MOZZARELLA mozzarella cheese, tomato, basil and vinaigrette £4.00
CARCIOFINI FRITTI fried artichoke hearts £3.50
CARPACCIO CON RUCCOLA thinly sliced raw beef, parmesan and ruccola salad £5.50

### ZUPPE E PASTA - SOUPS AND PASTA
ZUPPA DI PESCE fresh fish soup £2.50
GNOCCHI AL FUNGHI PORCINI dumplings with wild mushroom sauce £6.00
SPAGHETTI VONGOLE baby clam sauce £6.00

### MANZO - BEEF
FILETTO TUO E MIO fillet steak, cream, brandy and mushrooms £12.50
COSTATA PIZZAIOLA entrecote, tomato, garlic and wine £10.50
FILETTO AL PEPE fillet steak with peppercorns £12.50

### VITELLO - VEAL
SCALOPPINA AL LIMONE veal, lemon and wine £7.00
SALTIMBOCCA ALL ROMANA veal, parma ham and marsala wine £7.50
FEGATO ALL SALVIA calves liver, butter and sage £8.50

### POLLO - CHICKEN
POLLO SOPRESA chicken breast filled with parma ham and mozzarella £7.75
POLLO GENOVESE chicken breast, cream, brandy, basil and mushrooms £6.75
POLLO AL LIMONE chicken breast with lemon and white wine sauce £7.50

### PESCE - FISH
FRITTO MISTO DI MARE mixed fried seafood £8.50
TROTA ALL SALVIA trout with lemon, sage and wine £6.50
GAMBERONI ALLA GRIGLIA grilled pacific prawns, garlic and wine £9.00

potatoes included with all main dishes
fresh vegetables per selection £1.00 or selection of three vegetables £2.00

### DOLCI E FORMAGGI - SWEET OR CHEESE £3.00

### CAFE - COFFEE £1.00

Tuo e Mio is a popular Italian restaurant in the centre of Canterbury. Chef Yuri Mula offers a broad range of Italian home cooking, specialising in fresh pastas, local fish and shellfish. The kitchen staff even pick their own wild mushrooms during the season.

There are no longer any set price menus available, but the lunchtime specials mean that you can still eat well for around £10.00. A small selection from the à la carte appears opposite, with supplementary dishes such as Halibut with Salsa Verde (£12.50), Skate with Black Butter and Capers (£10.50), Fillet of Sea Bream with Tomato and Basil (£11.50) or Veal Chop with Sage and Rosemary (£12.50).

Directions: Tuo e Mio is situated opposite King's School in the Northgate, approximately 5 minutes walk from the main cathedral entrance.

### USEFUL INFORMATION

**SERVING TIMES:**
Lunch 12pm-2.30pm (Wed-Sun)
Dinner 7pm-10.45pm (Tues-Sat)
        7pm-10pm (Sun)
**CLOSED:** all day Mon & Tues lunch
**SEATING CAPACITY:** 70
**C/C:** V, MC, S, D, AE, DC

**NUMBER OF WINES:** 50
**HOUSE WINE:** £8.50
**RESERVATIONS:** advisable
**OUTDOOR EATING:** no
**CHILDREN:** welcome
**OFF-STREET PARKING:** no

# COMME ÇA

Tel: (01243) 788724

67 Broyle Road, Chichester, West Sussex, PO19 4BD

## A SELECTION FROM THE A LA CARTE MENU

Les Aumonières aux Deux Fromages £4.65
*Goat's cheese with spinach and honey and Brie with gooseberry
wrapped individually in filo pastry and served with a Savoy cabbage butter sauce*
Melon Beau Rivage £4.65
*Melon, prawns and avocado glazed with a spicy mango dressing*
Salade Camargaise de Mozzarella et Poivrons Doux £4.65
*Fresh mozzarella accompanied by cold grilled sweet peppers, avocado and tomatoes,
flavoured with balsamic and cumin vinaigrette*
Parfait de Foie de Volaille à l'Armagnac £4.65
*A Normandy chicken liver parfait flavoured with Armagnac
and presented with a cranberry jelly*
Salade d'Epinards et d'Endives aux Oranges et Magret de Canard Fumé £4.65
*Fresh chicory and spinach leaves tossed with sesame seeds and orange segments
and fine slices of smoked duck breast*

~ ~ ~ ~ ~

Papillote de Métan d'Alaska au Coulis de Choux Vert £10.25
*Baked fillet of halibut in filo pastry served with a creamy Savoy cabbage sauce*
Médaillons de Lotte au Jus d'Agrumes de Sèville £10.25
*Grilled medallions of monkfish accompanied by Citrus beurre blanc and orange zest*
Sole Comme Ça £12.25
*Spécialité de la Maison: Fillets of Dover sole served on or off the bone*
Médaillons de Filet de Boeuf Poêlé à l'Estragon £11.25
*Pan-fried fillet of beef flambéd with Madeira
and presented with an aromatic tarragon and mushroom cream sauce*
Selle d'Agneau au Romarin et Porto £11.25
*Boneless rack of lamb roasted with a Provincial herb crust
and served with a rosemary and port sauce*
Terrine de Pommes de Terre au Roquefort et Noix Gaule £9.75
*Baked terrine of potatoes and spinach layered with a mousse of Roquefort cheese and
walnuts, accompanied by a yellow pepper coulis*

~ ~ ~ ~ ~

Mousse au Chocolat Noir £4.45
*Dark chocolate mousse flavoured with Mandarin Impériale*
Gâteau de Fromage à l'Orange £4.45
*Orange cheesecake accompanied by a mandarin coulis*
Petit Sablé de Framboises Fraîches £4.45
*Shortbread pastry layers filled with fresh raspberries, accompanied by their own fruit coulis*
Prèlat de Chocolat Fondant et Café £4.45
*Layer of coffee biscuit filled with a fine chocolate mousse, served with coffee beans sauce*

Comme Ça is an elegant restaurant and bar that has built up an enviable reputation for fine French cuisine over the last eleven years.

Its proximity to the Chichester Festival Theatre means that the restaurant is extremely popular before and after the performances, so that despite the two spacious dining areas and the extra room provided during the summer by the delightful upper and lower terraces with their pergolas, fountains, flower beds and hanging baskets, it is always best to book.

Chef patron Michel Navet's extensive *carte* (a small selection is featured on the facing page) changes just twice a year, although there will always be three or four specials in the evening to choose from. Pre and after-theatre set price menus are available (£15.25 for 2 courses and £17.95 for 3 courses) and a traditional French family lunch is served on Sundays (£16.75 for 3 courses, children's menu £7.50).

The bar menu on the blackboard is also extremely good, though they do try to discourage dining in the bar area in the evenings.

Directions: Comme Ça is located just north of Chichester town centre on the A286 to or from Midhurst. The restaurant is situated on the opposite side of the road to the barracks and the Festival Theatre, roughly midway between the two.

### USEFUL INFORMATION

**SERVING TIMES:**
Lunch 12pm-2pm (Tues-Sun)
Dinner 5.45pm-10.30pm (Tues-Sat)
**CLOSED:** Sun night & all day Mon
**SEATING CAPACITY:** 80 in the restaurant, 20 in the bar
**C/C:** V, MC, S, D, AE
**OUTDOOR EATING:** yes

**NUMBER OF WINES:** 150
**HOUSE WINE:** £9.85
**RESERVATIONS:** advisable, but essential at weekends
**CHILDREN:** welcome
**OFF-STREET PARKING:** yes
**NO SMOKING** in the restaurant, but permitted in the bar area

# PLATTERS RESTAURANT
Tel: (01243) 530430
15 Southgate, Chichester, West Sussex, PO19 1ES

## A LA CARTE DINNER MENU

### TO START

PEAR AND STILTON PLATTER  £3.75
A terrine of fresh pear & blue stilton served on a port & redcurrant sauce
SCALLOP & LEEK TART  £4.95
Filo tartlet filled with butter fried leeks & scallops, served on a white butter sauce
CARPACCIO OF BEEF  £4.95
Wafer thin slice of raw fillet steak, shavings of fresh parmesan, basil & olive oil
MUSHROOM PLATTER  £3.95
Fricassée of mixed mushrooms in a cream & sherry sauce in a puff pastry case
SALMON AND SOLE ROULADE  £4.25
Fresh sole fillets wrapped around salmon mousse, poached & served chilled

### MIDDLE BITS

RACK OF LAMB  £14.25
Roast rack of English lamb, glazed with apricot & set on a light curried cream sauce
BEEF PLATTER  £13.95
Medallions of beef fillet pan-fried to your liking, set on a dark cherry sauce
SPINACH CREPES  £9.95
Crêpes made with fresh spinach stuffed with a mixture of wild & white mushrooms bound in a gruyère cheese sauce
CHICKEN PLATTER  £12.25
Roast breast of chicken filled with caramelised apples served with a rich cider sauce
PIGEON PLATTER  £12.95
Pan-fried breasts of wood pigeon, de-glaced with sloe gin on a bed of puy lentils
HALIBUT PLATTER  £13.95
Fillet of halibut poached in a rich fish stock & laid over a bed of cockles, mussels & prawns in a saffron jus
FILLET OF COD  £11.25
Baked fillet of cod set on a bed of steamed leeks on a roast tomato & garlic passata

### TO FINISH

CRÊME BRÛLÉE  £3.75
MEDLEY OF FRUIT SORBETS - Elderflower, Orange, Blackcurrant  £3.75
APRICOT & PEACH SCHNAPPS ICE CREAM  £3.75
in a Brandy Snap Basket
MEDLEY OF HOME-MADE ICE CREAMS  £3.75
Apricot, Pineapple, Strawberry
PEAR TATIN TART  £3.75
WHITE CHOCOLATE, HONEY AND ALMOND MOUSSE  £3.75
A PLATTER OF FINE CHEESES  £4.95

# CHICHESTER 31

Chef/proprietor Nik Westacott has come a long way since he started his catering career in a large London hotel washing up 20,000 glasses every night. In 1991 he founded Platters, an intimate town centre restaurant set up on a shoestring in the middle of a deep recession. Everyone thought he was crazy but, by offering "fresh food cooked with imagination", it worked.

Wild ingredients are a passion with Nik and though he will regularly go out to pick mushrooms, sloes and samphire, he stubbornly refuses to buy them! He is joined on his hunting trips by two Welsh springer spaniels who are of course hopeless at finding mushrooms, but great company.

The à la carte dinner menu featured opposite changes monthly and is supplemented by a daily-changing lunchtime table d'hôte (£6.95 for a single course, £9.95 for two courses or £12.95 for three courses).

Directions: Located at the bottom of South Street, Platters is 100 yards north of the railway station - opposite the Bedford Hotel and Magistrates' Courts.

## USEFUL INFORMATION

**SERVING TIMES:**
Lunch 12.15pm-2pm (Tues-Sat)
Dinner 7pm-after theatre (Thur-Sat)
**CLOSED:** all day Sun & Mon, plus Tues & Wed nights
**SEATING CAPACITY:** 30
**C/C:** V, MC, S, D
**OUTDOOR EATING:** yes

**NUMBER OF WINES:** 110
**HOUSE WINE:** £8.95
**RESERVATIONS:** essential
**OFF-STREET PARKING:** no but there is a public car park to the rear
**CHILDREN:** welcome
**NO WHEELCHAIR ACCESS**

# THE CROWN INN
## Tel: (01428) 682255
The Green, Petworth Road, Chiddingfold, Surrey, GU8 4TX

### A SMALL SELECTION FROM OUR A LA CARTE MENU

#### *Hors D'Oeuvres*

FANFARE OF MELON  £3.25
with pink grapefruit segments, sorbet & port & redcurrant coulis

STILTON FILLED MUSHROOMS  £5.80
baked, on a garlic cream & port sauce

PARFAIT OF SMOKED HADDOCK  £3.95
on frizzie salad, with sun-dried tomatoes, lemon & herb dressing & bruschetta

#### *Main Courses*

ROAST COD FILLET WITH SMOKED BACON  £8.95
on a rosemary scented clam broth with parsley mash

ROAST WOOD PIGEON  £9.75
on braised cracked wheat & bacon with glazed baby onions, garlic, mushrooms, sage & Madeira wine jus

PORK TENDERLOIN IN SPICY PANCAKE  £11.95
pork fillet rolled in Indian spices, onion & apple, wrapped in a crêpe and baked, with a dariole of rice served with mint, cucumber, tomato and yoghurt chutney

GLAZED BREAST OF DUCK  £11.95
sliced on a bed of Bok-choy in a plum, ginger and Szechuan pepper flavoured duck gravy

#### *Desserts*

BAKED BANANA MARTINIQUE  £3.50
sliced banana, glazed with rum sabayon sauce and served with a coconut basket filled with vanilla ice cream

MIXED CHEESE PLATTER  £4.50
selection of cheeses with celery, grapes and assorted biscuits

BAKED SAUTERNES CUSTARD  £3.50
with armagnac prunes

The Crown Inn has occupied the southern tip of Chiddingfold's picturesque village green since the late 13th century and these days offers period accommodation, cream teas, traditional bar snacks and full à la carte dining.

The restaurant is a handsomely panelled room with high fireplaces, tapestries and windows decorated with original Chiddingfold stained glass. The menu (a small selection from which is featured on the facing page) is changed seasonally.

Light meals are served in the bar area, with daily specials on the blackboard such as Grilled Sardines and Salad (£4.25) or Cornish Pasty with Vegetable and Onion Gravy (£5.25).

Directions: The Crown Inn is situated on the village green at Chiddingfold, approximately four miles to the south of Milford on the main A283 to Petworth.

### USEFUL INFORMATION

**SERVING TIMES:**
Lunch 12pm-2.30pm (Tues-Sun)
Dinner 7pm-9.30pm (Tues-Sun)
**CLOSED FOR FOOD:** all day Mon
**SEATING CAPACITY:** 50 in the restaurant, 40 in the bar
**C/C:** V, MC, S, D, AE, DC
**OUTDOOR EATING:** yes

**NUMBER OF WINES:** 30
**HOUSE WINE:** £7.90
**RESERVATIONS:** advisable for the restaurant
**OFF-STREET PARKING:** yes
**CHILDREN:** welcome
**ACCOMMODATION:** 8 rooms (B&B sgl fr £47, dbl £57-£90)

# THE CASTLE INN
### Tel: (01892) 870247
Chiddingstone, near Edenbridge, Kent, TN8 7AH

### A LA CARTE RESTAURANT MENU

*Marinaded Squid Salad* £5.75
*Giant King Prawns* with Mayonnaise or Garlic Butter £9.50
*A Plate of Smoked Scottish Salmon* with Brown Bread & Butter £8.50
*Home-made Chicken Liver Pâté* with Toast £5.25
*One Dozen Snails* £9.75
*Deep-fried Goujons of Sole* with Tartare Sauce £7.95
*A Warm Scallop Salad* £7.35
*Sevruga Caviar - 30 grams* on Crushed Ice with Toast £29.90
*Fish Soup* with Croûtons, Rouille & Grated Cheese (for two) £9.75

\* \* \* \* \*

*Dublin Bay Prawns* flambéed with Brandy
in Tomato, Onion & White Wine Sauce on Rice £13.25
*Lobster Newburg* for two persons £29.50
*Halibut Steak* with Herb Butter £9.85
*Dover Sole Grilled* Meunière or Colbert £14.75
*Fillet Steak* £12.95 *Sirloin Steak* £10.85 *T Bone Steak* £10.75
*Breast of Duck* with an Orange Sauce £10.45
*Tournedos* with a Mushroom, Red Wine & French Mustard Sauce £14.25
*Fillet of Beef with Stilton Sauce* £14.25
*Veal Escalope* Sautéed in Butter £10.85
*Chateaubriand* for 2 Persons with a Béarnaise Sauce £27.50
*Chicken Breast* in a Cream, Mushroom & Button Onion Sauce £9.45

All our main course prices include a selection of season vegetables and potatoes or a salad

\* \* \* \* \*

*Desserts*
From the Table d'Hôte Menu £5.45

The 15th century Castle Inn at Chiddingstone is an historic "restaurant with bars" and as such must be one of the most photographed restaurants in the country. Set in the idyllic village of Chiddingstone, the building forms part of a unique row of timbered houses.

The village street remains exceptionally unspoilt and the houses, with their mullions and casement windows, their picturesque roofs and projecting upper storeys, are attractive examples of 14th to 17th century domestic architecture. The National Trust liked it so much that in 1939 they bought the entire village for the princely sum of £25,000.

The restaurant's *carte* opposite changes every 3 to 4 weeks and is supplemented by various fixed price menus: a 3-course luncheon £13.50, Sunday lunch £15.50 for 2 courses, a 3-course dinner £22.50 and a 2-course Fireside Menu for £10.95. The home-made bar food is also excellent.

Directions: The Castle Inn is easily found on the bend in the centre of the village of Chiddingstone, which lies approximately 4 miles to the east of Edenbridge. The village is clearly signposted from the surrounding roads.

### USEFUL INFORMATION

**SERVING TIMES:**
Lunch 12pm-2pm (every day)
Dinner 7.30pm-9.30pm (every day)
**SEATING CAPACITY:** 57 in the restaurant, 45 in the bars
**C/C:** V, MC, S, D, AE, DC
**OUTDOOR EATING:** yes, for both the restaurant and the bar

**NUMBER OF WINES:** 150
**HOUSE WINE:** £9.75
**RESERVATIONS:** essential for the restaurant
**OFF-STREET PARKING:** no
**CHILDREN:** very welcome
**ACCOMMODATION:** there are two B&B's next door

# THE WHITE HORSE INN
### Tel: (01243) 535219
Chilgrove, near Chichester, West Sussex, PO18 9HX

*Fixed Price A La Carte Dinner Menu £23.50*
*A reduction of £4 will be made for persons not eating an hors d'oeuvre*

\*\*\*\*

Tonight's Appetiser

\*\*\*\*\*

Dominique's Home-made Soup

Pan-fried Fillet of Red Mullet with an Orange & Chive Salad

Scotch Smoked Salmon served with a Poached Egg and
Sprinkled with Black Pepper

Chilled Gazpacho

Carpaccio of Marinaded Fillet of Beef with Fresh Parmesan and
a Balsamic Dressing

Confit of Duck with Glazed Shallots

Poached Oysters glazed with a Champagne Sabayon on a Bed of Leeks

\*\*\*\*

Duo of Barbary Duck and Local Wood Pigeon's Breasts with
a Jasmine and Sultana Sauce

Fresh Monkfish with a Light Cream and Grain Mustard Sauce

Fillet of English Lamb set on a Mango and Mint Sauce

Chinese Style Port Ragoût with Summer Vegetables

Grilled Calves Liver on a Marmalade of Red Onions with a Madeira Sauce

Crêpe Gâteau with Wild Rice and Mushrooms (Vegetarian)

\*\*\*\*\*

A selection of Fresh Vegetables and Potatoes is served
to accompany the Main Course

\*\*\*\*

Dessert Selection or Cheese Platter

Just for once, I am not even going to mention the excellent food. I will concentrate instead on this dining pub's wine list. I recall describing a certain hotel's 900 bins as "serious" in one of our other editions. I think that must make Barry Phillips' wine list "critical", with around 2650 wines at the last count.

A huge leather-bound black book is brought to your table as the principal list. An even larger red book follows on - *The Red List* is a collection of old wines, rarities, Magnums, Grands Formats, First Growth Clarets, Château d'Yquem and Domaine de la Romanée-Conti. Philistine that I am, I spent a few minutes flicking through the pages for the most expensive. I have to report that I found the Château Petrus 1990 (priced at £5750.00 for the double Magnum) rather amusing!

I like the idea behind the "Mystery House Wine". If you can guess the variety of grape and country of origin correctly, there is no charge. If you guess incorrectly, they charge you £17.50. You write your answer on a postcard during your meal and the result appears on your bill.

Directions: The White Horse Inn is easily found, set back from the B2141 in the village of Chilgrove, roughly equidistant from the three major towns of Petersfield, Midhurst and Chichester.

### USEFUL INFORMATION

**SERVING TIMES:**
Lunch 12pm-2pm (Tues-Sun)
Dinner 7pm-9.30pm (Tues-Sat)
**RESTAURANT CLOSED:** Sun night, all day Mon, all Feb & last week Oct
**SEATING CAPACITY:** 75 in the restaurant, 20 in the bar
**C/C:** V, MC, S, D, AE, DC

**NUMBER OF WINES:** 2650-ish!
**HOUSE WINE:** £11.50
**RESERVATIONS:** advisable
**OFF-STREET PARKING:** yes
**CHILDREN:** by arrangement
**OUTDOOR EATING:** yes
**ACCOMMODATION:** 48 rooms (B&B single £35, double £79)

# THE GRIFFINS HEAD

Tel: (01304) 840325
Chillenden, near Canterbury, Kent, CT3 1PS

## EVENING MENU

### STARTERS

Home-made Vegetable Soup £2.50
Home-made Pâté £2.95
Stilton & Bacon Salad £3.50
Avocado with Grilled Brie £3.25
Garlic Mushrooms £2.75
Grilled Sardines £3.25
Marinated Anchovy Fillets £4.50
Warm Salad of Scallops & Bacon £4.50

### MAIN COURSES

Grilled Whole Plaice £7.95
Local Sea Bass (for two people) £27.00
Salmon Steak Grilled in Butter £8.75
Aberdeen Angus Scotch Fillet Steak £12.50
Aberdeen Angus Scotch Rump Steak £8.95
Barnsley Lamb Chops £8.95
Half a Roast Duck Served with Raspberry Sauce £9.95
Breast of Chicken Stuffed with Bacon, Mushrooms & Cream Cheese £8.75
Pork Chop with a Dijon Cream Sauce £8.50
Spinach & Cream Cheese Pasta Bake with a Side Salad £6.95
Liver & Bacon £7.50

### LUNCHTIME FEATURES

Cottage Pie £3.85
Chicken & Leek Pie £5.95
Lasagne £3.95
Fisherman's Pie £5.95
Ploughman's - Cheddar, Brie or Stilton £3.85
Salmon Fishcakes £5.95

*All main courses are served with a selection of mixed vegetables*

# CHILLENDEN 39

A visit to this excellent dining pub requires careful planning and a good deal of spare time - I know exactly where it is and it still takes me two hours to find it! One glance at the map on the back of their business card should explain what I mean (and if you think that my set of directions below dodge the issue, then I can assure you that they give equally confusing instructions over the telephone). The main piece of advice - don't leave home without their number.

However, your patience will be rewarded. Although still a Shepherd Neame tenancy, this country inn has been run impeccably (not to mention eccentrically) for the last 12 years by Jeremy (front of house - the eccentric part) and Karen (in the kitchen - the impeccable part) Copestake.

The blackboard menu changes daily and is more "snacky" at lunchtimes (the prices reflect this). There is also an unusually good champagne list, with around a dozen different varieties to explore.

Directions: Difficult at the best of times! From Canterbury, take the A2 towards Dover and turn left onto the B2046. Follow the signs to Nonington, go through this village and Chillenden should be about 1fi miles further along the road.

## USEFUL INFORMATION

**SERVING TIMES:**
Lunch 12pm-2pm (every day)
Dinner 7pm-930pm (Mon-Sat)
**CLOSED FOR FOOD:** Sunday night
**SEATING CAPACITY:** 70
**C/C:** V, MC, S, D, AE

**NUMBER OF WINES:** 50
**HOUSE WINE:** £10.00
**RESERVATIONS:** advisable
**OFF-STREET PARKING:** yes
**OUTDOOR EATING:** yes

# BAILIFFSCOURT HOTEL

Tel: (01903) 723511

Climping, near Littlehampton, West Sussex, BN17 5RW

---

A selection from the dinner menu

£32.50

*Assiette of Marinated and House Smoked Salmon
with Creamed Cucumber and Dill Salad*

*Beef Tomato dressed in a Pesto Sauce garnished with fresh
Parmesan Shavings and toasted with Pine Kernels*

*Boudin of Chicken Mousseline with Foie Gras and Green Peppercorns
on a Salad of Artichoke Hearts and Raspberry Vinegar*

*Warm Confit of Duck Leg on Seasonal Leaves
with Truffle Oil Dressing*

*Oven Baked Guinea Fowl with Peppered Swedes and Madeira Jus*

*Roast Rack of Lamb in Sweet Garlic Sauce with Soused Button Mushrooms*

*Fillet of Seabass on a Creamed Sauce of Basil with House-made Noodles
(£2.50 supplement)*

*Roulade of Pork Tenderloin filled with Calves' Kidney with Balsamic
Vinegar and Braised Baby Onions*

*Gateau of Celeriac and Pistachio Nuts on Honey and Rosemary*

*Roasted Peach in Almond and Grenadine Caramel*

*Baked Cream of Vanilla and Coconut with Confit of Kumquats*

*Brioche and Prune Pudding with Drambuie and Apple Sauce*

*Freshly Filtered Coffee with Cream and Petits Fours*

Described lovingly as 'The Genuine Fake', Bailiffscourt is unique. An illusionary shroud from the medieval age, dating back to a remarkably recent 1927, harmoniously envelopes the trappings of an altogether more modern era. The result is a quite stunning, luxury hotel.

The restaurant has a simple elegance that invites you to enjoy the classical and modern cuisine for which it has become renowned. In the evening an à la carte is offered. It is described as 'constantly evolving to allow for seasonal variations' and an example is featured opposite.

At lunch a slightly less extensive table d'hôte operates (2 or 3 courses at £14.50 and £18.50 respectively), and this is supplemented by a good range of imaginative bar snacks which are perfect for those after a less formal meal.

Directions: Climping is found just to the west of Littlehampton. Bailiffscourt is signposted from the A259.

## USEFUL INFORMATION

**SERVING TIMES:**
Lunch 12pm-2pm (every day)
Dinner 7pm-9.45pm (every day)
**SEATING CAPACITY:** 54
**C/C:** V, MC, S, D, AE, DC
**CHILDREN:** welcome
**DRESS CODE:** jacket preferred
**OUTDOOR EATING:** yes

**NUMBER OF WINES:** 175
**HOUSE WINE:** £13.95
**OFF-STREET PARKING:** yes
**NO SMOKING** in the restaurant
**RESERVATIONS:** advisable, but compulsory at weekends
**ACCOMMODATION:** 27 rooms (single fr £120, double fr £135)

# STANE STREET HOLLOW
Tel: (01798) 872819
Codmore Hill, Pulborough, West Sussex, RH20 1BG

*A selection from the A La Carte*

**SAUMON FUME A LA MODE DE CONCARNEAU £6.00**
Slices of home-smoked salmon filled with a tuna fish mousse
and served on a tossed leaf salad

**BOUCHEE AUX FRUITS DE MER £6.00**
Vol-au-vent filled with a fresh fish and prawns, served
with a cream sauce flavoured with fresh tarragon

**CREPE FARCIS AUX RIS D'AGNEAU ET GIROLLES £5.50**
Pancake filled with lamb sweetbreads and chantrelles, served
with a madeira sauce

~ ~ ~ ~ ~

**CUISSE DE CANARD FUME £12.00**
A boned, home-smoked leg of duckling filled with a coarse
pork farcis, roasted and served with a plum compote and red wine sauce

**POULET FARCIS FLORENTINE £11.50**
Boned leg of chicken filled with spinach and garlic, wrapped in
bacon and baked in puff pastry

**CHATREUSE DE COURGETTE £10.50**
A light courgette mousse flavoured with a little cheese and
served with a red pepper sauce

A platter of fresh vegetables and potatoes are included with the main courses

**A BLACKBERRY BOMBE £5.00**
Crushed meringue mixed with a blackberry compote and fresh cream,
chilled and served with a blackberry purée

**PROFITEROLES AU CHOCOLAT £5.00**
Small buns of choux pastry filled with a white chocolate mousse
and served with a dark chocolate sauce

**NOUGAT GLACE £5.00**
A parfait glacé flavoured with almonds and honey, served
with an orange sauce

It is at once apparent that Stane Street Hollow is somewhere a little bit special. More like a family home than a restaurant, you wander up the garden path to the front door of a beautifully converted pair of 16th century cottages, to then be seated in one of the intimate little dining rooms, feeling more like a friend dropping in for dinner than a paying customer. For 22 years Réne and Ann Kaiser-Young have been welcoming guests here, and long may it continue.

Using home-grown herbs, vegetables and soft fruits whenever possible, eggs laid in the back garden, and home-smoked hams, salmon, chickens and ducks, Réne prepares 'peasant style' continental country cooking. The à la carte menu, a small selection from which is shown opposite, changes monthly, but is supplemented by weekly fish specials such as Fillets of lemon sole filled with a salmon mousse, poached and served with a lobster sauce (£13), and Bass fillet poached in white wine and served on a bed of fresh fennel with a light cream sauce (£14).

A weekly table d'hôte luncheon menu (2 or 3 courses at £12.50 or £15.50) features a choice of two dishes with each course. On Sundays it is slightly more expensive (£15.50 and £18.50), but offers a traditional roast dish.

Directions: Leaving Pulborough on the A29 towards Billingshurst, the restaurant is found on the left after about 2 miles.

### USEFUL INFORMATION

**SERVING TIMES:**
Lunch 12.30pm-1.15pm (Wed-Fri + Sun)
Dinner 7.15pm-9.15pm (Wed-Sat)
**CLOSED:** Sunday evening, Saturday lunch, and all day Monday & Tuesday
**SEATING CAPACITY:** 30
**C/C:** V, MC, S, D

**NUMBER OF WINES:** 100
**CHILDREN:** welcome
**OFF-STREET PARKING:** yes
**NO SMOKING** in the restaurant
**OUTDOOR EATING:** no
**RESERVATIONS:** advisable

# THE WITHIES INN
### Tel: (01483) 421158
Withies Lane, Compton, Near Guildford, Surrey, GU3 1JA

## RESTAURANT MENU

**Hors d'Oeuvres**

Home-made Fisherman's Broth £3.50
Withies 'Soupe du Jour' £3.00
Deep-fried Whitebait £4.50
Seafood Crêpe Mornay £4.95
Melon & Parma Ham £6.25
Prawns with Mayonnaise Dip £3.95
Mushrooms in Garlic Butter £4.25
Home-made Withies Pâté £3.75

Mediterranean Prawns £8.25
Avocado with Seafood £6.75
Hot or Cold Artichoke £3.50
Paw Paw with Fresh Crab £6.75
Pan-fried Sardines with Lemon £4.95
Smoked Salmon £7.25
Arbroath Smokies with Lemon
 Mayonnaise £4.25

**Fish to your choice**

Fresh Scotch Salmon £12.95
Whole Local Trout £8.50
Scampi Meunière, Mushrooms £11.95
Poached Halibut with Prawns in a
 Brandy Sauce £14.00
Dover Sole £ market price

**Cold with Salad**

Home-cooked Gammon £8.95
Scotch Sirloin of Beef £10.95
Fresh Salmon Salad £13.95
~ ~ ~ ~ ~
Green Salad £2.20
Mixed Salad £2.20

**Entrées**

Individual Fillet of Beef
 Wellington £13.95
Half a Roast Duckling with Orange
 or Peach Sauce £12.50
Escalope of Veal Marsala £10.75
Roasted Rack of Lamb
 with Rosemary £12.50
Tournedos Rossini or
 au Poivre £13.95
Steak Diane Flambé £14.50
Chicken Kiev £9.25
Boeuf Stroganoff £10.50
Home-made Steak, Kidney &
 Mushroom Pie £9.75

**From the Chargrill**

Sirloin Steak £11.50
Rump Steak £9.75
Fillet Steak £12.50
T-Bone Steak £13.50
Grilled Calves Liver with Bacon &
 Onions £12.50

**Extras**

Vegetables - mostly £1.10 per choice
Spinach £2.00
Jacket Potato with Sour Cream
 & Chives £2.20

The Withies Inn is a traditional country pub whose buildings date from the 16th century. It has been unobtrusively modernised to accommodate a first-class restaurant with low beams and an intimate atmosphere. Weather permitting, an attractive pergola allows summer dining in the delightful garden.

The daily specials in the restaurant might include fresh crab (£8), scallops (£8.25), six County Clare oysters (£9) or asparagus (£8) as starters, and main courses such as sea bass (£18), grouse (£16), whole lobster (£25) or roast suckling pig (£18).

Bar snacks are also available. Ploughmans (from £3.75), a selection of sandwiches (from £3.25), jacket potatoes with a variety of fillings (from £4) and dishes such as Cumberland sausage with mashed potato, onion and gravy (£4.25) and a seafood platter (£6.50) are some of the most popular choices.

Directions: The Withies Inn is situated just to the east of Compton, which lies on the B3000 about 3 miles to the south-west of Guildford and can be reached from both the A3 and the A3100. Look out for the signposts to the inn.

### USEFUL INFORMATION

**SERVING TIMES:**
Lunch 12pm-2pm (rest: every day)
    12pm-2.30pm (bar: every day)
Dinner 7pm-10pm (both: Mon-Sat)
**CLOSED FOR FOOD:** Sun night
**SEATING CAPACITY:** 65 in the restaurant, 30 in the bar
**C/C:** V, MC, S, D, AE, DC

**NUMBER OF WINES:** 85
**HOUSE WINE:** £9.95
**RESERVATIONS:** advisable, but essential at weekends
**OUTDOOR EATING:** yes
**OFF-STREET PARKING:** yes
**CHILDREN:** welcome

# THE OLD VINE

Tel: (01892) 782271

Cousley Wood, Wadhurst, East Sussex, TN5 6ER

## A SELECTION FROM THE RESTAURANT MENU

### To Start

Cream of Wild Mushrooms & Chive Soup £2.95
Mozzarella, Basil & Beef Tomato Salad £3.05
Warm Smoked Mackerel Fillet accompanied by Potato
& Red Onion £2.95
Balls of Galia Melon laced in Crême de Menthe £3.15
Deep-fried Mushrooms filled with Chicken Liver Pâté
& Cranberry Jelly £3.45
Souffléd Stilton Fritters with Dijon & Mayonnaise £3.50
Smoked Salmon Pasta in a Creamy Wine Sauce £4.50
Deep-fried Calamari with a Bacon & Tomato Dip £3.45
Trio of Melon with Forest Fruits Sorbet £3.00

### Main Courses

Cajun-style Chicken on a bed of Fruit Rice £7.10
Poached Halibut Steak in a Tomato & Caper Sauce
with Sea Asparagus £8.05
Pan-fried Calves Liver flamed in Vodka and finished with
Onion & White Wine Vinegar £8.75
Vegetable Tartlet on a pool of Stilton & Celery Sauce £6.95
Grilled 6oz Fillet Steak stuffed with Mussels in a Prawn
& Brandy Sauce £11.00
Duck Breast with Mango & Cream Sauce £12.95
Poached Salmon & Monkfish wrapped in Puff Pastry £9.95
Pork Escalope with a Creamy Wholegrain Mustard Sauce £9.95
Braised Lamb Neck Fillet in a Mint & Redcurrant Gravy £8.15
Char-grilled Chicken Suprême marinaded with Limes,
Ginger & Garlic £7.95
Seared Tuna Steak with Black Peppercorns on Creamed Potato
with Asparagus Sauce £9.95
8oz fillet steak £13.95     8oz sirloin steak £10.50

The Old Vine at Cousley Wood is a picturesque country inn on the border between Kent and East Sussex. Dating back to the 16th century, the heavily-beamed pub is full of period character and offers a choice of imaginative restaurant cuisine and more straightforward bar fayre.

The restaurant menu featured on the facing page is a mixture of the ten or so daily specials and the blackboard menu which, paradoxically, remains fairly static. In the bar area you can expect dishes such as Pan-fried Lamb's Liver with Bacon & Onion Gravy (£5.85), Baked Pepper stuffed with Rice, Lentils, Walnuts, Celery & Apple, topped with Onion Sauce (£5.75), Steak & Kidney Pie (£5.95) or Seafood Fettucini (£6.75). Their selection of speciality sausages (all priced at £5.25) are extremely popular - varieties include Wild Boar with Apple, Venison with Wild Mushroom & Cranberry, or perhaps the Boar & Bison Banger.

Directions: The Old Vine is easily found in the centre of the village of Cousley Wood, which lies approximately 5 miles to the south-east of Tunbridge Wells on the B2100 which links Lamberhurst to Wadhurst.

### USEFUL INFORMATION

**SERVING TIMES:**
Lunch 12pm-2.15pm (Mon-Sat)
12pm-2pm (Sunday)
Dinner 6.30pm-9.30pm (Mon-Sat)
7pm-9pm (Sunday)
**SEATING CAPACITY:** 45 in the restaurant, 60 in the bar
**C/C:** V, MC, S, D
**OFF-STREET PARKING:** yes

**NUMBER OF WINES:** 33
**HOUSE WINE:** £7.65
**RESERVATIONS:** advisable, especially at weekends
**CHILDREN:** welcome, but not in the restaurant after 8pm
**NO SMOKING** area available
**OUTDOOR EATING:** yes

# OCKENDEN MANOR
### Tel: (01444) 416111
Ockenden Lane, Cuckfield, West Sussex, RH17 5LD

*A selection from the à la carte*

Bisque of Chichester Crab and Cornish Mussels
enriched with Saffron and Cognac
**£6.50**

Six Whitstable Rock Oysters
served with Shallot Vinegar, Lemon and Buttered Wholemeal Bread
**£8.95**

Charlotte of Goat's Cheese and Provençale Vegetables
served on a coulis of Red, Yellow and Green Peppers
**£7.95**

Breast of Sussex Wood Pigeon
roasted, sliced and served on a Field Mushroom
filled with Tarragon Mousse, White Wine and Truffle Sauce
**£8.25**

~ ~ ~

Cutlet of Monkfish roasted and coated with a Saffron, Caper,
Tomato and Butter Sauce
**£18.50**

A Whole Scotch Lobster, dressed and served with Mayonnaise, Minted Jersey
Royal Potatoes and a Salad of Mixed Leaves and Garlic Croûtons
tossed in Red Wine Vinaigrette
**£32.50**

Haunch of Ashdown Venison, roasted, sliced and served on Celeriac and Potato
Rosti with Raspberry Vinegar and Butter Sauce
**£19.25**

The centre cut of Beef Fillet, pan-fried and served with puréed Shallots on
Madeira Wine and Truffle Sauce
**£27.95**

Puff Pastry Case filled with Goat's Cheese, Tomato and Thyme Fondue
and Black Olives
**£17.75**

Built as a private residence for the Michel family in 1520, Ockenden Manor is now an elegant hotel situated in its own gardens in the picturesque Tudor village of Cuckfield. The dining room itself, with original oak-panelling and a highly ornate painted ceiling, effuses the tasteful luxury of a bygone era. Service is warm yet reassuringly unobtrusive, and the modern English cuisine prepared by Head Chef Geoff Welch is quite superb.

In addition to the seasonal à la carte, a daily table d'hôte is offered at dinner (3 courses £29.50, and £32.50 on Saturday) and a monthly table d'hôte at luncheon (2/3 courses £15.50/18.50) - perhaps Home-cured Gravadlax with a Whitstable Rock Oyster and Pickled Cucumber to start, Skate Wing braised in Merrydown Cider with chopped Apple, Chives and Cream to follow, and Banana and Ginger Brûlée with Langue de Chat Biscuits to finish! The somewhat lighter garden menu (two courses £9.95) is only available during the more reliable English summer months (or should that be days?).

The à la carte desserts are £6.25 each, a selection of English farmhouse cheeses £7.25, and coffee with petits fours £3.50.

Directions: Cuckfield is a few miles west of Haywards Heath on the A272. Ockenden Manor is found at the end of Ockenden Lane which runs off the main high street in the middle of the village.

### USEFUL INFORMATION

**SERVING TIMES:**
Lunch 12.30pm-2pm (every day)
Dinner 7.30pm-9.30pm (Mon-Sat)
       7.30pm-9pm (Sunday)
**SEATING CAPACITY:** 45
**C/C:** V, MC, S, D, AE, DC
**OUTDOOR EATING:** yes
**DRESS CODE:** smart casual

**NUMBER OF WINES:** 200
**HOUSE WINE:** £12.50
**RESERVATIONS:** advisable, but compulsory at weekends
**OFF-STREET PARKING:** yes
**NO SMOKING** in the restaurant
**ACCOMMODATION:** 22 rooms
(B&B single £85, double fr £105)

# THE DOVE INN
Tel: (01227) 751360
Plum Pudding Lane, Dargate, Near Faversham, Kent, ME13 9HB

## BLACKBOARD SPECIALS

Cherry Tomato & Basil Soup £3.25
(D) Broad Bean, Leek & Bacon Soup £3.25
(D) Chicken Liver Parfait & Onion Marmalade £4.50
(D) Smoked Haddock Fishcakes £4.50
on a Lightly Curried Sauce
Salad of Avocado, Bacon & Spinach £4.25
(D) Pan-fried Crevettes & Garden Herbs £4.50
Grilled Goat's Cheese £3.95
with Plum Tomatoes & Pesto
Salad Niçoise £4.50

~ ~ ~ ~ ~

Braised Poussin Portuguese -style £8.50
Cold Poached Salmon with Plum Tomato £6.75
(D) Pan-fried Entrecote Steak £10.00
with Bacon & Mushroom Sauce
(D) Fillet of Salmon with Provençale Vegetables £8.50
(D) Roast Breast of Duck £11.00
on a Confit of Onion, Scented with Thyme
Poached Breast of Chicken £8.50
with Pasta & Parmesan
Whole Pan-fried Plaice £8.00
(D) Grilled Fillet of Swordfish £10.50
with Tomato & Sweet Pepper Coulis
Grilled Mackerel with Sun-dried Tomatoes £6.95

~ ~ ~ ~ ~

Parfait Nelusko £4.00
Iced Grand Marnier Soufflé £4.00
Orange & Lemon Crème Brûlée £3.25
Apricot Sorbet set in a Kirsch Parfait £4.00
Basket of Ice Cream or Sorbet with Seasonal Fruit £3.50

(D) indicates that the dish might be available only at dinner

It would be very easy to drive past this plain Victorian roadside pub, but that would be to miss out on some of Nigel Morris' excellent modern British cooking and his wife Bridget's warm welcome.

The Dove Inn is still very much a country pub with local drinkers mixing with the growing number of diners. It's best to book in advance since the dining area seats just twenty people.

Like the cooking the decor is unpretentious, with simple country furniture on wooden floors and old sepia prints telling the history of the pub on the walls. The menu is changing all the time (and tends to be somewhat shorter at lunch), depending on the quality of the fresh local produce on offer that day.

Directions: The Dove is located in the small village of Dargate, approximately 3 miles to the south-west of Whitstable. Simply follow the signposts to Dargate from the main A299 which links the M2 at junction 7 with Whitstable.

### USEFUL INFORMATION

**SERVING TIMES:**
Lunch 12pm-2pm (summer: every day)
      12pm-2pm (winter: Tues-Sat)
Dinner 7pm-9pm (Tues-Sat)
**CLOSED FOR FOOD:** Sun night and Mon night (summer); Sun night and all day Mon (winter, exc Bank Hols)
**SEATING CAPACITY:** 20

**NUMBER OF WINES:** 12
**HOUSE WINE:** £7.25
**C/C:** V, MC, S, D
**RESERVATIONS:** advisable
**OFF-STREET PARKING:** yes
**OUTDOOR EATING:** yes
**CHILDREN:** welcome
**NO WHEELCHAIR ACCESS**

# PARTNERS & SONS
Tel: (01306) 882826
2-4 West Street, Dorking, Surrey, RH4 1BL

Cappuccino of Roasted Lobster £ 4.95

Terrine of Baby Leeks, Smoked Trout and Smoked Eel
with a Spring Water Vinaigrette £ 5.95

Carpaccio of English Lamb rolled in Fresh Herbs
with Marinated and Roasted Mediterranean Vegetables £ 5.95

Char-grilled Fillet of Fresh Shark and Salsa Dressing and Rocket Salad £ 5.50

Millefeuille of Vegetables with a Saffron Dressing £ 5.50

A Salad of Crab towered with Roast Sweet Peppers £ 6.50

*****

Fillet of Wild Salmon on a Bed of Samphire with a Chervil Butter Sauce £ 15.50

Baked Whole Lemon Sole filled with a Crab Mousse with Sauce Vierge £ 17.95

Pavé of Scotch Beef with Dauphinoise Potatoes,
Creamed Parsley and a Balsamic Jus £ 15.50

Peppered Best End of Lamb with Puy Lentils
Parmesan Polenta and a Rich Mint Jus £ 16.50

Pan-fried Breast of Chicken with a Fondant Potato,
Summer Vegetables and Morel Mushrooms £ 14.95

Confit Leg and Roasted Breast of Duck
with Crispy Vegetables and an Orange and Jasmine Tea Sauce £ 15.95

Tranche of Calves' Liver with a Sauce of Lime £ 13.95

Open Lasagne of Tomato Salsa and Buffalo Mozzarella
surrounded with Baby Vegetables £ 7.95

*****

Char-grilled Fruit Salad with a Lemon Bavarois £ 4.95

Chocolate Teardrop filled with White Chocolate Mousse
served with Bitter Orange Sauce £ 5.50

Tulip Basket filled with Strawberry and Black Pepper Ice Cream £ 5.50

Tartlet of Gooseberries and Nuts with a Lemon Thyme Syrup £ 5.50

Poached and Glazed Tamarillos with a Passion Fruit Sorbet £ 4.95

Assiette of British Cheese £ 4.50

Partners & Sons has been open since March 1997 and is quickly gaining an excellent reputation for their brand of modern English cuisine "with a Mediterranean touch" - lots of virgin olive oil and herbs.

The oak beamed building dates from the 17th century and the restaurant operates on three floors (the ground floor is non-smoking). The walls, rag-rolled in a terracotta hue, are adorned with old prints and there are always fresh flowers on the tables.

The à la carte menu featured opposite changes every four to six weeks and is served for both luncheon and dinner. A seasonal midweek menu is also available, with a choice of three dishes at each course and a set price of £12.50 for two courses.

Directions: Partners & Sons is easily found on the one-way system in West Street, amongst the town's many antique shops.

## USEFUL INFORMATION

**SERVING TIMES:**
Lunch 12pm-2.30pm (Wed-Mon)
Dinner 7pm-10.30pm (Wed-Mon)
**CLOSED:** all day Tues
**SEATING CAPACITY:** 70
**C/C:** V, MC, S, D, AE, DC
**NO SMOKING** area available

**NUMBER OF WINES:** 53
**HOUSE WINE:** £11.00
**RESERVATIONS:** advisable
**OUTDOOR EATING:** no
**CHILDREN:** welcome
**OFF-STREET PARKING:** no, but the Waitrose car park is nearby

# THE GEORGE AND DRAGON
Tel: (01403) 741320
Dragons's Green, Shipley, near Horsham, West Sussex, RH13 7JE

## TODAY'S SPECIALS

### STARTERS

HOME-MADE CHICKEN & LEEK SOUP £2.25
CRISPY COATED MUSHROOMS & DIPS £3.25
DEEP-FRIED BRIE & CRANBERRY SAUCE £3.75
LARGE PRAWNS IN FILO PASTRY & DIP £5.95

*All the above are served with hot French bread*

### MAIN COURSES

ENGLISH ROAST BEEF & YORKSHIRE PUDDING, ROAST POTATOES & FRESH VEGETABLES £5.95
HALF SHOULDER OF ENGLISH ROAST LAMB, ROAST POTATOES & FRESH VEGETABLES £9.95
LAMB & APRICOT PIE, CHIPS & FRESH VEG £5.50
PORK CHOP WITH HONEY & MUSTARD SAUCE, CHIPS & VEG £5.50
BACON & ONION PLAIT, CHIPS & VEG £5.50
STEAK CASSEROLE, DUMPLING, NEW POTATOES & VEG £6.50
CHICKEN & MUSHROOM PIE, CHIPS & VEG £5.50
MIXED MEAT KEBABS, SALAD & CHIPS £6.50
CRISPY COATED CHICKEN BREAST WITH SWEET & SOUR SAUCE, RICE & SALAD £6.25
TUNA, SWEETCORN & CHEESE PASTA BAKE, SALAD & NEW POTATOES £5.50
COD IN BATTER, CHIPS & PEAS £5.25
MUSHROOM & SPINACH LASAGNE, SALAD & FRENCH BREAD £5.25
VEGGIE KORMA, SALAD, RICE & NAN BREAD £5.25

### HOME-MADE PUDDINGS

SPOTTED DICK, APPLE PIE, TREACLE & WALNUT TART, BANOFFI PIE, BAKEWELL TART
*All served with custard or cream* £2.25 each

A SELECTION OF SORBETS £2.50 each

Don't be put off by the large monumental cross and gravestone in the front garden, nor by its cheery history of the local boy with white hair and pink eyes who, falsely accused of theft, drowned himself. The George and Dragon is a wonderful, traditional country pub dating back to the 16th century. Still very much a local, it enjoys a healthy reputation for serving real ales and deliciously huge portions of home-made food.

A basic pub menu offering all the familiar favourites like jacket potatoes (from £2.50), sandwiches (from £1.60) and ploughmans (£4.25) is supplemented by blackboard daily specials, a selection from which is featured opposite.

I would also like to hereby vouch for their 'famously large home-made chips'. Let's just say, if you were to serve a proportionally sized fried egg with one, the yoke would be bigger than an average dinner plate. They are, however, delicious and so my advice would be don't eat for a week before ordering!

Directions: About six miles south of Horsham on the A24, take the A272 towards Billingshurst. After about a mile turn right following the signpost to Dragon's Green. Continue for about 500 yards and the pub is on the left.

### USEFUL INFORMATION

**SERVING TIMES:**
Lunch 12pm-2pm (Mon-Sat)
      12pm-3pm (Sunday)
Dinner 6.30pm-9.30pm (Mon-Sat)
**CLOSED:** Sunday evening
**SEATING CAPACITY:** 32
**C/C:** not accepted

**NUMBER OF WINES:** 15
**HOUSE WINE:** £6.50
**OUTDOOR EATING:** yes
**OFF-STREET PARKING:** yes
**CHILDREN:** welcome
**RESERVATIONS:** advisable

# THE CRICKETERS

Tel: (01798) 342473

Duncton, near Petworth, West Sussex, GU28 0LB

## BLACKBOARD SPECIALS

### STARTERS

Home-made Celery and Stilton Soup with Fresh Bread £2.50
Garlic Mushrooms on Toast £3.95
Smooth Chicken Liver Pâté with Toast £4.25
Crispy-coated Brie and Redcurrant Jelly £4.25
Deep-fried Whitebait £4.25
Salad Niçoise £4.50

### MAIN COURSES

Traditional Cod in Batter and Chips £6.75
Deep-fried Wholetail Breaded Scampi £7.25
Breast of Chicken with Bacon and Mushrooms £7.95
Roasted Salmon Fillet and Pink Peppercorn Sauce £8.95
Duncton Mill Trout with Beurre Blanc and Sun-dried Tomatoes £8.95
Crispy Duck with Shoestring Noodles and Stir-fried Vegetables £8.95
Smoked Haddock Fillet with Poached Egg & Grain Mustard Sauce £8.95
8oz Sirloin Steak £10.95   8oz Fillet Steak £13.95
Half Shoulder of Lamb with Rosemary and Redcurrant £11.50
Whole Fresh Mullet with Spring Onions and Ginger £9.95
Whole Lobster Salad £10.95
Fanned Avocado and King Prawns £8.50
Tiger Prawn Kebabs and Salad £6.95
Grilled Tuna Steak with a Parsley Butter Sauce £8.95

### PUDDINGS

Normandy Apple Tart £3.00     Gabriella's Pudding £3.00
Deep Apple Pie £3.00          Summer Pudding £3.00
French Pear Tart £3.00        Treacle Tart £3.00
Cheeseboard £3.75             Ice-Creams £2.75

The Cricketers is a 15th century traditional country pub in the heart of the South Downs which, as its name might suggest, has strong links with the game of cricket. Indeed, in Victorian times, it was once owned by John Wisden, founder of the famous almanac. Nowadays it is a monument to the sport, with various trophies, sets of cigarette cards, old prints and manuscripts adorning the walls.

The summer months see The Cricketers at its best, as the inn has one of the prettiest pub gardens in the country. Fresh food is high on the agenda and the blackboard menu opposite changes all the time, with less snacks and more of an à la carte feel in the evenings.

But beware! A word of advice for those of you visiting for the first time... if you own a mobile phone, leave it in the car. Your normally friendly and mild-mannered host bears an obsessive hatred of the annoying little things and can turn rather nasty.

Directions: The Cricketers is approximately 3 miles to the south of Petworth on the main A285 Petworth to Chichester road.

## USEFUL INFORMATION

**SERVING TIMES:**
Lunch 12pm-2pm (every day)
Dinner 6.30pm-9.30pm (Tues-Thur)
   7pm-9.30pm (Fri & Sat)
**CLOSED FOR FOOD:** Sunday night and Monday night
**SEATING CAPACITY:** 20 in the restaurant, 30 in the bar

**NUMBER OF WINES:** 35
**HOUSE WINE:** £8.95
**RESERVATIONS:** advisable
**OUTDOOR EATING:** yes
**C/C:** V, MC, S, D
**OFF-STREET PARKING:** yes
**CHILDREN:** welcome

# THE KENTISH RIFLEMAN
Tel: (01732) 810727
Dunks Green, near Tonbridge, Kent, TN11 9RU

*A selection from the evening menu*

## STARTERS

Soup of the Day...broccoli & courgette £2.50

Three Cheese Pasta - a hot dish of pasta in a rich cheddar and stilton sauce topped with parmesan £2.95

Mussels Provençale, served with crusty bread £2.95

Goujons of Plaice £2.95

## MAIN COURSES

10oz Prime Scottish Rump Steak £9.75

8oz Prime Scottish Fillet Steak £11.95

Lamb's Liver, pan-fried with bacon £6.95

Rifleman Steak - strips of fillet steak sautéed with bacon, mushrooms and onions and finished with red wine and cream £8.50

Dijon Chicken - boneless breast of chicken stuffed with cheese and coated with French Dijon mustard sauce £7.95

Chicken Fillets, sautéed with mango, peppers and ginger £7.95

Grilled Halibut Steak with lemon butter £8.95

Grilled Duck Breast with blackcurrant and burgundy sauce £8.95

Pork Tenderloin with a green peppercorn and mushroom sauce £7.95

Home-made Steak, Mushroom & Ale Pie £6.50

Served with a selection of vegetables or a mixed salad

The Kentish Rifleman is a traditional 16th century country inn with exposed beams and an open fire, enjoying a tranquil setting on a pretty village green in the heart of Kent.

Whilst still very much a pub for the local community, The Kentish Rifleman nevertheless has an excellent reputation for its food, and attracts customers from far afield. The evening menu shown opposite is supplemented by daily blackboard specials such as Avocado & Prawn Salad (£3.95) or Spinach & Ricotta Tortellini Provençale (£2.95) to start, and Grilled Lamb Chops glazed with Orange, Honey & Redcurrant (£7.95) to follow.

At lunchtime there is a bar menu offering a good range of lighter meals. These include ploughman's (£3.95), salads (£4.95) and sandwiches, as well as hot dishes like Scampi & Chips (£5.50). Lunch specials are again shown on the blackboard.

Directions: Head north from Tonbridge on the A227 and after about a mile, when the road bends sharply left, head straight on. Continue for about another mile. Go straight over the first crossroads, and the pub is a short distance further along on the right.

## USEFUL INFORMATION

**SERVING TIMES:**
Lunch 12pm-2pm (Tues-Sun)
Dinner 7pm-9.30pm (Tues-Sat)
**CLOSED:** Sunday evening and all day Monday
**SEATING CAPACITY:** 54
**C/C:** V, MC, S, D

**NUMBER OF WINES:** 18
**HOUSE WINE:** £7.50
**OFF-STREET PARKING:** yes
**RESERVATIONS:** advisable, but compulsory at weekends
**OUTDOOR EATING:** yes

# THE SUN INN
### Tel: (01483) 200242
The Common, Dunsfold, Surrey, GU8 4LE

## TYPICAL MIDWEEK MENU

Home-made Farmhouse Vegetable Soup  £2.75

Smoked Mackerel Terrine  £4.75
with toast & salad

Avocado Mousse  £4.75
with salad & tortilla chips

Welsh Rarebit  £3.25
with Guinness, cheese & mustard

\* \* \* \* \*

Chilled Chicken & Apricot Pie  £6.25
with new potatoes & crisp salad

Quiche Lorraine  £5.75
with french fries & a crisp salad

Shepherd's Pie  £6.50
served with fresh vegetables

Venison Sausages  £5.75
simmered in red wine, bacon & mushrooms
served with vegetables

Pork Steak Dijonnaise  £7.95
wine, cream & mustard served with vegetables

Prime Gammon Steak  £7.25
served with vegetables

Poached Fillet of Salmon  £8.25
nestled on a watercress sauce

Fresh Grilled Sea Bass  £7.95
with ginger, spring onions, soy sauce & garlic

Rump Steak  £10.95
charcoal-grilled with field mushrooms
served with french fries & vegetables

The Sun Inn is a pretty country pub on the picturesque village common at Dunsfold in the heart of the Surrey countryside. Its classical Georgian façade conceals the main dining area within, a 15th century converted barn with a vaulted ceiling. During the summer months, a marquee is erected in the garden to provide shade for diners.

The menu, which changes daily, is written up on a blackboard in the bar and tends to be slightly more exotic at weekends than during the rest of the week. Good home-made bar snacks are also available.

The pub hosts live music once a month, mostly jazz or blues. Since these events are generally planned ad hoc, it is best to telephone beforehand to find out when the bands will be playing.

Directions: The Sun Inn is located in Dunsfold, approximately 9 miles due south of Guildford and 2 miles to the east of Chiddingfold. The village is signposted from the A283, A281 and B2130.

## USEFUL INFORMATION

**SERVING TIMES:**
Lunch 12pm-2.15pm (Mon-Sat)
    12pm-2.30pm (Sunday)
Dinner 7pm-10pm (Mon-Sat)
    7pm-9.30pm (Sunday)
**SEATING CAPACITY:** 22 in the dining room, 46 in the bar
**C/C:** V, MC, AE

**NUMBER OF WINES:** 32
**HOUSE WINE:** £7.50
**OFF-STREET PARKING:** yes
**RESERVATIONS:** advisable at the weekend & Bank Holidays
**CHILDREN:** welcome
**OUTDOOR EATING:** yes

# THE DOWNLAND HOTEL
Tel: (01323) 732689
37 Lewes Road, Eastbourne, East Sussex, BN21 2BU

## A La Carte Dinner Menu

### Starters

Salad of seared beef, green beans & truffle, hazelnut vinaigrette £7.50
Assiette gourmande of smoked salmon & langoustine, crême fraîche £7.50
Cannelloni of lobster & snapper, beurre blanc £6.50
Millefeuille of foie gras & roast shallot, wild mushroom jus £9.50
Bavarois of goats cheese & bacon, balsamic tomato & rocket salad £4.50
Ballotine of chicken & asparagus, warm stilton sauce £5.00
Cup of melon & exotica, syrup of armagnac £4.50
Today's soup £3.50

### Main Courses

Seared turbot & red mullet, saffron risotto, roast vegetables £14.50
Trellis of salmon, sole & seabass, saffron risotto, peppercorn hollandaise £15.50
Sauté of lobster & mediterranean prawns, cheese sabayon, ravioli of wild mushroom £22.50
Noisettes of venison, port wine & black pepper jus, caramelised shallots, foie gras £16.50
Fillet of lamb, mint & courgette crust, devilled couscous £14.50
Breast of duckling filled with raspberries, glazed with black pepper & caramel, sauce cassis £15.00
Grilled fillet of beef, fried leeks & shiitake, mustard sauce £15.50
Rosette of chicken & stilton, with seared bacon & polenta medallions £13.00

### Desserts

Basket of fruits with lemon sorbet, vanilla & nutmeg ice cream £4.00
Lemon tart with sauce cassis £4.00
Warm chocolate mousse with toffee ice cream £4.00
Mango crème brûlée with sweet lime syrup £4.00
Warm banana liqueur sponge, Galliano sauce £4.00

# EASTBOURNE

At first sight you could be forgiven for thinking that this quintessentially English seaside hotel has been included in this guide by mistake. Despite its residential location and rather plain exterior, The Downland Hotel is in fact home to one of the area's best restaurants.

Neither should you allow yourself to be alarmed by the owners' large collection of headgear as you sip your pre-dinner drink in the bar. One glance at the à la carte menu on the facing page should be sufficient to put your mind at rest and, once your curiosity has been aroused, Patrick Faulkner's modern British cooking will tempt you back time after time.

As Patrick so modestly puts it, *"your initial expectations might be lower, but then you'll be blown away by my food"*. Quite.

Directions: From London or Brighton, take the A22 towards Eastbourne. At the Willingdon roundabout follow the sign to the "Seafront" and the hotel is roughly 2 miles further along this road.

## USEFUL INFORMATION

**SERVING TIMES:**
Dinner 6.30pm-9pm (Tues-Sat)
**CLOSED:** every lunchtime and all day Sunday and Monday
**SEATING CAPACITY:** 35
**C/C:** V, MC, D, AE, DC
**OFF-STREET PARKING:** yes

**NUMBER OF WINES:** 38
**HOUSE WINE:** £9.95
**RESERVATIONS:** essential
**OUTDOOR EATING:** no
**CHILDREN:** over 10 yrs only
**ACCOMMODATION:** 14 rooms
(B&B sgl fr £37.50, dbl fr £59)

# GRAVETYE MANOR
### Tel: (01342) 810567
Near East Grinstead, West Sussex, RH19 4LJ

## First Courses

*Thai Spiced Fish Soup*    £12.50
with shellfish, squid ink noodles and bean sprout stir-fry.

*Ballotine of Foie Gras*    £16.00
green bean salad, spicy orange reduction and toasted brioche.

*Goat's Cheese and Hazelnut Ravioli*    £11.00
baby spinach, spiced tomato and apple crisps.

*Sweet Pepper Tian with Roast Hebridean Scallops*    £15.00
balsamic and basil oil dressing.

*Light Tomato Jelly*    £12.50
with summer vegetables, truffle and pea sprout.

## Main Courses

*Roast Native Lobster*    £29.50
with tortellinis, ginger braised vegetables and white Port sauce.

*Pan-Fried Fillets of John Dory*    £24.50
crushed crab potatoes, tomato, red pepper and basil purées.

*Trio of Iranian Caviars*    £48.00
with warm new potatoes, marinated salmon and crème fraîche, or served traditionally.

*Warm Tartlet of Forest Mushrooms*    £18.00
with quail eggs, creamed leeks, asparagus and Madeira.

*Roast Rump of Lamb*    £25.00
spiced couscous, baby aubergines with lamb sauce and rosemary oil.

*Young Roast Pigeon*    £23.00
ravioli of forest mushrooms, Parma ham and sage.

## Desserts

*Baked Lemon Soufflé Pudding*    £9.00
local double cream.

*Tian of Dark Chocolate with Mascarpone*    £10.50
raspberries and crisp fraise biscuits.

*Gravetye's Home-made Ice Creams and Sorbets*    £6.50

Gravetye Manor is a 16th century Elizabethan stone mansion that occupies a glorious site with fine southerly views. William Robinson, one of the greatest gardeners of all time, bought the manor and the 1,000 acres on which it stands in 1884 and it was here that he pioneered the English Natural Garden.

Gravetye is now a luxurious country house hotel and proud member of Relais et Chateaux. Their restaurant is one of the very best to be found in the English countryside, where head chef Mark Raffan inspires "thoroughly modern cuisine with a classic touch".

In addition to the selection from the *carte* opposite, two three-course fixed price menus with a choice of three dishes at each course are offered, costing £24 for luncheon and £30 for dinner (VAT is *excluded* from all prices).

Directions: From the M23 take exit 10 onto the A264 towards East Grinstead. After 2 miles, at the roundabout, take the 3rd exit (B2028) signposted to Haywards Heath and Brighton. Pass through Turners Hill and Gravetye Manor will be signposted to your left.

## USEFUL INFORMATION

**SERVING TIMES:**
Lunch 12.30pm-1.45pm (every day)
Dinner 7pm-9.30pm (Mon-Sat)
   7pm-9pm (Sunday)
**SEATING CAPACITY:** 40
**C/C:** V, MC, S, D
**OFF-STREET PARKING:** yes
**NO SMOKING** in the restaurant
**OUTDOOR EATING:** no

**NUMBER OF WINES:** 500
**HOUSE WINE:** £16.50
**RESERVATIONS:** essential
**CHILDREN:** welcome (over 7 yrs)
**DRESS CODE:** jacket and tie preferred in the evening
**ACCOMMODATION:** 18 rooms (from £140 + VAT per room)

# TOTTINGTON MANOR
Tel: (01903) 815757
Edburton, near Henfield, Sussex, BN5 9LJ

### A selection from the A La Carte

### STARTERS

| | |
|---|---|
| FRESH ASPARAGUS either with Hollandaise, Butter or Sundried Tomato Vinaigrette | £5.80 |
| CAESAR SALAD prepared at your table with Anchovies, Smoked Bacon, Croûtons and Shaved Parmesan Cheese and Caesar Dressing | £4.75 |
| CHICKEN SATAY Skewers of Chicken in spicy Peanut Sauce, chargrilled | £4.85 |
| SEARED SCALLOPS resting on young Spinach Leaves with Smoked Bacon and Garlic Butter | £7.40 |
| CURED ITALIAN HAM with Seasonal Melon and Ground Ginger or with Rocket and Shaved Parmesan | £5.80 |
| MILLEFEUILLE OF WHITE CRAB MEAT layered with Springs finest Oak Smoked Salmon in a Brandy flavoured Marie Rose Sauce | £7.15 |
| WARM DUCK CONFIT on a Salad of Fine Beans and Baby Beetroot | £4.85 |
| SHELLFISH BISQUE a rich Lobster and Crab Soup enhanced with Cognac, Spring Onions and Crab Parcels | £4.40 |

### MAIN COURSE SALADS

| | |
|---|---|
| SMOKED SALMON, CRAB AND PRAWN SALAD Slices of Springs Smoked Oak Salmon with White Crab Meat and peeled Tiger Prawns served with Marie Rose Sauce and Granary Bread | £13.50 |
| VEGETARIAN SALAD Fresh Asparagus with roasted Mediterranean Vegetables Mozzarella & marinated Black Olives served with Garlic & Parmesan Bread | £9.20 |

### MAIN COURSES

| | |
|---|---|
| ROQUEFORT, SOUR CREAM AND ONION TART with a warm salad of Cherry Tomatoes and New Potatoes | £7.80 |
| WARM SALMON AND CRAB SAUSAGE resting on young Spinach Leaves with Fennel and Ginger Sauce and turned New Potatoes | £9.40 |
| DEEP-FRIED GOUJONS OF BRILL TEMPURA with a roasted red pepper purée accompanied by Tempura Vegetables with Chilli Sauce | £10.80 |
| ESCALOPE OF VEAL chargrilled, served with Lemon, Asparagus and Minted New Potatoes | £13.95 |
| MARINATED LEG OF LAMB Truffled Potatoes, Savoury Beef Tomato with Aubergine, Creamed Spinach, Red Wine, Rosemary and Garlic Jus | £13.40 |
| 10oz PRIME SCOTTISH RIB-EYE STEAK Chargrilled with Tomato, Mushrooms, Onion Rings, Jacket Potato or French Fries | £12.95 |
| CALVES LIVER pan-fried with Sage, Red Onion Marmalade and Bubble and Squeak | £11.40 |
| 8oz PRIME SCOTTISH FILLET STEAK topped with Blue Cheese, Red Wine Sauce, deep-fried Onion Rings, Anna Potatoes and Fine Green Beans | £14.25 |

A SELECTION OF FRESH FISH DISHES ARE AVAILABLE DAILY

Tottington Manor is a beautiful 16th century family-run hotel which boasts an excellent reputation for the quality of chef proprietor David Miller's cuisine, and the relaxed and friendly atmosphere in which it may be enjoyed. The tastefully extended restaurant is complemented by magnificent views over the South Downs.

A small selection from the extensive lunchtime à la carte is shown opposite (a reduced version is offered in the evening), and variety comes in the form of daily blackboard specials which incorporate game in season and lots of fresh fish and seafood. A table d'hôte menu (2 or 3 courses at £20.50 or £25, including a half bottle of house wine) is also offered at dinner, and this changes every two or three days.

A weekly dessert menu may feature Passion Fruit Mousse with Fresh Mango and Passion Fruit Coulis (£4.80), Dark and White Chocolate Truffle Torte with Raspberries and Cassis (£5), or Treacle Tart and Ice Cream (£4).

Directions: Only 7 miles away from Brighton, Edburton is signposted off the A2037 about 3 miles south of Henfield.

## USEFUL INFORMATION

**SERVING TIMES:**
Lunch 12pm-2pm (Mon-Sat)
    12pm-2.30pm (Sunday)
Dinner 7pm-9.15pm (Mon-Sat)
**CLOSED:** Sunday evening
**SEATING CAPACITY:** 4 dining areas seating 55, 45, 25, & 12 respectively
**C/C:** V, MC, S, D, AE, DC
**NO SMOKING** tables available

**NUMBER OF WINES:** 80
**HOUSE WINE:** £9.95
**OFF-STREET PARKING:** yes
**RESERVATIONS:** advisable
**CHILDREN:** only over 5 years
**OUTDOOR EATING:** yes
**DRESS CODE:** smart
**ACCOMMODATION:** 6 rooms
(B&B single fr £45, double fr £65)

# HAXTED MILL
Tel: (01732) 862914
Haxted Road, Edenbridge, Kent, TN8 6PU

### Appetisers

| | |
|---|---|
| Soup of the day | £3.75 |
| Sautéed scallops with garlic | £7.50 |
| Mussels with bacon, leeks & cream | £5.25 |
| Char-grilled whole prawns with lime - coriander marinade | £7.25 |
| Crab & avocado tian | £5.95 |
| Deep-fried goats' cheese | £5.25 |
| Anti pasto, mozzarella, ham, artichokes, olives & asparagus | £5.75 |
| Roast red peppers, tomato, basil & mozzarella tart | £4.75 |
| Lasagne of scallops & prawns | £7.25 |
| Home-made pâté with onion marmalade | £5.75 |
| Hot chicken liver & bacon salad | £5.25 |
| Smoked salmon | £5.75 |

### Pasta

| | |
|---|---|
| Spaghetti, bacon & parmesan cheese | £4.25/5.75 |
| Tagliatelle, leeks, mushrooms & cream | £4.25/5.75 |

### Fresh Fish, Seafood & Meat

| | |
|---|---|
| Grilled fi lobster with lemon chive sauce | £14.95 |
| Char-grilled fish of the day flamed in pernod & bronze fennel | £11.95 |
| Casserole of seafood Thai style | £15.00 |
| Sautéed monkfish tail with dill | £13.95 |
| Seared fillet of salmon, tomato & coriander salsa | £9.95 |
| Lemon sole simply sautéed in the pan, beurre blanc | £10.95 |
| Fruits de mer, crab, lobster, langoustines, prawns & shrimps | £17.00 |
| Sautéed filet mignon, girolles port sauce | £15.00 |
| Char-grilled marinated chicken breast with oregano & lemon | £9.95 |
| Grilled rump of lamb, mint & basil pesto | £11.95 |
| Casserole of Tuscan squab, smoked bacon, and mushrooms in a red wine sauce | £14.95 |
| Sautéed lamb's liver, crispy fried onions & mash potatoes | £10.95 |

### Desserts

| | |
|---|---|
| Blackberry & apple pie with vanilla ice cream | £5.00 |
| Chocolate, orange mousse with chocolate tuille | £5.00 |
| Raspberry pithivier | £5.00 |
| Lemon sorbet with a shot of vodka | £4.00 |
| Sticky walnut tart with vanilla ice cream | £4.50 |

During the summer this already popular brasserie really buzzes with atmosphere, as the large terrace overflows with diners enjoying great food and the idyllic riverside setting next to the historic Haxted Mill. However, if you do reserve an outside table rather than one inside, be warned, for in the words of owner David Peak 'if it pours with rain, don't show up because you haven't got a table'. Though I'm not sure that he used the word 'pours'!

Originally the barns that serviced the old mill, the upstairs dining area with its uncomplicated chairs, tables and place settings has a deliberately simple charm. Fish and seafood, for which the restaurant is particularly renowned, are bought on a daily basis, as are all the vegetables and salads. The single menu has a seasonal flavour to it but actually changes weekly, and in the summer lighter lunches are also offered. Sunday lunch is a set menu with two or three courses (£10.95 and £15.95).

The home-made desserts are delicious, the coffee (£1.10) is to die for, and the wine list is appropriately imaginative. I was recommended the Fat Bastard Chardonnay, but maybe they were just trying to tell me something.

Directions: From Edenbridge High Street or the B2028 follow the signs to Haxted Mill.

### USEFUL INFORMATION

**SERVING TIMES:**
Lunch 12pm-2pm (Tues-Sun)
Dinner 7pm-10pm (Tues-Sat)
**CLOSED:** Sunday evening and all day Monday
**SEATING CAPACITY:** 50 in the winter, 90 in the summer
**C/C:** V, MC, S, D
**OUTDOOR EATING:** yes

**NUMBER OF WINES:** 60
**HOUSE WINE:** £8.95
**OFF-STREET PARKING:** yes
**CHILDREN:** welcome
**WHEELCHAIR ACCESS** to the downstairs and terrace only
**RESERVATIONS:** advisable, but compulsory at weekends & during the summer months

# HONOURS MILL RESTAURANT
Tel: (01732) 866757
87 High Street, Edenbridge, Kent, TN8 5AU

### Three Course Menu at £32.75

**Chilled Tomato and Basil Soup**
with Fresh Water Crayfish Tails
**Warm Sausage of Smoked Haddock and Dill**
with a Mild Curry Sauce
**Terrine of Foie Gras**
with a Port Jelly
**Sautéed Squid and Shellfish**
with Roast Tomatoes, drizzled with a Green Basil Olive Oil
**Blinis**
with Smoked Salmon and Soured Cream topped with Caviar
**Marinated Salmon**
on a bed of Summer Leaves with a Poached Egg
**Fish and Shellfish**
depending on the market of the day

### MAIN COURSES

**Medallion of Tuna**
Spiced and Seared with a Fresh Lime Sauce
**Grilled Scotch Rib of Beef**
with Red Wine and Wild Mushrooms
**Sautéed Magret of Duck**
on a Confit and Foie Gras Mash with a Raspberry Vinegar Sauce
**Best End of Lamb**
with a Rosemary and Lemon Stuffing wrapped in Puff Pastry
**Poached Breast of Chicken**
Stuffed with a Chicken Mousse and Lobster
with a Fresh Water Crayfish and Butter Sauce
**Fricassé of Rabbit**
with morrels, Shallots and Garlic

### DESSERTS

**Platter of French and English Cheeses**
or
**Selection from the Dessert Menu**

### COFFEE AND PETITS FOURS

Bought eleven years ago, proprietor Neville Goodhew has transformed a derelict mill into a quite stunning restaurant. The immaculate downstairs bar and lounge area is full of character, complete with brick floors, exposed beams and a wooden balcony overlooking a lily-covered mill pond. As if that is not enough, the original mill wheels have been restored like a museum exhibit and now sit proudly behind glass in the central spiral staircase which leads up to the beautiful dining area.

The cuisine is modern French and menus range from a very good value lunchtime table d'hôte (3 courses £15.50 available Tuesday to Friday) to the more expensive seasonal à la carte featured opposite. An evening table d'hôte also runs during the week (3 courses £26) but includes a half bottle of house wine. Both of these set menus change every two weeks. There is also a seasonal Sunday lunch (3 course £23.50).

Seasonal desserts may include Rhubarb Tart with an Almond flavoured Egg Custard, A light Vanilla Bavarois served with fresh Peaches, or a Crème Brûlée of Raspberries.

Directions: Easily found at the bottom end of Edenbridge High Street.

## USEFUL INFORMATION

**SERVING TIMES:**
Lunch 12.15pm-2pm (Tues-Fri, + Sun)
Dinner 7.15pm-10pm (Tues-Sat)
**CLOSED:** all day Monday, and Saturday lunch and Sunday evening
**SEATING CAPACITY:** 38
**C/C:** V, MC, S, D
**OFF-STREET PARKING:** no

**NUMBER OF WINES:** 150
**HOUSE WINE:** £10.15
**OUTDOOR EATING:** no, but drinks may be taken on the balcony
**RESERVATIONS:** advisable
**CHILDREN:** welcome
**NO WHEELCHAIR ACCESS**

# THE WOOLPACK
Tel: (01252) 703106
Elstead, near Godalming, Surrey, GU8 6HD

## *Starters*

Home-made cream of broccoli soup with bread  £2.75
Hot breaded Camembert with port & cranberry sauce  £4.75
Baked goat's cheese served with garlic, mango & chives  £4.75
Mushroom stroganoff served with paprika, wine & cream  £4.75
Shell-on prawns in chilli & garlic butter  £4.75
Deep-fried calamari served with garlic mayonnaise  £4.50
Local smoked trout served with salad & bread  £4.50
Avocado served with prawns & crabsticks, salad & bread  £4.75
Mussels in herb & garlic butter  £4.50
Farmhouse pâté served with salad & bread  £4.25
Home-made hummus served with pitta bread & salad  £3.95
Mustard-breaded turkey strips with orange & cranberry  £4.75
Scottish smoked salmon served with bread & salad  £5.95
Seafood bowl with prawns & crabsticks, salad & bread  £4.75

## *Main Courses*

Chicken tikka served with rice, salad, pitta & dippy-dippy  £7.25
Lamb steak in red Martini, ginger & orange  £8.95
Gammon steak in rum, pineapple & peppers  £8.75
Turkey escalope in vermouth, tarragon & mushrooms  £8.95
Pork korma (mild, contains nuts)  £6.95
Chicken casseroled in sweet basil, coconut & lime  £6.95
Lamb casseroled in port, thyme & mushrooms  £6.95
Macaroni served with creamy vegetables, salad & bread  £6.50
Lemon sole in pernod & fennel  £8.95
Beef casseroled in Guinness & orange  £6.95
Rump steak, plain  £10.50
Rump steak with Stilton & mustard sauce  £12.00

The Woolpack at Elstead has long been regarded as one of *the* dining pubs in the area and, judging by the number of meals they serve each week, it has lost none of its appeal. The 18th century building is divided into three main dining areas which seat over one hundred guests in comfort and there is a pretty garden with picnic tables for outdoor eating during the summer months.

Although it is busy most of the time (it's worth noting that you are not allowed to book tables), the atmosphere is relaxed and friendly. The menu (a typical example of what's on offer appears on the facing page) is chalked up on a large blackboard next to the salad bar, where more straightforward bar food such as ploughmans and jacket potatoes are served.

The chef's traditional home-made pies, such as Steak & Kidney, Chicken & Ham or Cod & Prawn, are perennial favourites. All are served with a choice of three fresh vegetables and cost £7.10 each.

Directions: The Woolpack is easily found in the centre of Elstead on the B3001, which links the A3 (about 5 miles south-west of Guildford) with Farnham.

### USEFUL INFORMATION

**SERVING TIMES:**
Lunch 12pm-2pm (every day)
Dinner 7pm-9.45pm (Mon-Sat)
7pm-9pm (Sun)
**SEATING CAPACITY:** 100+
**C/C:** V, MC, S, D, AE, DC

**NUMBER OF WINES:** 26
**HOUSE WINE:** £5.25 (fi litre)
**RESERVATIONS:** not available
**OUTDOOR EATING:** yes
**OFF-STREET PARKING:** yes
**CHILDREN:** welcome

# THE ELSTED INN
Tel: (01730) 813662
Elsted Marsh, Near Midhurst, West Sussex, GU29 0JT

## DAILY MENU

**Starters & Small Dishes**
Creamy Onion Soup £3.00
Smoked Salmon Pâté £4.00
Garlic Mushrooms £3.75
Stuffed Garlic Mushrooms £3.75
Egg Florentine £3.75
Coronation Chicken £5.00
Italian Salami Platter £5.00
Mixed Rollmops £5.00
Greek Salad £5.00
Salad Niçoise £5.00
Macaroni Cheese £4.50
Chilli & Toast £5.00

**Large & Small Dishes**
New Green Mussels with Garlic or Cheese £5.50/£11.00
King Prawns with Garlic or Lemon £5.75/£11.50
Smoked Salmon as starter £5.75
Large with Salad £10.25

**Desserts £3.50**
Banana Mousse with Raspberry Coulis
Bread & Butter Pudding
Marlborough Tart
Chocolate Mousse
Fresh Fruit Pavlova
Strawberries & Cream

**Main Dishes**
Fresh Lemon Sole £8.95
Large Local Trout £8.75
Fresh Selsey Crab Salad or Gratin £8.25
Spaghetti Vongole £7.50
Pasta Provençale £7.50
Spinach & Mushroom Roulade £7.50
Meaty Stuffed Marrow £7.50
Turkey & Mushroom Casserole £7.50
Beef with Red Wine £7.50
Beef in Beer Pie £7.75
Braised Lamb's Liver & Bacon £7.50
Sausages with Mustard Sauce £7.50
Lamb with Courgette & Mint £7.50
Guinea Fowl with Port Wine Sauce £8.50
Roast Lamb with Garlic & Rosemary £7.50
Lasagne & Salad £7.50
Salad Board (Ham, Beef, Lamb or Salmon) £7.50
Pan-fried Lamb's Kidneys with Mustard & Port £7.75

**Home-made Ice Creams**
**£2.50**

The Elsted Inn is a traditional Sussex country pub that serves good home-made dishes using locally produced ingredients wherever possible. The style of food has been loosely described as "Granny cooking" and the blackboard menu can change as much as twice a day. The pub is divided into two friendly and cosy bars with simple country furniture on wooden floors (one exclusively for diners and the other very much still a meeting-place for locals).

They serve a wide choice of local game, their cream is Jersey cream from a local farm (who also supply the asparagus and soft fruits in season), the bread is hand-made at the National Trust bakery at Slindon, local sausages come from Ron, eggs are free-range only, the wholemeal flour is ground at the mill at the Weald and Down Museum, chickens and ducks are mostly free-range from a local farm, the hams are home-cooked in the pub (and served in decent slices, not slivers) and real mutton in the Winter "comes courtesy of my aunt's noble herd of Jacob's sheep in Hampshire".

Directions: From Midhurst take the A272 towards Petersfield. After about 3 miles, take the left turning to Elsted and Harting. The pub is located in Elsted Marsh, just under 2 miles further along this road, on the left just before the railway bridge.

### USEFUL INFORMATION

**SERVING TIMES:**
Lunch 12pm-2pm (every day)
Dinner 7pm-9.30pm (Mon-Thur)
  7pm-10pm (Fri & Sat)
  7pm-9pm (Sun)
**SEATING CAPACITY:** 24 in the dining room, 20 in the bar
**C/C:** V, MC, S, D

**NUMBER OF WINES:** 17
**HOUSE WINE:** £8.95
**RESERVATIONS:** essential
**OFF-STREET PARKING:** yes
**OUTDOOR EATING:** yes
**CHILDREN:** welcome
**ACCOMMODATION:** will be available soon - please ring

# THE WINDMILL INN
Tel: (01483) 277566
Pitch Hill, Ewhurst, Surrey, GU6 7NN

## Starters

Carrot and Orange Soup £3.25
*served with Crusty Bread*

Scottish Smoked Salmon and Asparagus Roulades £4.75

Millefeuille of Sea Scallops £6.95
*on a Pool of Ginger Cream Sauce*

Pan-fried Foie Gras £5.95
*topped with Wild Mushrooms served on a piece of Fried Bread*

Grilled Goats' Cheese rolled in Almonds £4.95
*served on a bed of Mixed Leaves*

Warm Chicken and Bacon Salad £4.20
*drizzled in Wholegrain Mustard Dressing*

Fanned Avocado £3.95
*with a Strawberry Vinaigrette*

## Main Course

Local Marinated Venison £11.50
*served with a Berry Coulis*

Oven-roasted Duck Breast £15.20
*served with Baked Plums and garnished with Sweet Potatoes*

8oz Beef Fillet £19.00
*served with Wild Mushrooms and Truffle Sauce*

Local Rainbow Trout Fillet £11.75
*with Cauliflower and Onion au Gratin on a bed of Lemon Noodles*

Beef Steak Tomato £8.50
*on a bed of Vine Leaves stuffed with Stir-fried Vegetables and garnished with Sautéed Potatoes*

Roasted Chicken Breast £12.50
*stuffed with Brie, served with a Cheese and Leek Sauce and sprinkled with Smoked Salmon*

Monkfish served with Scallops £13.95
*in a Cream Sauce garnished with Asparagus Spears*

The Windmill Inn is an isolated country pub with stunning panoramic views across the Weald of Sussex. On exceptionally clear days the locals claim that you can see the English Channel in the distance through "Worthing Gap". The day of my visit I had stupidly forgotten to bring along my Patrick Moore telescope kit, so I wouldn't know.

The modern conservatory restaurant makes the most of its wonderful views and offers a good choice of home-made dishes. In season game is a speciality with venison, rabbit and pheasant bagged by the owners themselves.

The bar food menu is also worthy of a mention, comprising a mixture of imaginative dishes, such as Duck with Orange & Peach Sauce (£6.00), and more standard ones, such as Steak and Kidney Pie (£5.50), King Prawns with Garlic Butter (£7.50) or Toad in the Hole (£4.95).

Directions: Ewhurst is approximately 6 miles south-east of Guildford. To get to The Windmill, take the B2127 from Cranleigh towards Ewhurst and Forest Green. At the roundabout just after Ewhurst, go straight across (signposted to Shere) and the pub is fl mile along this road on your left.

### USEFUL INFORMATION

**RESTAURANT SERVING TIMES:**
Lunch 12pm-2.30pm (Wed-Fri)
    12pm-3pm (Sat-Sun)
Dinner 7.30pm-9.30pm (Tues-Sat)
**RESTAURANT CLOSED:** Sun night, all day Monday, and Tues lunch
(bar snacks every day except Sun night)
**SEATING CAPACITY:** 32 in the restaurant, 40 in the bar

**NUMBER OF WINES:** 50
**HOUSE WINE:** £8.95
**C/C:** V, MC, S, D
**RESERVATIONS:** advisable, but essential at weekends
**OFF-STREET PARKING:** yes
**OUTDOOR EATING:** yes
**CHILDREN:** welcome

# SEVENS

Tel: (01252) 715345

7 The Borough, Farnham, Surrey, GU9 7NA

## A SELECTION FROM THE A LA CARTE MENU

| | |
|---|---|
| GRILLED SARDINES WITH LIME VINAIGRETTE | £ 3.50 |
| PATE OF THE DAY | £ 3.25 |
| MEDITERRANEAN PRAWNS WITH AIOLI | £ 4.25 |
| DEEP-FRIED FISH GOUJONS WITH HOME-MADE TARTARE SAUCE | £ 3.80 |
| DEEP FRIED BRIE WITH CRANBERRY SAUCE | £ 3.30 |
| WARM CHICKEN LIVERS ON A BED OF LETTUCE WITH RASPBERRY VINAIGRETTE | £ 3.75 |
| STUFFED MUSHROOMS WITH STILTON AND WALNUTS | £ 3.50 |
| SEVENS' CAESAR SALAD | £ 3.25 |
| DIM SUM WITH ORIENTAL DIP | £ 3.75 |
| POTATO SKINS WITH TOMATO AND MOZZARELLA | £ 3.20 |

\*\*\*\*\*\*\*\*\*\*\*\*\*\*\*\*\*\*\*\*\*\*\*\*\*\*\*\*\*\*\*\*\*\*\*\*\*\*

| | |
|---|---|
| WARM CHICKEN SALAD WITH A LEMON DRESSING | £ 6.50 |
| FILLET OF PORK IN BRANDY CREAM AND GREEN PEPPERCORN SAUCE | £ 7.75 |
| THAI SPICED FISH ON A BED OF FRESH PASTA | £ 6.75 |
| WARM LEEK AND CHEESE TARTLET WITH TOMATO COULIS | £ 5.25 |
| PENNE ARRABIATA (SPICY TOMATO, CHILLI AND BASIL) | £ 5.25 |
| CHARCOAL GRILLED LAMB STEAK MARINATED IN LEMON, GARLIC AND ROSEMARY | £ 8.25 |
| GRILLED FILLET OF SALMON IN A PRAWN AND DILL SAUCE | £ 6.75 |
| CHARCOAL GRILLED SIRLOIN STEAK WITH GARLIC BUTTER | £ 8.75 |
| WITH PEPPER SAUCE | £ 9.75 |
| ROAST DUCK IN A MARSALA AND CHERRY SAUCE | £ 9.75 |
| CHARCOAL GRILLED BREAST OF CHICKEN WITH TARRAGON AND LIME BUTTER ON A BED OF WILD RICE | £ 6.95 |
| BEEF WELLINGTON WITH A BEARNAISE SAUCE | £11.50 |

\*\*\*\*\*\*\*\*\*\*\*\*\*\*\*\*\*\*\*\*\*\*\*\*\*\*\*\*\*\*\*\*\*\*\*\*\*\*

| | |
|---|---|
| SELECTION OF SWEETS | £ 2.50 |

Despite the inexorable rise of the "gastro-chains" in Farnham, one independent eatery has stood its ground for over 20 years. Sevens is a family-run wine bar and bistro housed in an 18th century beamed black-and-white building in the centre of town. The downstairs bar is air-conditioned and leads through to a well-hidden garden where barbecues are served during the summer.

The upstairs bistro/restaurant is well known locally for its steaks, fresh fish and vegetarian specialities. The à la carte menu featured opposite is changed every four weeks and is supplemented by evening specials such as Char-grilled Mahi Mahi (£8.75 - a meaty white fish from New Zealand) or Grilled Red Bream and Red Pesto (£7.50).

Directions: Sevens can be found in the centre of town on the principal shopping thoroughfare.

## USEFUL INFORMATION

**SERVING TIMES:**
Lunch 12pm-2.30pm (Mon-Sat)
Dinner 6.30pm-10.30pm (Mon-Thur)
6.30pm-11pm (Fri, Sat)
**CLOSED:** all day Sunday
**SEATING CAPACITY:** 80 in the restaurant, 30 in the bar
**C/C:** V, MC, S, D

**NUMBER OF WINES:** 80
**HOUSE WINE:** £8.40
**RESERVATIONS:** advisable
**OFF-STREET PARKING:** no
**NO WHEELCHAIR ACCESS**
**NO SMOKING** area available
**CHILDREN:** welcome
**OUTDOOR EATING:** yes

# THE ALBION TAVERN
### Tel: (01795) 591411
Front Brents, Faversham Creek, Faversham, Kent, ME13 7DH

## A SELECTION FROM THE BLACKBOARD

### Starters & Snacks

Fish Soup, Aioli & Croûtons £3.25
Fresh Smoked Mackerel £3.25
Roquefort & Nut Terrine £3.25
Mixed Leaf Salad & Toasted Goats Cheese £4.25
Warm Salad of Squid & Garlic £4.50
New Zealand Garlic Mussels garnished with Garlic Butter £4.50
Warm Salad of Chicken Livers with Wild Mushrooms £4.25
Mushroom & Prawn in a Chilli & Coriander Sauce £4.25
Smoked Trout Fillet with Lemon, Cucumber & Yoghurt £4.25
Smoked Haddock & Asparagus Pancake in a Cream Sauce £4.25
Warm Salad of Black Pudding with Parma Ham & Walnut £4.25

### Main Courses

Monkfish, Crab & Spinach Wellington with a Seafood & Tomato Sauce £11.75
Local Dressed Crab served with New Potatoes & Salad £8.25
A Variety of 3 Sausages with Melted Onions, Mashed Potatoes & Gravy £6.95
Beef, Mushroom & Ale Pie with Potatoes & Vegetables £6.95
Spinach, Mushroom & Stilton Pancake served with Salad £6.25
Pan-fried Sirloin Steak with a Celery, Stilton & Walnut Sauce £11.95
Meatloaf of British Beef & Mushrooms with a Wild Mushroom Sauce £6.75
Loin of Lamb Fillet with Garlic, Rosemary & Blackcurrant Sauce £10.25
Baked Stuffed Chicken Breast wrapped in Bacon
with White Wine, Mushrooms & Cream Sauce £8.25
Slow Roast Duck Legs with Pear & a Rich Fruity Sauce £8.95
Artichoke & Red Onion Flan served with Saffron Mayonnaise £6.25
Baked Marrow stuffed with Minced Lamb with a Tomato & Mozzarella Topping £7.25

### Desserts

Dark Chocolate Pudding with White Chocolate & Amaretto Sauce £3.50
Steamed Date & Apple Pudding £3.15
Individual Apricot & Shortbread Tartlet served with Apricot & Cointreau Sauce
& Greek Yoghurt Cream £3.50
Albion Glory - Mango Sorbet & Vanilla Ice Cream with Fresh Fruit & Fruit Coulis,
a Dash of Cream & Two Biscuits £2.95
Brown Bread & Rum Ice Cream £2.95
Selection of Mature French & English Cheeses with Biscuits £3.50

The Albion is a traditional Kentish pub tucked away beside Faversham Creek near the centre of town. The one main room is divided into two dining areas by the central bar and it remains a meeting-place where locals gather for a drink. The Albion is still very much a pub, but one with excellent food.

The plain wooden tables and chairs are surrounded by nautical memorabilia - prints of sailing vessels, shells on the walls, oars on the ceiling. However the rather intriguing fishing net turned out to be nothing more than an old hammock. The proximity of the Shepherd Neame brewery had obviously taken its toll on me.

When Patrick Coevoet took over at the helm three years ago, the pub was completely run down. These days it is probably wise to book beforehand to avoid disappointment as the imaginative blackboard menu (with around 6 to 8 specials that change every week) now draws the crowds from miles around.

Directions: Beside the Shepherd Neame brewery, take the small road across the bridge, bear right and The Albion's car park is on your right.

## USEFUL INFORMATION

**SERVING TIMES:**
Lunch 12pm-2pm (every day)
Dinner 7pm-9.30pm (Mon-Thur)
        7pm-10pm (Fri & Sat)
        7pm-9pm (Sun)
**SEATING CAPACITY:** 30
**C/C:** V, MC, S, D

**NUMBER OF WINES:** 11
**HOUSE WINE:** £7.95
**RESERVATIONS:** advisable, but essential at weekends
**OUTDOOR EATING:** yes
**CHILDREN:** welcome
**OFF-STREET PARKING:** yes

# READ'S

Tel: (01795) 535344
Mummery Court, Painter's Forstal, Faversham, Kent, ME13 0EE

## Fixed-price A La Carte £32.50

### First Courses

FRESH BROWN & WHITE CRABMEAT, LAYERED WITH SUSHI RICE
ON A FRESH PEA PUREE WITH A LOBSTER VINAIGRETTE

"BORSTCH A LA RUSSE", A RUSSIAN SOUP PREPARED FROM
ROASTED DUCKLING, BEETROOT AND A JULIENNE OF VEGETABLES

A HOT RISOTTO OF UNDYED SMOKED HADDOCK
WITH BROAD BEANS AND SHAVINGS OF PARMESAN CHEESE

A GATEAU OF LIGHTLY SMOKED SCOTTISH SALMON
LAYERED WITH A CUCUMBER AND LEMON MOUSSE

A GOOSE EGG SCRAMBLED WITH FOIE GRAS IN A BUTTER PUFF PASTRY
TARTLET ON A MADEIRA WINE SAUCE

### Main Courses

A FILLET OF FRESH WHITSTABLE TURBOT ON A BED OF SHIITAKE
MUSHROOMS WITH A WARM GINGER & SOY VINAIGRETTE

LAMB, LAMB, LAMB & LAMB - CHOICE ROASTED CUTS FROM THE BEST END,
SADDLE, FILLET AND KIDNEY OF NEW SEASON ROMNEY MARSH LAMB

SESAME COATED DUCK BREAST
WITH A SPICED PLUM SAUCE & GINGER STIR-FRIED VEGETABLES

A SAUTEED BREAST OF CORN-FED CHICKEN WITH ENGLISH GREEN,
FRENCH WHITE AND WATER ASPARAGUS WITH FRESH MORELS

AN UNTRADITIONAL LOBSTER "BOUILLABAISSE"
WITH A CREME FRAICHE AND SPRING ONION BROTH (£6 SUPP)

### Desserts & Cheeses

A HOT DRAMBUIE SOUFFLE WITH FRESH RASPBERRIES

THE CHOCOHOLICS ANONYMOUS - A COMBINATION OF CHOCOLATE
MOUSSE, CHOCOLATE MARQUISE, BITTER CHOCOLATE SORBET, LAYERED
CHOCOLATE TRUFFLE CAKE SERVED WITH WHITE CHOCOLATE ICE CREAM

AN APRICOT MOUSSE SERVED WITH A COMPOTE OF FRESH APRICOTS
AND A SHARP RASPBERRY SORBET

READ'S HOME-MADE JELLY AND ICE CREAM

A CHOICE FROM OUR BASKET OF BRITISH CHEESE
SERVED WITH GRAPES, BISCUITS & BREAD

Over the past twenty years, Read's has established itself as one of finest restaurants in the South-East of England. Chef/patron David Pitchford's classically based modern British cooking features on a fixed-price *carte* that changes every six weeks or so, whilst his wife Rona takes charge front of house.

Three-course set-price menus are available at both lunch (£17.50) and dinner (£20) and they have devised an innovative *Tasting Menu* which enables you to sample smaller portions of several of their dishes. If ordered, it must be for the whole table and is priced at £36 per person.

The menu cards have a specially commissioned Ronald Searle cartoon on their covers and include humourous quotations relating to food in general. One of those pearls of wisdom, Miss Piggy's *"Never eat more than you can lift"*, should certainly be heeded at all times.

Directions: Read's is easily found in the village of Painter's Forstal, signposted from the A2 and A251, approximately 2 miles to the south-west of Faversham.

### USEFUL INFORMATION

**SERVING TIMES:**
Lunch 12pm-2pm (Tues-Sat)
Dinner 7pm-10pm (Tues-Sat)
**CLOSED:** all day Sun & Mon
**SEATING CAPACITY:** 40
**C/C:** V, MC, S, D, AE, DC

**NUMBER OF WINES:** 300
**HOUSE WINE:** £14.00
**RESERVATIONS:** essential
**OFF-STREET PARKING:** yes
**OUTDOOR EATING:** yes

# THE RED LION
Tel: (01428) 643112
The Green, Fernhurst, West Sussex, GU27 3HY

## BAR SPECIALS

Camembert en croûte with gooseberry conserve  £4.25
Whole prawns sautéed in garlic butter  £4.25
Baked avocado with crab  £4.50
Mushrooms with a garlic stuffing topped with brie  £4.95
Fresh samphire & prawns tossed in garlic butter  £4.95
Mixed Mediterranean seafood cocktail  £4.95
Herring fillets marinated in a trio of sauces  £4.50

Breaded Scottish scampi with chips, salad or peas  £6.95
Steak, kidney, Guinness & mushroom pie  £7.25
Home-cooked ham, egg, bubble & squeak  £6.25
Stincotto - shank of pork with honey & Meux mustard  £9.50
Pancakes stuffed with spinach, mushrooms & garlic  £4.95
Fresh pasta with artichokes, peppers & sun-dried tomatoes  £5.95
Roast shoulder of lamb with red wine, garlic & garden herbs  £9.75
Braised local rabbit with white wine & prunes  £6.95
Coronation chicken with savoury rice & salad  £6.95
Diced breast of turkey in a spicy yoghurt & coconut sauce  £7.25
Irish bake - layers of potato with bacon, spinach & onions  £6.25

## A LA CARTE
*Evenings only - not Sunday*

Scotch sirloin steak  £9.95
   or with garlic or Dijon sauce  £12.50
Poached smoked haddock with a coriander & lime rosti
   & a mornay sauce  £7.50
Smoked fillet of pork with an apple & apricot sauce  £8.95
Oriental beef with baby corn, peppers & spring onions  £6.95
Tuna steak with pink peppercorns & port wine sauce  £7.25
Local pink trout with a mint & orange sauce  £7.95

The Red Lion is a traditional 16th century country pub tucked away near the village green by St. Margaret's Church in the village of Fernhurst. Not exclusively a restaurant and not exactly an ale-house, it is essentially a local pub (the oldest in the village) with extremely good food.

It is also the adopted home of *"101 Uses for a John Major"*, a book written by the satirical cartoonist Patrick Wright, whose son Joe is the chef here. The atmosphere is very friendly, as befits a pub that recently put a mock doodlebug through its roof to join in the VE-Day celebrations.

The bar food shown on the facing page is written up on the blackboard and changes daily, with à la carte dishes available every evening (except Sunday) served from 7pm until 10pm.

Directions: The village of Fernhurst is located about 4 miles to the south of Haslemere on the main A286 Haslemere to Midhurst road. In the village take the turning towards Lurgashall and the Red Lion can be found opposite the village green after approximately 800 yards.

### USEFUL INFORMATION

**SERVING TIMES:**
Lunch 10.30am-2.30pm (every day)
Dinner 5.30pm-10.30pm (every day)
**SEATING CAPACITY:** 30 in the restaurant, 20 in the bar area
**C/C:** V, MC, S, D, AE
**NO SMOKING** areas available

**NUMBER OF WINES:** 50
**HOUSE WINE:** £9.35
**RESERVATIONS:** advisable
**OFF-STREET PARKING:** yes
**OUTDOOR EATING:** yes
**CHILDREN:** welcome

# THE GRIFFIN INN
Tel: (01825) 722890
Fletching, near Uckfield, East Sussex, TN22 3SS

A selection from the evening à la carte

## Starters
Terrine of pork & chicken liver with home-made chutney £4.95
Tomato fish broth with mullet, cod & coly with aioli & croutons £4.95
Salad of quails' eggs, crispy bacon & parmesan £4.95
Steamed asparagus with a lemon beurre blanc £4.95

## Mains
Char-grilled Scottish fillet of beef with a roasted red onion and tomato confit £15.95
Pan-fried Barbary duck breast, served on char-grilled Italian vegetables with a sweetened plum sauce £13.95
Thai king shrimps wok-fried with spinach, chillies, lemongrass and coriander £12.50
Large mushrooms with char-grilled aubergines, courgettes, tomatoes and bocconcini cheese drizzled with pesto £7.95
Roasted rack of new season's lamb filled with avocado and air-dried ham, finished with a mint vinegar £13.95
Thai green vegetable curry with bok choy potatoes, served with jasmine rice £6.95
Freshly caught local crab mayonnaise with Jersey Royals and organic leaves £10.50
Pan-fried free-range calves' liver and roasted red onion confit with crispy prosciutto £11.95

## Puddings
£3.95 each
Grapefruit & orange marmalade ice cream
Strawberry meringue roulade
Steamed treacle sponge pudding & custard
Filo basket filled with plums & apricots roasted in amaretto
A selection of English farmhouse cheeses £4.95

Owned by the Pullan family (of Ebury Wine Bars renown) for over eighteen years, the Griffin Inn enjoys a pleasant village location in the heart of East Sussex countryside.

Over the past three years James Pullan has successfully injected a youthful excitement into both the atmosphere and the cuisine, without ever losing touch with the more traditional delights of a country pub. Everything here is home-made and wherever possible sourced locally - the village butcher, fish from Newhaven, wonderful cheeses from the Sussex High Weald Dairy, and so on.

The bar and restaurant menus change daily to accommodate a modern British cuisine, strong on fish from the Pacific Rim, with deftly innovative touches courtesy of the team of eight chefs who come from all over the world. As one might expect, the wine list is very extensive and carefully researched, with a good selection of lesser known single estate Italian wines being particularly worthy of mention. There are also weekly wine specials and twelve house wines by the glass.

Directions: Signposted from the A272 and A275, Fletching is about 3 miles west of Uckfield. The Griffin is at the top end of the high street.

## USEFUL INFORMATION

**SERVING TIMES:**
Lunch 12pm-2.45pm (every day)
Dinner 7pm-10pm (Mon-Sat)
**CLOSED:** Sunday evening in the restaurant (bar menu available)
**SEATING CAPACITY:** 70 in the restaurant, 50 in the bar
**C/C:** V, MC, S, D, AE
**CHILDREN:** welcome

**NUMBER OF WINES:** 150
**HOUSE WINE:** £9.50
**RESERVATIONS:** advisable, but compulsory at weekends
**OUTDOOR EATING:** yes
**OFF-STREET PARKING:** yes
**ACCOMMODATION:** 4 rooms
(B&B single £45, double £75)

# BASSETTS RESTAURANT

Tel: (01892) 750635
37 High Street, Frant, East Sussex, TN3 9DT

### DINNER MENU

Chilled gazpacho soup

Fish brawn terrine with marinated cucumber

Irish potato bread with poached asparagus and a hollandaise sauce

Smoked duck, pancetta lardons and pine kernels on a leaf salad with a horseradish dressing

Sweet potato and goat cheese brûlée with walnut and rosemary bread

Coarse pâté of rabbit and hare with a radish and watercress salad

\* \* \*

Grilled fillets of sea bream with roast capsicums and a 'beurre rouge' sauce

Crisp pastry millefeuilles with sautéed mignons of beef and a grain mustard sauce

Baked globe artichoke filled with spinach and mushrooms wrapped in a puff pastry lattice served with a white wine butter sauce

Pan-fried calves liver and bacon on a bed of crushed potato with a cask ale and onion jus

Roast supreme of maize-fed chicken stuffed with a morel farçi on a cream infused jus

Roast chump of lamb served with Bassetts mint jelly and a red wine jus

All served with a selection of fresh vegetables

\* \* \*

Dessert

A selection of British farmhouse cheeses

Filter coffee and petits fours

£27.50

Bassetts is a delightfully intimate restaurant found tucked away in the picturesque village of Frant. A comfortable lounge leads into an elegant dining area with low ceilings, exposed beams and a large stone fireplace decorated by several hundred bottles of wine.

The cuisine, described by owner Nicholas Mott as 'modern European', is superb. The evening table d'hôte menu, a sample of which appears opposite, changes monthly to accommodate seasonal variations and is fairly priced at £27.50 (3 courses and coffee). The lunch menu is also a table d'hôte offering three choices at each course (2 or 3 courses £13.50 and £16.50). The dessert menu features home-made ice creams and sorbets, as well as rich dishes such as Mango bavarois on a collage of exotic fruits laced with vodka, or Sussex curd tart studded with sultanas and apricot coulis.

There are regular Gourmet Evenings (5 courses £32.50) and Magic Nights (no mushrooms allowed!) when a magician performs at the tables. These are both very popular so book early.

Directions: The village of Frant is about 3 miles south of Royal Tunbridge Wells on the A267. Follow the signs to Frant High Street and Bassetts is easily found opposite the church.

## USEFUL INFORMATION

**SERVING TIMES:**
Lunch 12.30pm-1.30pm (Tues-Sat)
Dinner 7.30pm-9pm (Tues-Sat)
**CLOSED:** Sunday and Monday
**SEATING CAPACITY:** 28
**C/C:** V, MC
**CHILDREN:** welcome

**NUMBER OF WINES:** 70
**HOUSE WINE:** £9.50
**RESERVATIONS:** advisable
**OUTDOOR EATING:** no
**OFF-STREET PARKING:** no
**NO SMOKING** in the restaurant, but allowed in the lounge

# INN ON THE LAKE
Tel: (01483) 415575
Ockford Road, Godalming, Surrey, GU7 1RH

### A Selection From Our A La Carte Menu

**To Start**

Slithers of Chilled Galia Melon £4.25
*enhanced with an English Strawberry Soup & Timbale of Berries*

Rillette of Salmon & Monkfish £5.85
*finished with a Spiced Mustard Cream*

Terrine of Rabbit & Bacon £5.20
*with Sweet Pickled Vegetables*

Warm Leek, Stilton & Pine Kernel Flan £5.00
*crisp Continental Leaves & Roast Tomato Coulis*

**Main Courses**

Escalope of Sea Bass, Champ & Citrus Cream £14.65
*with a hint of Rosemary*

Breasts of Local Pigeon £11.95
*set on Savoy Cabbage, Redcurrant Sauce & Parisienne Potatoes*

Roast Baby Chicken £11.15
*served with Chateau Potatoes, Carrots & Beans finished with a Mild Thyme Jus*

Loin of Venison marinated in Red Wine & Garlic £13.95
*set on Bubble & Squeak*

Ravioli of Goats' Cheese £9.50
*set in a pool of Sweet Pepper Coulis*

Warm Salad of Oyster Mushrooms £9.95
*flambéed with Port & Orange Segments*

**Desserts**

Rich Chocolate Tarte £3.95
*with Orange flavoured Custard*

Baked Apple in a Crisp Golden Cage £3.95
*& crunch Apple Pearls*

Poached Pear £3.95
*with Vanilla & Chocolate Sauce*

Plate of Cheeses £4.85
*accompanied by Celery, Apple & Grapes*

The Inn On The Lake is a part Tudor, part Georgian, part modern country house hotel set in two acres of landscaped gardens on the outskirts of Godalming.

The main restaurant, presided over by head chef Wayne Hatenboer, offers an à la carte menu that reflects the latest trends in modern British cooking. The menu changes seasonally and makes good use of the freshest local produce. The restaurant is housed in one of the hotel's modern extensions and features a fully functional pond stocked with koi carp as its centrepiece.

Snacks are served in the bar area and might include Warm Tomato & Mozzarella Salad (£4.75), Croque Monsieur (£4.25) or Fillet Steak (£15.95), and desserts such as Chocolate Terrine with Crème Anglaise (£3.45).

Directions: From the A3 take the A283 turn-off towards Milford. At Milford, turn left at the traffic lights on the A3100. Go under the railway bridge and the Inn On The Lake is located on your right at the mini-roundabout.

### USEFUL INFORMATION

**SERVING TIMES:**
Lunch 12pm-2pm (every day)
Dinner 7.30pm-9.30pm (Mon-Sat)
**CLOSED:** Sun night
**SEATING CAPACITY:** 65
**C/C:** V, MC, S, D, AE, DC
**NO SMOKING** area available
**OUTDOOR EATING:** yes

**NUMBER OF WINES:** 35
**HOUSE WINE:** £9.95
**RESERVATIONS:** advisable
**OFF-STREET PARKING:** yes
**CHILDREN:** welcome
**ACCOMMODATION:** 20 rooms
(B&B from £80 p.n. per room)

# THE COMPASSES INN
### Tel: (01483) 202506
### Station Road, Gomshall, Surrey, GU5 9LA

## To Start

Pan-seared Queenies & Prawns served with a Squid Ink Pasta
in an Olive Oil, Lime & Basil Dressing £4.95

A Warm Tartlet of Smoked Chicken with Mixed Salad Leaves,
dressed in a Split Oil & Balsamic Vinegar & garnished with Cherry Tomatoes
& Smoked Garlic £5.25

Home-made Soupe du Jour with Crusty Bread £2.95

Savoury Herb Crêpes filled with Wild Mushrooms & Brie,
glazed with Cream & Cheese, served with Crusty Bread £3.75

Eggs under a Crust - an Oven-baked Egg on a bed of Braised Leeks
& Grain Mustard, topped with Cheese & Breadcrumbs £3.50

## To Follow

Grilled Calves Liver on a Savoury Mash
with a Dubonnet & Orange Sauce £11.95

Roast Half of Duck
with a Port & Fresh Berry Sauce £8.95

Whole Grilled Lemon Sole
topped with Capers & Diced Peppers in a Lime Herb Butter £10.95

Fillet Steak au Poivre - a Prime Fillet Steak liberally sprinkled with Black
Pepper, then flamed in Brandy & finished with Cream £12.50

Penne Regata with a Fresh Tomato & Chilli Sauce,
garnished with Grilled Vegetables & Shavings of Parmesan Cheese £6.95

*All main courses are served with a selection of fresh seasonal vegetables &
baby new potatoes*

Built in 1830 and originally known as *God Encompasses*, this name was so frequently mispronounced as *Goat and Compasses* that it stuck. The word *Goat* has now been dropped and it is now simply known as *The Compasses*.

The picturesque Tillingbourne Stream runs between the pub and its popular beer garden, meaning that nature rules. After my visit, I had to pause at the door to allow a duck and her five ducklings to waddle past me into the bar. I didn't wait to see what they ordered.

The à la carte menu featured opposite changes monthly and is served in the restaurant every evening (except on Mondays). Good home-made pub food is available all day every day (again with the exception of Mondays when last orders are taken at 2.30pm), with dishes such as Steak and Kidney Pie (£5.95) or Fresh Salmon and Cod Fishcakes (£5.95). The blackboard specials change daily and might include Supreme of Chicken filled with Fresh Mango in a Spiced Tomato and Cream Sauce (£6.95) or perhaps a Fresh Crab and Seafood Medley served with a Granary Loaf (£9.95).

Directions: The Compasses Inn is situated midway between Guildford and Dorking on the main A25.

**USEFUL INFORMATION**

**SERVING TIMES:**
Lunch - bar food only
Dinner 7pm-9pm (Tues-Sun)
**RESTAURANT CLOSED:** Mon night and every lunchtime
**SEATING CAPACITY:** 50 in the restaurant, 30 in the bar
**C/C:** V, MC, S, D
**NO SMOKING** in the restaurant

**NUMBER OF WINES:** 21
**HOUSE WINE:** £7.95
**RESERVATIONS:** advisable for the weekends
**OFF-STREET PARKING:** yes
**OUTDOOR EATING:** yes
**CHILDREN:** welcome
**ACCOMMODATION:** 3 rooms (B&B from £45 for a double)

# CAFE DE PARIS
Tel: (01483) 534896
35 Castle Street, Guildford, Surrey, GU1 3UQ

### A SELECTION FROM THE A LA CARTE RESTAURANT MENU

**hors d'oeuvres**

Soupe de Poisson de la Mediterranée avec sa Rouille  £5.10
*Mediterranean-style fish soup with a piquant sauce, croûtons & grated cheese*
Salade de Caille aux Raisins  £5.10
*Quail off the bone, pan-fried with grapes & armagnac on a bed of salad*
Escargots à la Bourguignonne  £5.80
*Snails in garlic butter*
Rosti et Saumon Fumé, Sauce Aigre  £6.80
*Rosti potatoes & smoked salmon with sour cream*

**poissons**

Matelotte de Lotte Bourguignonne  £13.95
*Monkfish, pan-fried, finished in a shallot & red wine sauce*
Bouillabaisse Marseillaise  £22.50
*Traditional fish stew from Marseille with rock fishes, crabs, lobsters, etc.*

**viandes et volaille**

Côte de Veau "Normande" ou "au Beurre"  £12.20
*Veal chop in an apple & cream sauce, or plain*
Carré d'Agneau au Romarin  £13.95
*Individual rack of lamb with fresh rosemary sauce*
Côté de Boeuf Grillé (pour deux personnes)  £26.50
*Grilled rib of beef with a sauce of your choice (for two people)*

### LE CHEF VOUS PROPOSE POUR CE MOIS

Meurette d'Oeuf Poché aux Moules, au Curry  £6.80
*Soft poached egg in a cream curry sauce with mussels*
Tian de Sardines aux Epinards 'Provençale'  £6.80
*Grilled sardines on a bed of spinach, Provençale herbs & coulis*
Tranche de Foie Gras de Canard Poëlé à l'Armagnac  £7.80
*Pan-fried duck foie gras with Armagnac & fresh grapes*
* * * * *
Gâteau de Lotte aux Aubergines  £13.95
*Gateau of monkfish with aubergines, tapenade & coulis*
Canon d'Agneau Grillé, Crème d'Oignon à la Menthe Fraîche  £13.75
*Grilled fillet of lamb with cream of onion & fresh mint*
Rognons de Veau Poëlés à la Moutarde Ancienne  £13.95
*Pan-fried veal kidneys finished with seed mustard cream sauce*

Forget the super apex return to Paris on the Eurostar and head over to Guildford. True, the town lacks some of the beauty of the Left Bank and the Louvre, but if authentic French cuisine is the aim of the trip, you need look no further than the Cafe de Paris in Castle Street.

This authentic French restaurant and brasserie has been satisfying Surrey's Francophiles for the past nine years. Such is the draw of Thierry Niel's à la carte restaurant menu (featured opposite) that the chef's suggestions change every month to cater for the many regular customers.

The brasserie menu is equally tempting (particularly if your horse in the 3.35pm at Longchamp didn't oblige) with à la carte, blackboard and fixed price menus at all times. This £13.95 3-course set menu can be taken in either the restaurant or the brasserie (but not in the restaurant on Friday and Saturday evenings).

Directions: Follow the ringroad and turn left at the sign to the High Street (not Town Centre). Bear round to the right to avoid the pedestrianised area and take the second turning on the left into Castle Street. Cafe de Paris is on the first corner and the public car park 50 yards further along on your left.

### USEFUL INFORMATION

**SERVING TIMES:**
Lunch 12pm-2.30pm (Mon-Sat)
Dinner 6.30pm-11pm (Mon-Sat)
**CLOSED:** all day Sunday
**SEATING CAPACITY:** 30 in the restaurant, 20 in the brasserie
**C/C:** V, MC, S, AE
**OUTDOOR EATING:** no

**NUMBER OF WINES:** 100
**HOUSE WINE:** £12.20
**RESERVATIONS:** essential at all times for the restaurant (no bookings taken for the brasserie)
**CHILDREN:** welcome
**OFF-STREET PARKING:** no but there are 2 public car parks nearby

# THE GUN INN
### Tel: (01825) 872361
### Gun Hill, near Horam, East Sussex, TN21 0JU

## An Evening Selection

**Fillet Steak** £12.80
Succulent fillet (8oz approx) grilled to your choice
**Rump Steak** £7.80
Best rump (8oz approx) grilled to your choice
**Gammon Steak** £6.60
Thick gammon slice grilled and served with a pineapple ring

*Our steaks are served with a potato fritter, mushrooms, grilled tomato and salad garnish and chips, jacket potato or new potatoes*

**Seafood Platter** £6.60
Golden fried goujons of plaice, scampi, scallops and haddock
**Scampi Platter** £6.60
Premium scampi coated in crisp breadcrumb
**Chicken Fillets** £6.30
Strips of tender chicken coated with golden breadcrumbs
**Fillet Steak Wellington** £8.40
Fillet Steak wrapped in flaky puff pastry with pâté, mushrooms, onions and sherry
**Mr Robbins' Sausages** £5.20
Three delicately spiced, locally caught sausages
**Mrs Lucioni's Lasagne** £5.90
Minced beef in a spicy tomato sauce with pasta and cheese
**Alison's Haddock Pasta** £5.90
Smoked haddock and tagliatelle in a creamy sauce with prawns and mushrooms
**Vegetarian Lasagne** £5.90
Vegetables with pasta and cheese
**Cauliflower Cheese** £5.20
Fresh cauliflower with creamy cheese sauce (available when in season)

All the above are served with a salad garnish and either chips, jacket potato, new potatoes, garlic bread *or* a help yourself salad

# GUN HILL

Welcomed in the summer by an abundance of brightly coloured flowers in hanging baskets and large pots, and in the winter by roaring fires and cosy, low-beamed rooms, this 15th century inn is worth finding down gently winding lanes in the heart of idyllic East Sussex countryside.

I am glad to say that although the food here is very good, the traditional pub roots have not been forgotten, and dropping in for a beer and a quick bite to eat is not frowned upon. Children are welcome and there is even a menu for them, and French bread sandwiches and jacket potatoes are readily available.

The main menu is supplemented by daily blackboard specials such as Sussex Fidget Pie (£6.30) and Lamb, Rosemary and Apricot Pie (£6.30), as well as fresh fish from Newhaven. Desserts are all home-made and include regular favourites like Apple Pie or Cheesecake (£2.90 each) and seasonal specials shown on the blackboard.

Directions: Gun Hill lies between Horam and Hailsham and is signposted from the A267 and the A22.

## USEFUL INFORMATION

**SERVING TIMES:**
Lunch 12pm-2pm (every day)
Dinner 6pm-10pm (every day)
**SEATING CAPACITY:** 88
**C/C:** V, MC, S, D
**NO SMOKING** area available

**NUMBER OF WINES:** 30
**HOUSE WINE:** £7.50
**RESERVATIONS:** not taken
**OFF-STREET PARKING:** yes
**CHILDREN:** welcome
**OUTDOOR EATING:** yes

# THE WHITE HORSE

Tel: (01483) 208258
Hascombe, near Godalming, Surrey, GU8 4JA

## Menu

£22.00 per person

### Starters

Oriental Filo-wrapped Prawns in a Chilli Dip
Deep-fried Brie with Cranberry Sauce
Cod & Shrimp Fishcakes with a Parsley Sauce
Caesar Salad with Avocado & Croûtons
Fresh Asparagus served hot with Butter

### Main Courses

Grilled Salmon Steak stuffed with Spinach
in a light Cream & Grain Mustard Sauce
Veal Cordon Bleu
Veal Escalope stuffed with Ham & Cheese
Sautéed Calves' Liver with Fresh Sage & Butter
Skewered Charcoal-grilled chicken pieces
marinated in Honey, Ginger, Garlic & Fresh Coriander
on a bed of Rice with a Spicy Tomato Salsa
Lamb Noisettes in a Honey, Rosemary & Red Wine Sauce

### Desserts

Hazelnut & Raspberry Meringue £4.00
Chocolate Concorde £4.00
Blackcurrant & Apple Crumble £3.50
Treacle & Walnut Tart £4.00
Chocolate Truffle Cake £3.50

The White Horse is a traditional country pub well-known in the area for both its excellent restaurant and splendid home-made bar food.

When I tried to find out a little about the building's history, I was told *"this part here dates back to the 16th century, and that bit over there from last September"*, so I would imagine that their successful formula has lead to a certain amount of renovation and extension.

In addition to the set price menu featured opposite, there is an à la carte menu that features many interesting vegetarian choices, such as Cashew & Mushroom en Croûte witha Red Pepper Sauce (£10.50). Both menus are changed every couple of months.

The bar food blackboard might feature Dolcelatte Ploughman's (£4.50), Smoked Fish Platter (£6.25), Steak, Guinness & Mushroom Pie (£7.50), Salmon & Prawn Fishcakes (£7.95) or Thai Chicken Salad (£7.50).

Directions: The White Horse is easily found on the outskirts of the village of Hascombe on the B2130, approximately 3 miles south-east of Godalming.

### USEFUL INFORMATION

**SERVING TIMES:**
Lunch 12pm-2pm (Mon-Fri)
   (bar food served until 2.20pm)
   12pm-2.30pm (Sat & Sun)
Dinner 7pm-10pm (Mon-Sat)
   7pm-9.30pm (Sun, bar food only)
**RESTAURANT CLOSED:** Sun night
**SEATING CAPACITY:** 30 in the restaurant, 100 in the bar

**NUMBER OF WINES:** 32
**HOUSE WINE:** £7.50
**RESERVATIONS:** advisable
**C/C:** V, MC, S, D, AE, DC
**OUTDOOR EATING:** yes
**CHILDREN:** welcome
**OFF-STREET PARKING:** yes
**NO WHEELCHAIR ACCESS**

# FLEUR DE SEL
## Tel: (01428) 651462
### 23-27 Lower Street, Haslemere, Surrey, GU27 2NY

*A Selection from the A La Carte*
*(2 courses £21.00 - 3 courses £26.00)*

*Hors d'Oeuvre*

*Soupe de Poissons et ses Garnitures*
**Fish Bisque served with Croûtons, Rouille & Gruyère Cheese**

*Gâteau de Crabe de Cornwall et Crevettes à la Mangue*
**Cornish Crab and Prawn Cake with Mango Mayonnaise**

*Fond d'Artichaut Soufflé au Roquefort Sauce Mousseline*
**Artichoke Heart filled with Roquefort Soufflé**

\* \* \*

*Entrées*

*Filet de Daurade Soufflé Saumonette Sauce Vierge*
**Fillet of Sea Bream with Salmon Soufflé and Basil & Orange Sauce**

*Médaillons de Lotte Farçis aux Poivrons Doux et Coulis de Tomate*
**Medallions of Monkfish filled with Sweet Peppers**

*Canon D'Agneau en Croûte de Couscous Epicé*
**Loin of Lamb wrapped in Lightly Spiced Couscous**

*Canette de Gressingham Rôtie au Miel et Gingembre*
**Roast Crispy Duck with Honey and Ginger Sauce**

*Suprême de Poulet Farçis aux Langoustines et Pâtes Fraîches*
**Chicken Breast filled with Langoustines served with Fresh Pasta**

\* \* \*

*Plateau de Fromages*
**A Selection of Cheeses**
or
**Desserts**

*Sablé à la Mangue et aux Fraises*
**Shortcrust Biscuits with Mango and Strawberries**

*Crème Brûlée Citronelle*
**Lemon Grass Crème Brûlée**

*Nougat Glaçé au Miel de Provence et Fruits Rouges*
**Honey flavoured Iced Nougat with Summer Fruits**

# HASLEMERE 101

Fleur de Sel, Michel Perraud's renowned French restaurant, is a linked trio of three-hundred-year-old listed cottages set up on a raised pavement in the pretty village of Haslemere. Blue and lemon are the predominant colours, with fresh flowers and crisp white linen creating an elegant yet inviting ambience.

Michel could not have had a better apprenticeship, having spent six years in the 1980's as head chef at The Waterside Inn, Bray where his *modern-classical* cuisine brought the restaurant its highly-coveted third Michelin star.

The fixed price *carte* from his own kitchen generally gives a choice of eight dishes at each course (a small selection is shown opposite) and changes four times per year. Table d'hôte menus are also available - lunch is charged at £9.50 for 2 courses and £12.50 for 3 courses, whilst the dinner menu costs £12.50 for 2 courses or £16.50 for 3 courses (Tues-Thur only).

Directions: Fleur de Sel is easily found on the town's elevated terraced pavement known as Lower Street, approximately 400 yards from the town hall.

## USEFUL INFORMATION

**SERVING TIMES:**
Lunch 12pm-2pm (Tues-Fri, & Sun)
Dinner 7pm-10pm (Tues-Sat)
**CLOSED:** Sat lunch, Sun night and all day Monday
**SEATING CAPACITY:** 50
**C/C:** V, MC, S, D, AE

**NUMBER OF WINES:** 100
**HOUSE WINE:** £11.00
**RESERVATIONS:** advisable
**OFF-STREET PARKING:** no, but there is a public car park over the road (entrance in High Street)
**OUTDOOR EATING:** no

# BISTROT SAINT-PIERRE

Tel: (01444) 417755
65 The Broadway, Haywards Heath, West Sussex, RH16 3AS

## STARTERS
******

SLOW ROAST DUCK SALAD WITH COCONUT AND GINGER DRESSING
4.25

WARM SALAD OF CHILLI SALT SQUID, PEPPERS
AND FRESH CORIANDER LEAVES
4.50

GRILLED FLAT BREAD WITH HUMMUS, BABA GANOUJ AND TZATZIKI
3.95

CHEESE AND ONION WAFFLES WITH HERB MASCARPONE
AND ROAST TOMATOES
4.25

DEEP-FRIED GOATS CHEESE, WILD ROCKET AND TOMATO CHILLI JAM
4.50

SEARED TUNA BURGERS, AVOCADO SALSA AND ORIENTAL HERB OIL
4.50

## MAINS
******

CHAR-GRILLED RIB OF BEEF, BEARNAISE SAUCE
9.50

ROASTED RUMP OF LAMB, DEEP-FRIED AUBERGINE AND CUMIN LENTILS
8.75

PEPPERED CHICKEN STEAK WITH CHILLI ROAST ONIONS
AND DEEP-FRIED CABBAGE
7.95

ROAST RACK OF PORK WITH GARLIC POTATO MASH AND PESTO
8.50

SEARED COD WITH FRESH NOODLES AND COCONUT CURRY SAUCE
8.75

TOSSED NICOISE SALAD WITH FRESH GRILLED TUNA,
BALSAMIC DRESSING
8.75

There's a little bit of London chic and style about proprietor Paul Montalto and his restaurants. Bistrot Saint-Pierre is no exception. Modern without being brash, trendy but not aloof, it is popular and relaxed.

The same may be said about the cuisine, which as with that presented at the Dining Room (see page 152) reflects the innovative flair of Executive Chef Anthony Tobin, probably best known as one of those chefs on TV's *Ready, Steady, Cook* who can make a wonderful meal out of almost nothing. I took along a can of lager, a can of Guinness, a bottle of red wine and an Anadin to test him out. Unfortunately I was ignored, but left to my own devices I threw together a very nice hangover!

The seasonal à la carte shown opposite is supplemented by a great value weekly table d'hôte (2 courses £9.95).

Directions: Easily found in the centre of Haywards Heath on The Broadway.

### USEFUL INFORMATION

**SERVING TIMES:**
Lunch 12pm-2.30pm (Mon-Fri)
Dinner 6pm-11pm (Mon-Sat)
**CLOSED:** Saturday lunch and all day Sunday
**SEATING CAPACITY:** 70
**C/C:** V, MC, S, D, AE

**NUMBER OF WINES:** 20
**HOUSE WINE:** £6.95
**OUTDOOR EATING:** yes
**OFF-STREET PARKING:** no
**RESERVATIONS:** advisable
**DRESS CODE:** smart
**CHILDREN:** welcome

# THE SUNDIAL RESTAURANT
## Tel: (01323) 832217
Gardner Street, Herstmonceux, East Sussex, BN27 4LA

### A Selection from the A La Carte

#### Crustaces ~ Hors d'Oeuvres et Entrées Chaudes

LE DELICE D'ASPERGES AU SAUMON FUME £9.50
Fresh asparagus served with Scotch smoked salmon & hollandaise sauce
LA SALADE DU PRINTEMPS £12.50
Lobster, salmon, prawns, crab on a bed of rocket salad and avocado
LE CARPACCIO DE CANETON FUME AU PARMESAN £9.50
Marinated fillet of duck in olive oil vinaigrette
LA ROULADE DE BOEUF AU BLANC DE CRABE £9.50
Very thinly sliced fillet of beef, rolled with fresh white crab
LA PETITE BOUILLABAISSE A LA ROUILLE £9.50
A lovely fish soup with garlic croûtons
LES QUENELLES DE COQUILLE ST. JACQUES ET LOTTE £10.50
Scallops and monkfish mousse served with a lobster sauce
LES ROSETTES D'AVOCAT AUX MEDAILLONS DE LANGOUSTE £14.50
Avocado pear with all white lobster, served with a mousseline sauce
L'ASSIETTE DE SAUMON FUME £10.95
Freshly cut Scotch smoked salmon

#### Poissons ~ Volailles ~ Gibier et Viandes

LES PAUPIETTES DE SOLE BELLE SOPHIE £22.50
Two fillets of sole rolled in salmon, baked in the oven and decorated with lobster
LES ECREVISSES AUX TROIS EPICES £19.50
Crayfish sauté with herbs, served on a bed of risotto
LA SOLE LOCALE DOREE BELLE MEUNIERE £22.50
Local Dover sole gently pan-fried, served with tartare sauce
LES MEDAILLONS DE LANGOUSTE ET COQUILLE ST JACQUES £27.50
A lovely combination with lobster and scallops
LE CANETON ROTI SAUCE AUX FRAMBOISES £19.50
Boneless roast duckling, served with a delicious raspberry sauce
LES MEDAILLONS DE VEAU SUR AUBERGINE £19.50
Two veal fillets served with aubergine and a cream and Calvados sauce
LES MIGNONETTES DE BOEUF AU FOIE DE CANARD £19.50
Two prime Scotch fillets with fresh duck liver, in a tasty marrow-bone sauce
GROUSE VIGNERONNE £22.50
A delicious short season speciality

LES LEGUMES FRAIS DE LA SAISON OU LA SALADE PANACHEE £2.95

Much has happened in the restaurant industry since The Sundial opened over thirty years ago, and not all of it pleases chef proprietor Giuseppe Bertoli. Too many pubs masquerading as restaurants, too many microwaves and too much mediocrity are just a few bones of contention. And therein lies his enduring success - he is a premier chef specialising in French cuisine of the highest standard, and he doesn't pretend otherwise. When he and his charming wife Laure finally do retire, lovers of eating out in style will be all the poorer.

The main à la carte, a sample of which is shown opposite, changes every few weeks but always features daily specials such as delicious Belon Oysters (£8.50) and Le Loup de Mer Roti (£19.50). Set menus are also offered at lunch (3 courses £19.50, and on Sunday £22.50) and dinner (3 courses £27.50), whilst the more daring may elect Le Menu Gourmandaise de Signor Bertoli (a 5 course menu surprise £39.50). A fine selection of cheeses (£6.25) and a good choice of home-made desserts (£4.50) are complemented by an extensive wine list.

Directions: Conveniently located on the A271 at Herstmonceux, between Hailsham and Bexhill.

### USEFUL INFORMATION

**SERVING TIMES:**
Lunch 12pm-2pm (Tues-Fri)
12pm-2.30pm (Sat-Sun)
Dinner 7pm-9.30pm (Tues-Sat)
**CLOSED:** Sunday evening and all day Monday
**SEATING CAPACITY:** 50 in the restaurant, 22 in private dining-room
**C/C:** V, MC, S, D, AE, DC

**NUMBER OF WINES:** 250
**HOUSE WINE:** £12.25
**OFF-STREET PARKING:** yes
**OUTDOOR EATING:** yes
**RESERVATIONS:** advisable
**DRESS CODE:** smart casual
**NO SMOKING** in the restaurant, but allowed in the bar

# LANGSHOTT MANOR
Tel: (01293) 786680
Langshott, Horley, Surrey, RH6 9LN

### Dinner Menu

**Cream of Watercress Soup**
with Flaked Smoked Trout

**Potted Shrimp**
with Oriental Style Salad

**Guinea Fowl Terrine**

**Caesar Salad**
with Smoked Ham and Avocado

~ ~ ~

**Warm Red Pepper Mousse**
with Griddled Mediterranean Vegetables

**Grilled Baby Sole**
with Mussel and Saffron

**Best End of Lamb**
with Tarragon Mousse and Ratatouille

**Oriental Style Duck**
with Stir-fry Vegetables

**Calves Liver and Bacon**
with Creamed Onions and Sage

**Fillet of Beef**
with Mushroom and Herb Sauce and Confit of Garlic

~ ~ ~

**A Selection of Desserts**

Three Courses £32.50 including Coffee and Sweetmeats

Looking out across tranquil gardens and ponds whilst perhaps enjoying a pre-dinner gin and tonic, it is very hard to believe that Gatwick Airport, the M23 and the M25 are only a few miles away. There is little doubt that Langshott Manor, a beautifully restored grade 11 Elizabethan manor house, offers something rather special.

The restaurant itself is made up of two intimate dining rooms, light and airy in summer, cosy and warmed by roaring log fires in winter. The cuisine is modern European and the menus reflect a quality rather than a quantity of choice. The lunch menu (3 courses £24) is a smaller version of the dinner menu which appears opposite and both change weekly. Desserts may include Stewed Gooseberries with Stemmed Ginger Parfait, Chocolate Cheesecake with Orange Salad, and Hazelnut Tart.

Directions: From junction 9 of the M23 follow the signs to the A23 and Redhill. Continue north on the A23 for about 2 miles. At a large roundabout in Horley you will see the Chequer's Hotel on your left. Turn right down Ladbroke Road and after about a mile you will find the entrance on your right.

### USEFUL INFORMATION

**SERVING TIMES:**
Lunch 12.30pm-1.30pm (Sun-Fri)
Dinner 7pm-9.15pm (every day)
**CLOSED:** Saturday lunch
**SEATING CAPACITY:** 24
**C/C:** V, MC, S, D, AE, DC
**NO SMOKING** in the restaurant

**NUMBER OF WINES:** 50
**HOUSE WINE:** £12
**RESERVATIONS:** compulsory
**OUTDOOR EATING:** yes
**OFF-STREET PARKING:** yes
**ACCOMMODATION:** 10 rooms
(B&B single £105, double fr £135)

# DUKE WILLIAM INN
Tel: (01227) 721308
The Street, Ickham, near Littlebourne, Canterbury, Kent, CT3 1QP

## STARTERS

GRILLED BLACK PUDDING, TOPPED WITH CARAMELISED SHALLOTS, GARLIC & WILD MUSHROOMS, DEGLAZED WITH BALSAMIC VINEGAR & PORT WINE THEN FINISHED WITH A LITTLE CREAM £4.25

PIECES OF BRIE WRAPPED IN PARMA HAM, SET ON A CROUTON, BAKED & SERVED WITH REDCURRANT JELLY £5.95

SEAFOOD YORKSHIRE - INDIVIDUAL YORKSHIRE PUDDING SEASONED WITH SAFFRON, CUMIN, CREAM & A SELECTION OF SEAFOOD £4.95

FRESH RAVIOLINI STUFFED WITH FRESH CREPES, SERVED WITH A CREAM & ASPARAGUS SAUCE £5.75

## MAIN COURSES

GREEN LIP MUSSELS COOKED WITH MUSHROOMS, SPRING ONION, GARLIC, GINGER & FINISHED WITH CREAM, SERVED WITH EGG FRIED RICE £8.75

SALMON JAX STYLE - SERVED WITH A PUREE OF MANGO, BASIL, GINGER, LEMON ZEST & RASPBERRY VINEGAR £9.95

SPATCHCOCK POUSSIN BRUSHED WITH ENGLISH MUSTARD, GRILLED IN A SKILLET WITH BACON & CRANBERRY JELLY £6.95

PEPPERED CONFIT OF DUCK SERVED WITH GREEN PEPPERS, SHALLOTS, BRANDY, CREAM & JUS £13.75

BURGUNDY SIRLOIN STEAK - COATED IN GRUYERE CHEESE & GARNISHED WITH MUSHROOMS PROVENCALE £9.55

FILLET OF PORK QUEEN B - SAUTEED WITH HONEY, PINE NUTS & CREAM £9.25

WIENER SCHNITZEL - BREADCRUMBED VEAL ESCALOPE SAUTEED IN BUTTER & FINISHED WITH LEMON JUICE £10.75

HALF LEG OF LAMB (APPROX 2LB) SERVED ON A BED OF VEGETABLES WITH A RED WINE SAUCE. NB: MINIMUM OF 30 TO 45 MINUTES COOKING TIME IS REQUIRED £14.95

MIXED MUSHROOM STROGANOFF SERVED ON A BED OF RICE £9.25

What immediately drew me to The Duke William at Ickham was the saying printed at the foot of each page of their menu, *"A Day Without Wine Is Like A Day Without Sunshine"*. These people obviously know their stuff.

This 17th century inn is a traditional Kentish country pub that serves a phenomenal array of dishes. The à la carte restaurant menu on the facing page comprises just a tiny selection from their list. For example, there are 7 different ways to enjoy your avocado pear, 6 choices of mushrooms, 17 choices of fish dishes as a starter (38 for the main course!) and an unquantifiable number of variations to the style in which your breast of chicken might be prepared.

The whole experience is mind-boggling and I recommend that you take a speed reading course before your first visit.

Directions: The Duke William is easily found in the centre of Ickham village which is situated about 4 miles to the east of Canterbury and signposted from the main A257 Canterbury to Sandwich road.

### USEFUL INFORMATION

**SERVING TIMES:**
Lunch 12pm-2.30pm (Tues-Sun)
Dinner 6pm-10pm (Mon-Sat)
**CLOSED FOR FOOD:** Sunday night and Monday lunch
**SEATING CAPACITY:** 80 in the restaurant, 30 in the conservatory
**C/C:** V, MC, S, D, AE, DC

**NUMBER OF WINES:** 57
**HOUSE WINE:** £9.75
**RESERVATIONS:** advisable at the weekend
**NO SMOKING** areas available
**OFF-STREET PARKING:** yes
**CHILDREN:** welcome
**OUTDOOR EATING:** yes

# THE HUNGRY MONK
### Tel: (01323) 482178
Jevington, near Eastbourne, East Sussex, BN26 5QF

*Selected Dishes from our Seasonal Menus*

£24.00 inc. VAT

Yellow Pepper and Sage Soup with Fresh Parmesan
Warm Salad of Duck Livers, Lardons and Balsamic Onions
Red Mullet Mousse with Dill Hollandaise
Goats' Cheese and Sweet Pepper Tart
Three Cheeses in Filo with Cranberry Sauce
Ceviche of Scallops with Pancetta +£1.75
Watercress Salad with Hot Venison Sausages and pickled Walnuts

Fillet of Monkfish with Yellow Pepper and Prawn Sauce and Mangetout
Bouillabaisse of Salmon, Prawns, Scallops and Cod with Fennel and Pernod
Rack of English Lamb with Flageolet Beans, Redcurrant & Rosemary Sauce
Roast Stuffed Rabbit in Prosciutto with Mustard Sauce
Crisp Breast of Norfolk Duckling or Pink Breast of Barbary Duck with
Glazed Fruit and Vegetables and Madeira Sauce +£2.50
Medallions of Fillet Steak with Pink Peppercorn Sauce and Spinach +£2.50
Breast of Local Pheasant with Apple and Calvados Sauce

<u>Vegetarian:</u> Aubergine and Goats' Cheese Croustade with Fresh Tomato
Sauce served with a Green Salad or Green Beans

*All main courses are served with Fresh Vegetables and
Dauphinoise or New Potatoes*

A Glass of Dessert Wine
or
The Original Hungry Monk Banoffi Pie
Rice Pudding with Prunes in Armagnac
Lemon Tart with Cassis Sauce
Chocolate Hazelnut Meringue with Red Fruits
Brioche and Pear Pudding with Cream
Hungry Monk Sorbet
Hungry Monk Ice Cream
A Savoury of Parma Ham and Mushrooms on Toast
British Cheeses

Cafetière Coffee or Earl Grey Tea and Home-made Chocolates +£2

Dating back in part to the 12th century when three monks from a nearby monastery lived here, The Hungry Monk is a quite exceptional restaurant, full of charm and character with a worthy reputation for the excellence of its modern European cuisine. The interior is richly romantic and the four private dining rooms, each decorated with a certain amount of flair and individuality, offer the opportunity for even more intimate gatherings.

A young and enthusiastic team in the kitchen ensure that the high standards first set by the proprietors Nigel and Susan Mackenzie some 29 years ago are still maintained. Everything here is home-made and there is a strong, local emphasis - South Downs lamb, Newhaven fish, Sussex cheeses and so on. The seasonal menu changes every six weeks but special diets can be catered for in advance.

If you only try Banoffi Pie once more in your life, then try it here. For this is *the original*, and that's official!

Directions: About 3 miles west of Eastbourne on the A259 turn right towards Jevington. The Hungry Monk is easily found in the middle of the village.

### USEFUL INFORMATION

**SERVING TIMES:**
Lunch 12pm-2pm (Sunday)
Dinner 7pm-9.45pm (every day)
**CLOSED:** for lunch from Monday to Saturday
**SEATING CAPACITY:** 36 in the restaurant, between 2 and 16 in the 4 private dining rooms
**C/C:** AE

**NUMBER OF WINES:** 120
**HOUSE WINE:** £9
**NO SMOKING** in the restaurant
**RESERVATIONS:** compulsory
**CHILDREN:** over four years old are welcome
**OFF-STREET PARKING:** yes
**OUTDOOR EATING:** no, but there is a courtyard for drinks

# THE LIME TREE
### Tel: (01622) 859509
8-10 The Limes, The Square, Lenham, Maidstone, Kent, ME17 2PQ

## A SMALL SELECTION FROM OUR A LA CARTE MENU

### LES ENTREES
Consommé de Pintade £4.95
*Guinea fowl accompanied by herb quenelle & a paysan of seasonal vegetables*

Ravioles Vapeur an Crabe £6.75
*Home-made ravioli stuffed with crab presented with shellfish cappuccino & fennel julienne*

Charlotte de Homard et Sole £7.95
*A light lobster & sole mousse encased in smoked salmon accompanied by a parsley & dill oil*

### LES VIANDES
Tournedos de Boeuf £16.50
*Prime scotch beef pan-fried sliced around a croûte of polenta dressed with a shiitake mushroom sauce*

Suprême de Volaille £13.25
*Breast of chicken wrapped around a guinea fowl mousseline gently poached & presented sliced around a purée of Spinach with roast garlic, shallot & herb sauce*

### FLAMBE DISHES cooked at your table
Chateaubriand de la Maison £35.00
*Chef's special fillet steak - for two people*

### LES POISSONS ET CRUSTACES
Filet de Saumon d'Ecosse £13.95
*Roast fillet of fresh Scottish salmon served on a bed of wilted Spinach accompanied by light lobster stock thickened with butter*

Blanquette de Lotte £15.50
*Pan-fried monkfish tail accompanied by a saffron mussel stew*

Chausson de Bar £15.50
*Baked fillet of sea bass presented with a ginger and coriander sauce and a bouquet of glazed seasonal vegetables*

### METS VEGETARIANS
Tartelette aux Poireaux et Champignons de Bois £12.50
*Tartlet of leeks & oyster mushrooms topped with a herb crumble & dressed on a white wine & chive sauce*

The Lime Tree is an attractive family-run hotel situated in Lenham's picturesque village square. The building itself is steeped in history, the original timber-framed house dating back to the 14th century.

Their restaurant specialises in classic French and Continental cuisine, with an emphasis on fresh seafood.

The main à la carte menu, a selection from which appears opposite, changes every three to four months and is supplemented by a three-course table d'hôte menu, priced at £19.95 during the week and £21.95 on Saturdays. On Sundays a three-course luncheon menu is available (including a traditional roast dish) costing £14.95.

Directions: The village off Lenham is signposted from the A20, approximately midway between Maidstone and Ashford. The Lime Tree is at the far side of the village square opposite the church.

### USEFUL INFORMATION

**SERVING TIMES:**
Lunch 12pm-2pm (Sun-Fri)
Dinner 7pm-9.30pm (Mon-Sat)
**CLOSED:** Sat lunch & Sun night
**SEATING CAPACITY:** 60
**C/C:** V, MC, S, D, AE, DC
**NO SMOKING** in the restaurant
**OUTDOOR EATING:** yes

**NUMBER OF WINES:** 90
**HOUSE WINE:** £11.50
**RESERVATIONS:** advisable, but essential at weekends
**OFF-STREET PARKING:** yes
**CHILDREN:** welcome
**ACCOMMODATION:** 10 rooms (B&B sgl £42.50, dbl £56.50)

# THACKERY'S

Tel: (01273) 474634
3 Malling Street, Lewes, Sussex, BN7 2RA

2 Courses £18.00 or 3 Courses £21.50

*A selection from the main menu*

### TO START

**MUSSELS**
Cooked with Garlic, White Wine and Cream
**CRUNCHY TOPPED**
Cheesey Leek and Bacon Pot
**DEEP-FRIED CAMBAZOLA**
Served on a Warm Orange and Cranberry Sauce
**MIXED LEAF SALAD**
With Avocado, Sun-dried Tomatoes and Prawns topped with
Roasted Sunflower Seeds, served with Warm Olive Bread

### FOR YOUR MAIN COURSE

**TUNA STEAK**
Cooked Pink over charcoal finished with a Roasted Red Pepper Sauce
**FILLET OF SCOTTISH SALMON**
With Prawns in a Creamy Lemon Sauce
**MONK FISH**
With Garlic, Tomato & Basil
**ROAST HALF CRISPY DUCKLING**
With Kumquats and Stem Ginger flavoured with Five Spice
**PORK TENDERLOIN**
Cooked with Mushrooms, Grain Mustard, Honey and Cream
**THACKERY'S CARPETBAGGER STEAK**
A large Scotch Sirloin Steak stuffed with Smoked Oysters and Mushrooms
with an Onion Duxelle. Grilled over Charcoal and served in a Rich
Red Wine Sauce (£3.50 extra)

*All served with a Selection of Fresh Vegetables*

### SWEET COURSE

We offer a Daily Selection of home-made Desserts,
Home-made Ice Cream or Cheese

Situated in a row of 300 year old timbered cottages, Thackery's is an intimate restaurant renowned for its modern British cuisine.

The husband and wife team of Graham and Jaycee Funnell have built up a loyal following since opening some 14 years ago, and it really is a pleasure to dine here. The fixed price menu, a selection from which appears opposite, changes regularly to incorporate seasonal specialities. In addition to the main menu, a less expensive alternative is offered during the week (3 courses £16.50) when one may perhaps have Baked Avocado with Garlic Mushrooms topped with Melted Mozzarella to start, followed by Sussex Lamb Steak cooked pink over charcoal with Red Wine and Rosemary as a main course.

Desserts are all home-made with particular favourites being Graham's Amaretto Ice Cream, Fresh Fruit Pavlova, and hot cakes such as Apple and Walnut smothered in delicious Hot Toffee Fudge Sauce. Definitely not for those counting calories!

Directions: At the bottom of the hill in Lewes High Street, cross over the bridge and continue for about 200 yards along Cliffe High Street. At the T-junction you will see Thackery's opposite.

## USEFUL INFORMATION

**SERVING TIMES:**
Lunch in private dining room by appointment only
Dinner from 7pm (Tues-Sat)
**CLOSED:** Sunday and Monday
**SEATING CAPACITY:** 30 in the restaurant, 20 in the private dining room
**C/C:** V, MC, S, D, AE

**NUMBER OF WINES:** 60
**HOUSE WINE:** £8.50
**DRESS CODE:** smart casual
**RESERVATIONS:** advisable
**CHILDREN:** welcome early in the evening
**OFF-STREET PARKING:** no
**OUTDOOR EATING:** no

# KING WILLIAM IV
Tel: (01227) 721244
4 High Street, Littlebourne, Canterbury, Kent, CT3 1ST

### Starters

Gazpacho - A Chilled Spanish Soup £2.20
Beef Tomato, Basil and Mozzarella Salad £3.75
A Puff Pastry Box filled with Oyster and Button Mushrooms
and a Green Peppercorn Sauce £3.95
Home-made Beetroot Fettucini with Garlic, Chives and Olive Oil £3.95
Red Mullet Esquabeche - Grilled Fillets of Red Mullet
with Pickled Vegetables £3.95
Filo Basket of Mussels with Bacon and Brie £4.25

### Main Courses

House Smoked Chicken Breast with Roasted Peppers
on a bed of Salad with a Parmesan Dressing £7.50
Stuffed Savoy Cabbage Leaves filled with Wild Rice and Mixed Nuts
with a Tomato Sauce £6.75
Pan-fried Wild Boar Sausages with Dijon Mustard Mashed Potato
and Onion Gravy £7.25
Char-grilled Brochettes of Pork Fillet and Apricots,
Marinated in Honey and Rosemary with a Brandy Jus £7.95
Grilled Lamb Cutlets with Pesto Crust and a Red Wine Jus £7.95
Roasted Barbary Duck Breast on a Potato Rosti
with Caramelised Pear and a Blackcurrant Sauce £9.95
Char-grilled Beef Fillet Steak with Pomme Fondant, Parmesan
and Sautéed Mushrooms with a Thyme Jus £11.50

All Main Courses are Served with Potatoes and a Selection of Seasonal Vegetables

### Sweets

Walnut and Ricotta Cake £2.95
Apple and Thyme Tart Tatin with a Cinnamon Crème Anglaise £3.25
Summer Pudding with a Raspberry Coulis £3.25
Home-made Raspberry, Peach and Peach Schnapps Ice Cream
in a Brandy Snap Basket £3.25
Belgian Chocolate and Fresh Cherry Tart £3.25

Just a couple of miles from the medieval splendour of Canterbury, the King William IV belies its typical village inn appearance by offering excellent cuisine from a highly imaginative menu.

The inn was built in the late 18th century and, despite the foody nature of the business, is still a pub where the locals come for a drink. The dining area itself is decorated in a rustic style, with hop vines draped along the exposed beams and old pewter tankards hanging around invitingly.

The menu is constantly evolving, with at least two items changed every week. In addition to the *carte* on the facing page, a couple of blackboards show the daily fish specials, with dishes such as Roasted Monkfish Tail with Sautéed Mushrooms and Peppers and a Red Wine Jus (£8.50), Seared Steak of Cod with a Sweet Tomato Sauce (£7.95) or Char-grilled Salmon on a bed of Mangetout and Lemon Butter Sauce (£7.50).

Directions: 2 miles to the east of Canterbury, the King William IV is located in the centre of the village of Littlebourne on the main A257 Canterbury to Sandwich road.

## USEFUL INFORMATION

**SERVING TIMES:**
Lunch 12pm-2pm (every day)
Dinner 7pm-9.30pm (every day)
**SEATING CAPACITY:** 40
**C/C:** V, MC, S, D
**OUTDOOR EATING:** yes
**OFF-STREET PARKING:** yes

**NUMBER OF WINES:** 90
**HOUSE WINE:** £7.00
**RESERVATIONS:** advisable (as there are only 9 tables)
**ACCOMMODATION:** 7 rooms (B&B single £28, double £40)

# HORSTED PLACE

Tel: (01825) 750581
Little Horsted, near Uckfield, East Sussex, TN22 5TS

### A LA CARTE MENU

#### FIRST COURSE

**Pan-fried Scallops**
on sautéed Jerusalem artichoke and lobster dressing £9.80

**Confit of Duck Leg**
served on clay oven bread and azzupa dressing £7.50

**Fresh Noodles**
with smoked haddock and asparagus £7.00

**Strudel Pastry of Salmon and Leeks**
with a dill and sour cream dressing £6.50

**Warm Salad of Lamb's Lettuce**
with chive omelette and red wine dressing £4.50

#### MAIN COURSE

**Monkfish Tail**
wrapped in parma ham and basil on pease purée £19.50

**Saddle of Rabbit**
filled with shallots, brioche and lime leaf on shitake mushrooms £18.00

**Fillet of Beef**
with tomato, onion & coriander salsa, shallot rosti potato & pesto sauce £19.50

**Medallions of Pork**
with a tian of pork, prunes and hazelnuts £18.00

**Tartlet of Spinach and Mushrooms**
served on caramelised red onions and tomato butter sauce £14.00

**Salads**
Mixed Salad, Green Salad, or Curly Endive with Croûtons £3.50

Dating back to 1850 and one of the finest examples of Gothic revivalist architecture to be found in Britain, Horsted Place is now a luxurious country house hotel which stands proudly at the centre of its own beautiful estate.

The Pugin Restaurant offers a graceful setting in which to enjoy fine food. The classical English cuisine is elegantly yet simply prepared, drawing upon local produce whenever possible. The seasonal à la carte is shown opposite, and this is supplemented by daily table d'hôte menus available at both lunch (3 courses £17.95) and dinner (3 courses £30). These prices include coffee and mints.

The East Sussex National Golf Club, whose 10th fairway is overlooked by Horsted Place, also boasts a fine brasserie style restaurant named Hunningtons. Good value, fresh food is served at lunchtime and Friday and Saturday evenings (3 courses £19.95). Sunday lunch is especially popular.

Directions: Two miles south of Uckfield on the A22, turn right on to the A26 and the entrance to the hotel is a few hundred yards along on the right.

### USEFUL INFORMATION

**SERVING TIMES:**
Lunch 12.30pm-2pm (every day)
Dinner 7.30pm-9.30pm (every day)
**SEATING CAPACITY:** 40
**C/C:** V, MC, S, D, AE, DC
**CHILDREN:** welcome
**DRESS CODE:** jacket & tie preferred
**OUTDOOR EATING:** yes

**NUMBER OF WINES:** 80
**HOUSE WINE:** £12.50
**OFF-STREET PARKING:** yes
**NO SMOKING** in the restaurant
**RESERVATIONS:** advisable
**ACCOMMODATION:** 20 rooms
(B&B single £120, double £120)

# CISSWOOD HOUSE

**Tel: (01403) 891216**

Sandygate Lane, Lower Beeding, near Horsham, Sussex RH13 6NF

### A selection from the menu

#### STARTERS

SMOKED HADDOCK FEUILLETE WITH A LIGHT CREAM SAUCE WITH MUSHROOMS

SAFFRON GNOCCHI BAKED IN GORGONZOLA SAUCE

COLD POACHED SALMON WITH NEW POTATO SALAD

SPICY LAMB DUMPLINGS ON A BED OF SALAD WITH CORIANDER YOGHURT

SAUTEED TIGER PRAWNS WITH SPICY VERMICELLI NOODLE SALAD WITH LEMON AND GARLIC SAUCE (£1 supplement)

#### FISH COURSE

WHOLE DOVER SOLE GRILLED OR MEUNIERE (£2.50 supplement)

BAKED WHOLE SEABASS SCENTED WITH FENNEL & COOKED WITH OLIVE OIL

GRILLED HALIBUT FILLET TOPPED WITH CORIANDER AND LIME TARTARE AND FRESH HERB BREADCRUMBS

#### MEAT DISHES

NOISETTES OF LAMB SERVED WITH A WILD MUSHROOM DUXELLE

FRIED BREAST OF CHICKEN FILLET WITH FRESH HERBS, CHEESE, BACON AND SCENTED WITH GARLIC

HALF A CRISPY ROAST DUCK WITH APPLE SAUCE AND SAGE AND ONION STUFFING

PAILLARD OF VEAL WITH FRESH GARDEN HERBS

FILLET STEAK AU POIVRE

#### VEGETARIAN DISH

STUFFED HOME-GROWN PATTY PAN FILLED WITH LENTIL DE PUY AND MUSHROOMS WITH A CHEESE AND SAGE SAUCE

*All main courses are served with either a selection of fresh vegetables and potatoes or a seasonal salad*

Built in 1928 for the Chairman of Harrods, Sir Woodman Burbidge and his wife Cissily, and named after them, Cisswood House is now an elegant family-owned hotel and restaurant with an enviable reputation for its traditional French cuisine.

The chef/proprietor Othmar Illes personally selects and buys meat, fish, which is the house speciality, and vegetables from the London markets to ensure that the highest standards are maintained. An extensive menu, a small selection from which appears opposite, is offered at lunch (2 or 3 courses for £20.50 and £22.00 respectively) and dinner (2 or 3 courses for £21.50 and £24.50 respectively). Some dishes changes daily.

Desserts include a wonderful array of home-made sorbets and ice creams, as well as dishes such as Caramelised Banana encased in a fresh pancake with toffee sauce and vanilla ice cream, Praline Parfait with tulip biscuits, and Fresh Chocolate and Rum Mousse on a lake of coffee sauce. (Coffee and home-made petits fours are an additional £2.00)

Directions: Lower Beeding is a small village a few miles south-east of Horsham. From the A23 at Handcross, follow the A279 into Lower Beeding and where the road bears left, carry straight on. Cisswood House is a few hundred yards further along on the right.

## USEFUL INFORMATION

**SERVING TIMES:**
Lunch 12pm-2pm (Mon-Sat)
Dinner 7pm-9.15pm (Mon-Sat)
**CLOSED:** Sunday
**SEATING CAPACITY:** 70
**C/C:** V, MC, D, AE, DC
**OUTDOOR EATING:** no
**DRESS CODE:** smart casual

**NUMBER OF WINES:** 150
**HOUSE WINE:** £9.50
**RESERVATIONS:** advisable, but compulsory at weekends
**OFF-STREET PARKING:** yes
**ACCOMMODATION:** 34 rooms
(B&B single £75, double £95)

# JEREMY'S AT THE CRABTREE
Tel: (01403) 891257
Brighton Road, Lower Beeding, West Sussex, RH13 6PT

A typical three course dinner £25.00

### STARTERS

Ceviche with fresh coriander and a prawn dressing

Marinated mackerel and squid on crispy fennel salad

Stuffed tomatoes with roasted aubergine, feta and garlic on chicory salad

Gazpacho soup with fresh coriander

Chicken Balotine with oyster mushrooms and tarragon

### MAIN COURSES

Grilled & braised lamb with courgettes, sweet potato purée and a mild garlic cream

Pan-fried pigeon breast with bacon, celery & rocket in orange and sesame dressing

Goats' cheese, leek and baby spinach tart

Seared tuna with roasted peppers, tomato, cucumber & caper dressing

Fillets of plaice with Cornish crab on samphire with chive and ginger butter

### PUDDINGS

Apricot Pudding    Strawberry Millefeuilles    Lemon Tart
Chocolate Nemesis    Cashel Blue with biscuits

If you happen to be driving a little too quickly down the hill then it would be easy to miss The Crabtree, or to write it off as just another roadside pub. It would be your loss, because behind the rather inauspicious frontage is a jewel of a restaurant named Jeremy's.

There are no pretensions of grandeur here. The dining area spills into a friendly, flagstoned bar and the daily menus are hand-scrawled photocopies. But who cares? The atmosphere is lively, the food delicious, and during the week the value is exceptional.

The dinner menu featured opposite is supplemented by a daily à la carte and a set menu midweek (3 courses £12.50). Lunchtime specials include a two-course menu (£10.50) - perhaps Grilled Sardine with Lemon and Garlic on Tomato Salad, followed by Lime & Ginger Cheesecake - and a one-course menu (£6.50), which offers for example Seared Tuna on Salade Niçoise with a glass of Chardonnay. Bar snacks such as sandwiches (from £1.95) and ploughmans (from £4) are also available, Sunday lunch is £16.50, and theme evenings every Monday (2 courses £15) are very popular.

Directions: Lower Beeding is about 3 miles south-east of Horsham. Leaving the A23 at Handcross, follow the A279 to Lower Beeding and then bear left on the A281 towards Cowfold. Jeremy's is on the left after 200 yards.

### USEFUL INFORMATION

**SERVING TIMES:**
Lunch 12.30pm-2pm (every day)
Dinner 7.30pm-9pm (Mon-Sat)
**CLOSED:** Sunday evening
**SEATING CAPACITY:** 45 in the restaurant, 20 in the bar
**C/C:** V, MC, S, D, AE

**NUMBER OF WINES:** 40
**HOUSE WINE:** £10
**OFF-STREET PARKING:** yes
**NO SMOKING** area available
**RESERVATIONS:** advisable
**CHILDREN:** welcome
**OUTDOOR EATING:** yes

# THE CAMELLIA RESTAURANT
## Tel: (01403) 891711
South Lodge Hotel, Lower Beeding, near Horsham, West Sussex, RH13 6PS

*A selection from the A La Carte*

Cream of Asparagus and Watercress Soup
served with poached egg and crispy shallots
*Eight Pounds and fifty pence*

Pressed Terrine of Ham Hock and Potato
with parsley dressing
*Nine Pounds and fifty pence*

Ravioli of Smoked Haddock and Artichoke
with sauterne and caviar
*Ten Pounds and fifty pence*

*Main Courses*

Chargrilled Fresh Tuna
on olive potatoes with an oriental dressing
*Twenty~four Pounds and fifty pence*

Pan-fried Organic Beef Fillet
with home-smoked butter and oyster sauce
*Twenty~five Pounds*

Sautéed Monkfish
with artichoke brandade, cep veloute
*Twenty~four Pounds and fifty pence*

Breast of English Duckling
roasted with vanilla, apple and Calvados jus
*Twenty~three Pounds*

*Desserts*

Poached Fruits set in Muscat Jelly with vanilla syrup
*Eight Pounds*

South Lodge Assiette of Chocolate
*Eleven Pounds and fifty pence*

Prune and Armagnac Souffle with kirsch ice cream
*Eight Pounds*

Dating back to 1883 when it was built as a home for the Godman family, South Lodge is now a luxurious hotel which languishes contentedly in its own extensive gardens.

The Camellia Restaurant, complete with open fire, Victorian panelling and outstanding service is appropriately elegant without ever becoming too formal. Named after a 200 year old Camellia growing just outside, it overlooks the terrace and lawns where luncheon and dinner may be taken when the weather permits.

Head Chef Timothy Neal prepares traditional English cuisine with strong Mediterranean influences. The constantly evolving à la carte, which always indulges the chef's mushroom fetish by featuring a fungi of the day, is supplemented by daily table d'hôte menus offered at lunch (2/3 courses for £14.50/16.50, and Sunday lunch £19) and dinner (3/5 courses £25/32). There is also a daily vegetarian menu - perhaps Leek Tartlet with ratatouille and truffle to start (£6.50) and Chargrilled Vegetables with thyme rosti and mozzarella cheese to follow (£14).

Directions: Lower Beeding is a few miles south-east of Horsham. Leaving the A23 at Handcross, follow the A279 until it meets the A281. Turn left and the entrance to South Lodge is a short distance along on the right.

### USEFUL INFORMATION

**SERVING TIMES:**
Lunch 12pm-2.30pm (every day)
Dinner 7pm-10pm (every day)
**SEATING CAPACITY:** 45
**C/C:** V, MC, S, D, AE, DC
**NO SMOKING** in the restaurant
**OUTDOOR EATING:** yes
**DRESS CODE:** jacket & tie preferred

**NUMBER OF WINES:** 260
**HOUSE WINE:** £14.50
**RESERVATIONS:** advisable, but compulsory at weekends
**OFF-STREET PARKING:** yes
**ACCOMMODATION:** 39 rooms (single £120, double £145)

# THE MIDDLE HOUSE
Tel: (01435) 872146
Mayfield, East Sussex, TN20 6AB

### *A selection from the A La Carte*

**Singapore Crispy Duck £5.95**
*Crispy Duck served on a Pine Nut Mixed Leaf Salad with a Chinese Dressing*

**Cliquot Scallops £7.50**
*King Scallops Lightly Poached in a Champagne and Cream Sauce, garnished with Julienne of Crispy Leek*

**Jamaican Melon £5.00**
*Crown of Chilled Galia Melon filled with Mango and Fresh Ginger with a Spiced Rum Dressing*

**Parma Ham Paysanne £5.50**
*Italian Parma Ham with Roasted Vegetables Dressed with Balsamic Vinegar, Olive Oil and Fresh Basil*

**Brie en Croûte £4.95**
*Deep-fried French Brie Wrapped in Filo Pastry with a Sweet and Sour Blackberry and Port Chutney*

### ~ MAIN COURSES ~

**Sussex Lamb and Walnut Farcie £12.50**
*Boneless Rack of Lamb Roasted Pink with Rosemary and Garlic served on a Walnut Farcie with a Honey and Garlic Sauce*

**Five Spiced Duck £12.25**
*Half Chinese Spiced Duck in an Apricot and Ginger Glaze*

**Calves' Liver Jerez £11.95**
*Filled with Spinach and Tarragon, Sautéed Pink with Cream and Sherry*

**Ported Wild Boar £10.95**
*Wild Boar Steak in a Port Sauce served on a Garlic and Parsnip Rosti*

**Seafood Fricassé £13.50**
*Scotch Salmon and King Scallops cooked in a Chablis White Wine and Cream Sauce served with a Dill Rice Timbale*

Dating back to 1575, The Middle House is Grade 1 listed and described as 'one of the finest timber framed buildings in Sussex'. After many years as a private residence, it became a local inn in 1926 before undergoing substantial renovation in the late 1980's to become the luxury small hotel that it is today.

The restaurant itself is stunning. Incorporating the old private chapel, it boasts ornate carvings, oak-panelling from floor to ceiling, two open fires and sweeping views over the award-winning gardens and the Vale of Heathfield beyond. Drawing heavily from local suppliers and using only fresh produce, chef Russell Webb ensures that his cuisine is of the highest standard. The seasonal à la carte featured opposite is supplemented by excellent daily specials which always include a fine array of fish dishes.

For those after a less formal meal then the bar menu, complete with a large selection of blackboard specials, might well be the answer. The Sunday lunch (3 courses £14.95) and Wednesday Jazz Evenings (3 courses £14.95) are very popular.

Directions: Mayfield is about 8 miles south of Tunbridge Wells, just off the A267. The Middle House is easily found in the high street.

## USEFUL INFORMATION

**SERVING TIMES:**
Lunch 12pm-2pm (Mon-Sat)
　　　12pm-2.30pm (Sunday)
Dinner 7pm-9.30pm (every day)
**SEATING CAPACITY:** 60 in the restaurant, 50 in the bar
**C/C:** V, MC, S, D, AE, DC
**NO SMOKING** of pipes and cigars in the restaurant

**NUMBER OF WINES:** 60
**HOUSE WINE:** £8.95
**OFF-STREET PARKING:** yes
**RESERVATIONS:** advisable, but not available in the bar
**OUTDOOR EATING:** yes
**CHILDREN:** welcome
**ACCOMMODATION:** 9 rooms (B&B single £45, double fr £55)

# KING WILLIAM IV

Tel: (01372) 372590
Byttom Hill, Mickleham, near Dorking, Surrey, RH5 6EL

## MAIN COURSES

**Steak, Kidney and Mushroom Pie £6.95**
cooked in Guinness under a Crispy Pastry Topping

**Hot Poached Scottish Salmon £7.95**
with a White Wine and Mushroom Sauce

**Seafood Pie £6.95**
Cod, Cockles and Mussels under a Crispy Pastry Topping

**Tandoori Chicken £8.50**
served with Salad, Fresh Fruits, Minted Yoghurt and New Potatoes

**Cold Poached Scottish Salmon £7.95**
with a Strawberry and Avocado Salad and New Potatoes

**Pasta with Prawns £6.75**
in a Tomato, Pepper and Mushroom Sauce, served with a Salad

**Tostados (Mexican Style) £6.25**
Spicy Beans in Tomato Sauce, served with Crispy Corn Pancakes
with Salad and Guacamole

**Brie and Leek in Filo Pastry £6.50**
served with a choice of Salad or Fresh Vegetables and New Potatoes

**Italian-style Pasta £6.25**
in a Tomato, Pepper and Mushroom Sauce
served with a Salad and Parmesan

## HOME-MADE DESSERTS

**Bread and Butter Pudding £2.95**
with Ice Cream and Maple Syrup

**Fruit Crumble £2.95**
with Ice Cream

**Treacle Tart £2.95**
with Custard

**Cheese and Biscuits £3.50**

Originally an ale-house for Lord Beaverbrook's estate staff, The King William IV is an unusual and attractive free-house, part Victorian but principally dating from 1790. It has a unique position, perched on a hillside (alongside the main A24) with picturesque views from the lovely terraced garden across Norbury Park and the Mole Valley.

This historic inn is certainly more a pub than a restaurant, although a great deal of care and attention is nevertheless afforded the food. But don't expect a menu! The predominantly English and Mediterranean dishes are written up on the blackboard (although they are changed only twice a year) and are subject to considerable alteration if the pub is very busy (especially Sunday lunchtimes, Bank Holidays and "extremely hot days"). This is to ensure that the very high standard is maintained.

A couple of daily specials are normally available, such as Fillets of Red Mullet with Prawns, Almonds and Mushrooms (£7.50) or Baked Cod Steak with Leeks and Prawns in a Provençale sauce (£8.75).

Directions: From junction 9 on the M25 follow the A24 signposted to Dorking. Shortly before the village of Mickleham, the King William IV can be seen standing on the hill above the Frascati restaurant. Incidentally, the Frascati car park is a public car park and can be used at all times.

### USEFUL INFORMATION

**SERVING TIMES:**
Lunch 12pm-2pm (every day)
Dinner 7pm-9.30pm (Tues-Sun)
**CLOSED FOR FOOD:** Mon night
**SEATING CAPACITY:** 48 in the bar, 90 in the garden area
**C/C:** V, MC, S, D
**CHILDREN:** please telephone first

**NUMBER OF WINES:** 12
**HOUSE WINE:** £7.95
**RESERVATIONS:** limited
**OUTDOOR EATING:** yes
**NO WHEELCHAIR ACCESS**
**OFF-STREET PARKING:** no, but see "Directions" above

# THE ANGEL HOTEL
Tel: (01730) 812421
North Street, Midhurst, West Sussex, GU29 9DN

### THE COWDRAY ROOM

*~ a selection of dishes ~*

Terrine of Pork, Apricots & Pistachio with Beetroot Relish £6.50
Deep-fried Cornish Squid with Avocado & Chilli Salad £6.50
Paw Paw, Cracked Selsey Crab & Chilli Dressing £6.85
Seared Red Mullet, Couscous & Mediterranean Vegetables £7.50
Lobster, Avocado & Mango Salad £7.50
Pressed Ham Terrine, Asparagus & Truffle Salad £6.75

\* \* \* \* \*

Cold Poached Supreme of Scottish Salmon, Herb Mayonnaise £12.75
Roast Channel Cod with Asparagus, Tomato & Basil £12.00
Half a Devon Lobster Cold or Thermidor £15.50
Veal Cutlet with Polenta & Local Cèpes £13.00
Roast Yorkshire Grouse in the Traditional Style £16.00
Lamb Sweetbreads in Pastry Leaves, Tarragon Cream Sauce,
Baby Garden Carrots £13.00
Breast of Chicken with Chorizo Sausage & Roast Garlic £12.00
Grilled Rib of Aberdeen Angus Beef with Shallots and a
Burgundy Wine Sauce £12.00
Sage Gnocchi with Gorgonzola £12.00

Caesar Salad £3.50
Mixed or Green Salad £1.95
A Selection of Daily Vegetables & Potatoes £2.50
Pommes Frites or Minted New Potatoes £1.95

\* \* \* \* \*

Baked Vanilla Cheesecake with Caramelised Kumquats £5.50
Iced Nougat Glaces with Poached Fruit £5.25
Caramelised Banana Tart Flamed with Rum £6.50
Pear and Cardamom Crème Brûlée £4.95
Selection of Home-made Ice Creams & Sorbets £4.95

A fine example of an old English coaching inn, the Angel Hotel has been closely associated with the small town of Midhurst and the neighbouring Cowdray Estate since the 15th century. Sympathetically restored by the present proprietors Peter Crawford-Rolt and Nicholas Davies, the hotel offers elegant accommodation and enjoys an excellent reputation for the quality of its cuisine.

The Cowdray Room offers an à la carte at lunch and dinner featuring contemporary British dishes, complemented by those from the Continent and Caribbean. This changes daily and an example is shown on the facing page. A similar, but slightly less expensive version is served in the more relaxed atmosphere of the brasserie. Good value, daily table d'hôte menus are also available here at luncheon (2 courses £12.50) and dinner (3 courses £21.50).

Directions: Easily found in the middle of Midhurst on North Street.

## USEFUL INFORMATION

**SERVING TIMES:**
Lunch 12pm-2.30pm (every day)
Dinner 7pm-9.30pm (every day)
Brasserie 6pm-10pm (every day)
**SEATING CAPACITY:** 60 in the restaurant, 40 in the brasserie
**C/C:** V, MC, S, D, AE, DC
**DRESS CODE:** jacket & tie requested in the restaurant at dinner

**NUMBER OF WINES:** 122
**HOUSE WINE:** £11.75
**OFF-STREET PARKING:** yes
**RESERVATIONS:** advisable
**OUTDOOR EATING:** yes
**CHILDREN:** welcome
**ACCOMMODATION:** 28 rooms (B&B single fr £80, double fr £90)

# MAXINE'S

Tel: (01730) 816271
Red Lion Street, Midhurst, West Sussex, GU29 9PB

## A LA CARTE MENU

### Starters

Robert's Fish Soup with Rouille, Cheese and Croûtons £4.95

Gravadlax with Mustard and Dill Sauce £5.95

Crab Cakes with Tomato and Coriander Sauce £4.95

King Prawns fried in Garlic Butter £6.50

Goat's Cheese Bavarois with roasted Sweet and Sour Tomatoes £4.95

Prawns and Mango Salad with Avocado and Thai Sauce £5.95

### Main Courses

Fresh Fish of the Day £M.P.

Spicy King Prawns in Garlic Butter £12.95

Poached Salmon with Sorrel Sauce £9.95

Sirloin Steak with Peppercorns in White Wine Cream Sauce £10.50

Calf's Liver with Citrus Sauce £10.95

Lamb Fillet with Tarragon and Madeira Sauce £14.95

Sweetbreads with Prawns in a White Wine Sauce £11.50

Half a Crispy Duck with Raspberry Sauce £12.95

King Prawns with Coconut and Chilli served with Rice £12.50

### Puddings

Dutch Apple Pie served with Cream £4.50

Sticky Toffee Pudding with warm Butterscotch Sauce £4.50

Hazelnut Parfait £4.50

Meringue filled with fresh Fruit and Cream £4.50

Vanilla Ice Cream with Coffee Syrup £4.50

*Prices are inclusive of service and VAT*

# MIDHURST 133

Crisp white table linen welcomes you to Maxine's, an intimate continental restaurant housed in a 15th century black-and-white half-timbered building in the centre of Midhurst.

The Dutch husband and wife team of Robert and Marti de Jager have built up a loyal following over the past 17 years, with Robert in charge of the kitchen and Marti providing the very friendly, informal service front of house.

In addition to the à la carte menu on the facing page, a three-course set price menu is available (except on Saturday nights) costing £14.95 with a choice of four dishes at each course.

Directions: Maxine's can be found in Red Lion Street on the corner between Church Hill and the town square, not far from the Spread Eagle Hotel.

## USEFUL INFORMATION

**SERVING TIMES:**
Lunch 12pm-1.30pm (Wed-Sun)
Dinner 7pm-9.30pm (Wed-Sat)
**CLOSED:** Sunday night and all day Mondays & Tuesdays
**SEATING CAPACITY:** 24
**C/C:** V, MC, S, D, AE
**NO SMOKING** in the restaurant

**NUMBER OF WINES:** 60
**HOUSE WINE:** £9.95
**RESERVATIONS:** advisable
**OFF-STREET PARKING:** no
**OUTDOOR EATING:** no
**CHILDREN:** welcome
**NO WHEELCHAIR ACCESS**

# OLDE MANOR HOUSE
Tel: (01730) 812990
Church Hill, Midhurst, West Sussex, GU29 9NX

## A SELECTION FROM THE A LA CARTE MENU

Stir-fried Gamba Prawns
in a Thai Herb Cream Sauce

A Broth of Wild Mushrooms
finished with Chive Flocked Cream drizzled with Truffle Oil

Puff Pastry Tartelette
encasing Quenelles of Wild Salmon Mousse
upon a pool of Blood Orange and Coriander Beurre Blanc

Chicken Liver and Foie Gras Parfait
upon a Madeira Gelée

\* \* \* \* \*

Roasted Fillet of Wild Salmon
in a Nest of Samphire with a Bantry Bay Mussel Sauce

Tails of Monkfish
with a Tomato and Saffron Coulis

Prime Fillet of Scotch Beef
topped with a Red Onion and Grenadine Marmalade

Strips of Corn-fed Chicken Breast
in a Pernod and Cucumber Sauce inside a Crisp Pastry Chest

Roasted Canon of Lamb
carved upon Aubergine Caviar served with Roasted Garlic Cloves

Avocado Filled with Chestnuts and Cheese
baked in Lattice Pastry with Saffron Pilau

\* \* \* \* \*

Marquesse de Chocolat, Pistachio Nuts

Lemon Tart with Lemon Ice Cream

Fresh Mango
prepared at your table

A Selection of Cheeses

Olde Manor House is a 14th century black-and-white timbered town house restaurant serving cuisine based on a classical theme but adapted to include modern, international flavours.

The restaurant is well-known for classical dishes prepared at your table, such as Steak Tartare served with Traditional Seasonings, Chateaubriand with Sauce Béarnaise, Dover Sole Grilled or Poached and served with Lemon or Meunière, or a particular favourite of this author's (but it's a very long story that involves careering around the Yucatan Peninsula in a vain search for one) Roast Suckling Pig with Apple Sauce.

The restaurant enjoys a very formal atmosphere, with highly efficient service and general pampering. Post-prandial drinks can be taken in either the bar area or the more relaxed ambience of the conservatory.

Directions: Olde Manor House is located on Church Hill, between Midhurst's main road North Street and the town square.

### USEFUL INFORMATION

**SERVING TIMES:**
Lunch 12pm-2.30pm (Tues-Sun)
Dinner 7pm-10.30pm (Tues-Sat)
**CLOSED:** Sun night & all day Mon
**SEATING CAPACITY:** 60
**C/C:** V, MC, AE, DC

**NUMBER OF WINES:** 90
**HOUSE WINE:** £8.95
**RESERVATIONS:** advisable
**OUTDOOR EATING:** no
**CHILDREN:** welcome
**OFF-STREET PARKING:** no

# THE SPREAD EAGLE HOTEL
Tel: (01730) 816911
South Street, Midhurst, West Sussex, GU29 9NH

## FIXED PRICE A LA CARTE
## £28.50
*(includes canapé, coffee and petit four)*

Chilled Cucumber and Crayfish Soup

Spinach Mousse with a Tomato Butter Sauce and Crispy Fried Leeks

Home-Smoked Scottish Salmon with Salad Leaves and Lemon (£3 supp)

Pan-Fried Wood Pigeon with Braised Lentils and a Grain Mustard Sauce

Three Layer Fish Terrine wrapped in Spinach with a Brandy and Dill Relish

Bresaola of Angus Beef with Salad Leaves, Parmesan Cheese & Virgin Olive Oil

Home-Smoked Chicken and Quail Egg Salad with Artichoke and Pink Grapefruit

~ ~ ~ ~ ~

Poached Fillet of North Sea Turbot with Home-made Noodles and Samphire
with a Tarragon Mustard Sauce

Steamed Loch Fyne Salmon with Vegetable Ribbons & a light Red Pepper Sauce

Fillet of Aberdeen Angus Beef with Vegetables and a Rich Red Wine Sauce

Sautéed Calf Kidney with local Chantrelle Mushrooms, Caramelised Shallots,
Noisette Potatoes and a Herb Risotto

Roast Confit of Duck Leg with Sweet Red Cabbage, Celeriac,
Crushed Olive Potatoes and a Blackberry Sauce

Sautéed Pork Fillet cooked with Herbs and Salsify
with Sautéed Potatoes and a rich Madeira Sauce

Roasted Best End of Sussex Hill Lamb with Caramelised Shallots, Garlic,
Mushrooms, Bacon Lardons and Fondant Potatoes (£3 supp)

Double Scottish Beef Entrecôte Roasted Rare to Medium to enjoy at its best
with a Rich Red Wine Sauce (£8 supp for two people)

~ ~ ~ ~ ~

Warm Mirabelle Plum Soufflé with its own Compôte

A Marbled Raspberry Parfait served with Poached Peach in a Vanilla Syrup

Hot Blackberry and Apple Tart with Apple Sorbet and a Vanilla Sauce

Steamed Chocolate Sponge with Two Sauces of Orange Custard and Chocolate

Seasonal Berries served in a Brioche Loaf with Cinnamon Ice Cream

The Spread Eagle Hotel dates back to 1430 and was originally one of England's oldest coaching inns. The hotel's restaurant has built up an enviable reputation over the years and head chef Ken Jelfs' cooking continues to make the best use of Britain's great natural larder (his words, not mine).

The fixed price *carte*, an example of which appears on the facing page, presents a few modern twists on some old favourites. At lunchtimes a lighter à la carte menu breaks with tradition and offers dishes which can be taken either as smaller portions or as more substantial main meals.

These might include Salad of Citrus Marinated Chicken with Sliced New Potatoes, Croûtons and a Raspberry Vinegar Dressing (£4.95 or £8.50), A Platter of St. Danille Parma Ham with Galia Melon and Garden Salad (£5.20 or £9.50) or perhaps Home-made Loch Fyne Salmon and Chive Fishcakes with Lemon Butter, Timbale of Broccoli and New Potatoes (£5.20 or £8.45).

Directions: The hotel is easily found in South Street near the centre of town.

## USEFUL INFORMATION

**SERVING TIMES:**
Lunch 12pm-2pm (every day)
Dinner 7pm-9.30pm (Sun-Thur)
    7.30pm-10pm (Fri & Sat)
**SEATING CAPACITY:** 70
**C/C:** V, MC, S, D, AE, DC
**NO SMOKING** in the restaurant
**OUTDOOR EATING:** yes

**NUMBER OF WINES:** 320
**HOUSE WINE:** £9.50
**RESERVATIONS:** advisable
**OFF-STREET PARKING:** yes
**CHILDREN:** welcome
**NO WHEELCHAIR ACCESS**
**ACCOMMODATION:** 39 rooms
(B&B from £55 p.p. per night)

# THE BULL INN
### Tel: (01825) 722055
The Green, Newick, East Sussex, BN8 4LA

## Starters

| | |
|---|---|
| **Hot Wedges of Brie** | £4.25 |
| *served on a pool of Cumberland Sauce* | |
| **Avocado Pear** | £3.95 |
| *grilled with Prawns & Stilton* | |
| **Fan of Melon** | £3.25 |
| *set on a Strawberry Coulis* | |
| **Chef's Chicken Liver Pâté** | £3.45 |
| *served with Plum Compot & Toast* | |
| **Smoked Trout Fillet** | £4.45 |
| *served with tossed Salad & a Lemon and Peppercorn Dressing* | |

## Main Courses

| | |
|---|---|
| **Paupiettes of Plaice** | £9.95 |
| *lined with Oak-Smoked Salmon, poached and served with a Cheese Sauce* | |
| **Tronçon of Salmon** | £8.50 |
| *on a bed of ribboned courgettes with a Dill Sauce* | |
| **Roast Half Duckling** | £8.95 |
| *with a Grand Marnier Sauce & Oranges* | |
| **Braised Guinea Fowl** | £8.50 |
| *with red Pimento Sauce & Asparagus Spears* | |
| **Medallions of Pork** | £8.25 |
| *flamed in Brandy & served with a Pepper Sauce* | |
| **Rack of Lamb** | £9.75 |
| *served with a Redcurrant & Rosemary Sauce* | |
| **Veal Cordon Bleu** | £9.95 |
| *filled with Cheddar Cheese & Ham, breadcrumbed and served with a Sherry Sauce* | |

*Al our Main Course Dishes are served with Seasonal Vegetables and Potatoes*

The Bull Inn dates back to 1510 when it served as a resting place for weary pilgrims travelling from Winchester to Canterbury. Today it retains much of its 16th century character, with old oak beams, low ceilings and open fires. The popular restaurant that adjoins the bar area occupies the site of the old milking parlour.

Featured opposite is a small selection from the seasonal à la carte menu. This is supplemented by a good selection of steaks (from £8.95) and vegetarian dishes which appear with other daily specials shown on a blackboard.

There is also a Snack Menu for those after a lighter meal. This includes choices such as Steak, Kidney & Guinness Pie (£5.50), Cajun Chicken (£7.50) and Wholetail Scampi (£5.45) as well as traditional favourites like ploughman's (£3.95), jacket potatoes (from £3.50), salads and sandwiches. The Sunday roast offers an optional three courses for £10.95.

Directions: Newick is about 3 miles west of Uckfield on the A272. The Bull is at the top end of the village green.

## USEFUL INFORMATION

**SERVING TIMES:**
Lunch 12pm-2pm (every day)
Dinner 7pm-9pm (every day)
**SEATING CAPACITY:** 50 in the restaurant, 30 in the bar
**C/C:** V, MC, S, D, AE, DC
**CHILDREN:** welcome

**NUMBER OF WINES:** 20
**HOUSE WINE:** £7.95
**RESERVATIONS:** advisable, but compulsory at weekends
**OUTDOOR EATING:** yes
**OFF-STREET PARKING:** yes

# NEWICK PARK
Tel: (01825) 723633
Newick, East Sussex, BN8 4SB

## Starters

Assiette of Home Smoked Salmon served with a
Horseradish Cream and a Blini with Sevruga Caviar
£7.50

Salad of Pan-fried Foie Gras
with Fresh Summer Truffles and a Port Dressing
£8.25

Cappuccino of Lentils scented with Truffle Oil
£5.25

Roast Quail with a nest of Deep-fried Vegetables
with its own Egg
£6.50

## Main Courses

Roasted John Dory on a bed of Herbs & Olive Oil
topped with a Parmesan Galette
£18.25

Fillet of Beef served on a Rich Red Wine and Shallot Sauce
£18.95

Pan-fried Salmon on a Sorrel Sabayon
£16.95

Breast of Barbary Duck slowly roasted on a Fondue of
Spring Onions and a Plum & Armagnac Sauce
£17.50

Pan-fried Fillet of Veal served with its own Jus
£18.50

Assiette of South Downs Lamb
on a bed of Lentils served with a Garlic & Thyme Jus
£17.95

Michael and Virginia Childs spent the best part of six years renovating Newick Park and they have achieved that rare combination of understated luxury and genuine warmth. This proud Georgian house effuses charm from every corner and I could have sat in the lounge all day, sipping coffee and enjoying sweeping views over the 200 acre estate and on towards the South Downs themselves.

As one may expect the restaurant is beautiful. High ceilings, ornate trimmings and an elegant decor anticipate the culinary feast to come. The à la carte menu, which changes weekly, relies on quality rather than quantity of choice and an example is shown opposite. There is also a Gourmet Menu offering 5 courses for £25.

At luncheon a weekly table d'hôte (3 courses and coffee £17.50) is available together with a selection of lighter dishes.

Directions: From Newick, which lies about 3 miles west of Uckfield on the A272, turn south on the green and follow the signposts to Newick Park. At the first T-junction turn left and after a few hundred yards the entrance to the estate is found on your right.

## USEFUL INFORMATION

**SERVING TIMES:**
Lunch 12pm-2pm (every day)
Dinner 7pm-10pm (Mon-Sat)
**CLOSED:** Sunday night
**SEATING CAPACITY:** 45
**C/C:** V, MC, S, D, AE
**NO SMOKING** in the restaurant
**CHILDREN:** welcome

**NUMBER OF WINES:** 55
**HOUSE WINE:** £8.70
**RESERVATIONS:** advisable
**OUTDOOR EATING:** yes
**OFF-STREET PARKING:** yes
**ACCOMMODATION:** 13 rooms
(B&B single £95, double fr £160)

# THE BELL
Tel: (01342) 842989
Outwood Lane, Outwood, Redhill, Surrey, RH1 5PW

*A selection from the à la carte menu*

### STARTERS

**Thai Mushrooms £3.95**
Whole button mushrooms marinated in a home-made Thai sauce and baked in the oven, served warm with flour tortillas and a salad garnish
**Surrey Tartlet £3.95**
A home-made shortcrust pastry filled with cheese, onions, mushrooms and leeks, lightly seasoned with herbs. Served hot or cold with a salad garnish
**"The Bell" Duet Platter £7.95**
A deep-fried selection of spicy chicken breast fillets, jalapeno peppers, onion rings, prawn brochettes, Yakatori chicken, brie parcels & potato skins, served with garnish & dips
**Home-made Brie Parcels £3.90**
Fingers of brie coated in breadcrumbs then deep-fried, served with a choice of garlic mayonnaise or redcurrant dip and a salad garnish

### MAIN COURSES

**Chicken Fajita £9.50**
Tender strips of chicken marinated in red wine and cajun spices, sautéed with onions, mushrooms and peppers, served on a sizzling skillet. Accompanied with flour tortillas, tomato salsa, sour cream and guacamole
**Caribbean Lamb £8.65**
Medallions of lamb lightly griddled, served on a bed of stir-fried peppers, onions, aubergines and tomatoes, laced with a delicate rum & pineapple sauce. Served with sauté potatoes
**Misto di Mare £8.75**
A stir-fry combination of pasta, vegetables, smoked salmon, mussels, prawns & monkfish blended in a cream & white wine sauce, accompanied with garlic bread and salad
**Sautéed Monkfish £11.75**
Nuggets of monkfish wrapped in Scotch smoked salmon sautéed in a light garlic butter, served with a delicate lobster sauce, and a selection of fresh vegetables and potatoes
**Old Smokie Pie £8.50**
Smoked haddock, broccoli florets & sliced mushrooms in a creamy cheddar cheese sauce, topped with puff pastry. Served with fresh vegetables and potatoes
**Vegetable Bellington £6.95**
Fresh vegetables layered with cheese then enveloped in puff pastry, served on a spicy tomato sauce, with fresh vegetables and potatoes
**Warm Pasta Salad £7.95**
Vegetarian cheddar cheese, tomatoes, red peppers, mushrooms, penne pasta, sun-dried tomatoes, sliced black olives & onions lightly sautéed, then nestled on a bed of fresh salad in a crispy flour tortilla

# OUTWOOD 143

A quarter ton bronze bell hanging by the front door welcomes visitors to this traditional 17th century coaching inn at Outwood. The inside is charming, with an original inglenook fireplace, ceiling and wall beams cut from the timbers of a Charles II man-o'-war, and the occasional appearance by a ghostly grey lady who suffered a gruesome fate on the ancient hanging tree in the rear garden.

The food served here really is very good, enjoying an excellent reputation and offering a remarkable range of dishes. The seasonal à la carte takes a little over three days to read from cover to cover, and only a very small selection from it is shown opposite. For those of you who can't find anything there to take your fancy, or are simply put off by books with no pictures, then daily specials featuring another ten main courses and a handful of starters and desserts are written up on a large blackboard. I am almost too embarrassed to add that a bar menu is also available!

Directions: Outwood is a little village between the A22 and the M23 about 4 miles south-east of Redhill. From the A22 follow the signposts to Horne and then Outwood. At the T-junction on the village green turn right, and The Bell is about 150 yards further along.

## USEFUL INFORMATION

**SERVING TIMES:**
Lunch 12pm-2pm (Mon-Sat)
and all day 12pm-9pm (Sunday)
Dinner 6.30pm-9.30pm (every day)
Light snacks served all day (Mon-Fri)
**SEATING CAPACITY:** 74 in the restaurant, 44 in the bar
**C/C:** V, MC, S, D, AE

**NUMBER OF WINES:** 30
**HOUSE WINE:** £7.95
**OFF-STREET PARKING:** yes
**RESERVATIONS:** advisable, but compulsory at weekends
**OUTDOOR EATING:** yes
**CHILDREN:** welcome
**NO SMOKING** area available

# THE DUCK INN
## Tel: (01227) 830354
Pett Bottom, Bridge, near Canterbury, Kent, CT4 5PB

## A LA CARTE MENU

### Starters

Home-made leek & potato soup  £3.25
Pan-fried squid with spring onion mayonnaise  £3.95
Mussels steamed with cider & cream  £4.95
Smoked salmon parfait  £4.95
Course duck pâté  £3.95
Avocado pear with a Stilton & tomato vinaigrette  £3.45
Warm salad of chicken livers with a balsamic vinaigrette  £3.95

### Main Courses

Fillet steak bordelaise  £12.00
Poached supreme of chicken in a port & oyster sauce  £7.95
Barbary duck breast with orange & ginger  £9.00
Breast of pheasant with an apricot flambée  £7.25
Fillet of pork with pâté & a Dijon mustard cream sauce  £8.95
Lemon sole baked with white wine & mussels  £9.25
Smoked salmon baked with a herb cheese on a fresh tomato vinaigrette  £8.25
Soused whole mackerel with rosemary & red cabbage  £6.95
Gratin of avocado & mushroom with Gruyère cheese  £6.25

### Home-made Puddings

Crème caramel  £2.75
Caramelised oranges with hazelnut shortbread  £2.75
Date & walnut steamed pudding  £2.75
Walnut & maple syrup steamed pudding  £2.75
Treacle tart  £2.75
Real traditional creamy rice pudding  £2.75
Pears in red wine with almond shortbread  £2.75
Jam Roly Poly  £2.75
Irish whiskey chocolate fudge cake  £2.75
Strawberry crêpes  £2.75
Gooseberry & lemon tart  £2.75
Fruits of the forest with Cassis & flapjack  £2.75

# PETT BOTTOM 145

The Duck at Pett Bottom is a traditional 17th century country inn set in beautiful Kent countryside. The pub has links with Noel Coward and Ian Fleming, both of whom lived locally and drank regularly in the tiny public bar now known as *The James Bond Bar*. The celebrity status also extends to more recent times - shortly before my visit Marlon Brando had taken a few friends to dine in the restaurant and the table of four (plus child) ate their way through 7 starters, 7 main courses and 9 puddings, allegedly!

The à la carte menu changes every week according to the availability of fresh produce. The dishes opposite represent a typical weekend menu - the blackboard is condensed during the week and may only carry perhaps 4 starters and 6 mains. The bar food is equally good and might include Calamari Pan-fried in Garlic and Tomato (£3.95), Bacon Volcano Salad (£5.95) and a preposterous selection of home-made pies, such as Beef & Guinness, Chicken & Cider, or Lamb & Apricot (all £6.95).

Directions: The Duck Inn is located at Pett Bottom, approximately 4 miles to the south of Canterbury. To get there, take the first exit on the A2 east of Canterbury signposted to Bridge. Follow the road down to a crossroads and go straight across, signposted to Pett Bottom. Then take the second left under the railway bridge and follow this country lane for roughly 2 miles.

### USEFUL INFORMATION

**SERVING TIMES:**
Lunch 12pm-2.30pm (every day)
Dinner 6.30pm-10pm (Mon-Sat)
7pm-9pm (Sun)
**SEATING CAPACITY:** 30 in the restaurant, 20 in the bar
**C/C:** V, MC, S, D, AE, DC
**OUTDOOR EATING:** yes
**OFF-STREET PARKING:** yes

**NUMBER OF WINES:** 16
**HOUSE WINE:** £8.99
**RESERVATIONS:** advisable at the weekend
**NO SMOKING** area available
**CHILDREN:** welcome
**ACCOMMODATION:** 1 flatlet (B&B £20 per person per night)

# BADGERS

Tel: (01798) 342651
Coultershaw Bridge, Petworth, West Sussex, GU28 0JF

### Starters

Warm Smoked Salmon with Toasted Hazelnuts & a Balsamic Vinegar  £5.45
Fresh Gambas with a Spicy Sauce, Cucumber Dice & Spring Onions  £5.95
Chicken Liver Parfait with a Grape & Ginger Chutney  £4.95
Stir-fried Squid in Thai Spices & Coconut Milk  £5.45
Cold Duck Breast with an Oriental Salsa  £5.25
Tapas - a Selection of Seafoods  £5.95
Kidneys in a Sherry Sauce  £5.25

### Pasta

Tortellini with Smoked Salmon & Dill in a White Wine & Cream Sauce  £4.95
Rigatoni with Poached Salmon, Mushrooms & Spring Onions in a Cream Sauce  £5.45
Rigatoni with Fresh Vegetables, Stir-fried in Olive Oil & Herbs  £5.25

### Salads

Chicken Pan-fried with a Cajun Spice, Tossed with Sweet Capsicum Peppers, served on a Bed of Salad  £6.25
Tomato & Mozzarella Salad with Fresh Basil & Fresh Parmesan  £4.95
Greek Salad with Feta Cheese & Black Olives in a Lemon Dressing  £4.95

### Meats

Pan-fried Medallions of Lamb with a Tomato Fondue & Grilled Vegetables  £9.95
Half Shoulder of Lamb, Roasted with Rosemary with a Vegetable Sauce  £11.95
Roast Duck Breast with a Sherry, Ginger & Soy Sauce  £10.95
Pork Fillet Flambéed in Marsala with Wild Mushrooms  £9.95
Fillet Steak with Shallots & a Jus  £14.95
Fillet of Beef Stroganoff with Rice  £7.95
Bubble & Squeak, Ham & Eggs  £5.95

### Fish

Zarzuela - Spanish Casserole of Fish, Mussels, Gambas, Peppers & Squid  £13.95
Salmon en Papillote with a King Scallop, Tarragon & Pink Peppercorns  £11.95
Fish Pie with Mussels, Tiger Tails, Cod & Salmon, Topped with Potato  £6.95
Grilled Salmon Fillet Topped with a Sun-dried Tomato Pesto on a Bed of Aubergines & Sweet Red Peppers  £10.95
Baked Cod with a Herb Crust, Stir-fried Vegetables, Drizzled with Chilli Oil & Topped with Parmesan  £10.95
Cocquilles St. Jacques with a Side Salad  £10.95
Mussels in White Wine  £6.95

Badgers is a 19th century country dining pub with a seasonal menu that changes twice each year, specialising in fish during the Summer and game in Winter.

Three spacious, comfortable rooms and a pretty courtyard outside with a well make up the dining area, although the feel of the place is more like that of a brasserie.

The daily specials blackboard is very popular, offering dishes such as Pasta with Broccoli and a Blue Cheese Sauce (£4.95), Goat's Cheese on a Crouton with Dressed Salad (£4.95), Pasta with Scallops, Tiger Tails, Sweet Peppers and Fresh Basil (£8.95), Whole Red Mullet Casseroled in a Pot of Mediterranean Vegetables (£11.95), Hot and Spicy Lamb's Liver with Bacon, Peas and Coriander (£6.95), Risotto Cakes with Sun-dried Tomato and a Fresh Basil Pesto (£4.95) or Venison Sausages Braised in Red Wine and served with Red Cabbage and Creamed Potato (£6.95).

Directions: Badgers is set back a little from the main A285 Petworth to Chichester road, approximately 2 miles to the south of Petworth.

## USEFUL INFORMATION

**SERVING TIMES:**
Lunch 12pm-2.30pm (Mon-Fri)
 12pm-3pm (Sat & Sun)
 12pm-4pm (Sundays in Winter)
Dinner 7pm-10pm (Mon-Fri, & Sun)
 7pm-10.30pm (Sat)
**SEATING CAPACITY:** 60
**C/C:** V, MC
**OFF-STREET PARKING:** yes

**NUMBER OF WINES:** 50
**HOUSE WINE:** £9.95
**RESERVATIONS:** recommended at weekends
**OUTDOOR EATING:** yes
**CHILDREN:** welcome (over 6 yrs)
**ACCOMMODATION:** 3 rooms (B&B £70 per room including a Continental breakfast)

# THE DERING ARMS
## Tel: (01233) 840371
Pluckley, Ashford, Kent, TN27 0RR

**Starters**

Avocado - grilled with Stilton £3.25

Sussex smokies - smoked mackerel flaked into a creamy cheese sauce & browned under the grill £3.85

Soft herring roes - pan-fried with crispy smoked bacon & served on a bed of shredded lettuce £3.95

Chicken liver - sautéed with onion, bacon & mushrooms, finished with a brandy & cream sauce £3.95

**Main Courses**

Jim's Seafood Special £18.00 per person (min 2 people, 24 hrs notice required) - for example: fish soup; hot dishes of mackerel grilled with capers, soft roes with bacon, grilled sardines & rosemary; cold dish comprising lobster, crab, King prawns, prawns, shrimps & oysters; served with granary bread, salad & three home-made mayonnaise dips

Pie of the day £7.45

Skate wing served with caper butter £9.65

Grilled fillet of salmon, served with Pernod & lemon butter sauce £9.95

Local trout - pan-fried in butter with hazelnuts & lemon £10.65

Sirloin steak
 - plain £10.65
 - with garlic butter £10.65
 - or crushed black peppercorns £10.65
 - with green peppercorns, brandy & cream sauce £11.65

**Desserts**

Home-made fruit crumble £2.75

Oranges in caramel with Grand Marnier £2.75

Chocolate & chestnut slice with Cointreau £2.75

Lemon posset £2.95

Banana pancake served with fresh cream & vanilla ice cream £3.25

Pineapple Lisa - fresh pineapple, raspberries, fresh cream & vanilla ice cream, flamed with brandy £3.85

The Dering Arms is a traditional country inn that stands on what was once the Dering family estate, situated "within a bow-shot" of Pluckley railway station. The distinctive architecture of the building includes curved Dutch gables and 'Dering' windows.

The menu opposite remains virtually unchanged, so of most interest to discerning diners are the daily blackboard specials, predominantly their excellent fresh fish and seafood dishes. These might include starters of Provençale Fish Soup (£3.95) or Half a Dozen Oysters (£5.95), main courses such as Scallops in Garlic & Lemon Butter (£10.95), Grey Mullet with Garlic, Chilli & Olive Oil (£9.95), Monkfish in a Bacon & Orange Sauce (£10.95), Whole Lobster Salad (£16.95), Fillet of Red Bream Meunière (9.95) and Salmon Fishcake with Sorrel Sauce (£9.95), and perhaps a dessert such as Vanilla Cream Cheese Slice with Caramel Sauce & Roast Hazelnuts (£2.95).

Directions: Pluckley is approximately 5 miles to the north-west of Ashford on the B2077 and is signposted from the A20, A28 and A274. Once in the village, take the turning signposted to the railway station.

### USEFUL INFORMATION

**SERVING TIMES:**
Lunch 12pm-2pm (Tues-Sun)
Dinner 7pm-9.30pm (Tues-Thur)
    7pm-10pm (Fri & Sat)
**CLOSED FOR FOOD:** Sun night and all day Monday
**SEATING CAPACITY:** 26 in the restaurant, 12 in the bar
**C/C:** V, MC, AE

**NUMBER OF WINES:** 110
**HOUSE WINE:** £8.95
**RESERVATIONS:** advisable
**OUTDOOR EATING:** yes
**CHILDREN:** welcome
**OFF-STREET PARKING:** yes
**ACCOMMODATION:** 3 rooms
(B&B single £28, double £36)

# NUTFIELD PRIORY
Tel: (01737) 822066
Nutfield, Redhill, Surrey, RH1 4EN

## A Selection from the A La Carte

**PARFAIT OF SMOKED SALMON AND HERBS WITH SAUCE VERT**
*Eight pounds, ninety five pence*

**ROAST SCALLOPS, POLENTA MASH AND PARSLEY PESTO**
*Nine pounds, fifty pence*

**BOUILLON OF FOIE GRAS WITH TRUFFLE CONSOMME**
*Eight pounds, ninety five pence*

**OVEN BAKED CHEESE SOUFFLE**
*Nine pounds, fifty pence*

**VELOUTE OF WATERCRESS WITH OYSTER RAVIOLI**
*Six pounds, seventy five pence*

**WARM TART OF CORNISH CRAB WITH GAZPACHO VINAIGRETTE**
*Seven pounds, fifty pence*

~ ~ ~ ~

**ROAST FILLET OF SEABASS, CONFIT OF FENNEL, TOMATOES AND OLIVES**
*Twenty two pounds, fifty pence*

**NAVARIN OF LAMB WITH GARLIC AND THYME**
*Twenty two pounds*

**DOUBLE RIB OF BEEF SERVED WITH SAUCE PERIGOURDINE**
*Fifty seven pounds, fifty pence*

**GIGOT OF MONKFISH BOUILLABAISSE SAUCE AND GREEN ROUILI**
*Twenty one pounds, seventy five pence*

**ROAST BLACK LEG CHICKEN, ETUVEE OF LEEKS AND JUS OF CEPES**
*Twenty one pounds, seventy five pence*

**PAN-FRIED CALVES LIVER, SAFFRON POTATOES AND ALSACIAN BACON**
*Twenty two pounds*

**PAVE OF SCOTTISH SALMON, BOUILLON OF PEAS &NEW SEASON ONIONS**
*Nineteen pounds, seventy five pence*

Dating back to 1872 but recently restored to its former glory, Nutfield Priory stands proudly on Nutfield Ridge, basking in its gothic splendour and commanding lordly views across the rolling countryside below.

Fashioned after the Palace of Westminster, the Cloisters Restaurant enjoys an elegant grandeur which is complemented by its exquisite cuisine. The evening à la carte shown opposite carries a good selection of desserts such as Soufflé of Chocolate & Pistachio Nuts (£7.75), Millefeuille of Hazelnut, Praline & Raspberries (£6.75), and Baked Lemon Tart & Mascarpone (£6.75). A daily table d'hôte (3 courses at £22) is also available.

The à la carte is not presented at luncheon. Instead an excellent Menu du Jour is offered (2 or 3 courses at £13 and £16 respectively) with a choice of four dishes at each course.

Directions: Nutfield Priory is located 1 mile east of Redhill on the A25.

## USEFUL INFORMATION

**SERVING TIMES:**
Lunch 12.15pm-2pm (Sun-Fri)
Dinner 7pm-9.45pm (every day)
**CLOSED:** Saturday lunch
**SEATING CAPACITY:** 60
**C/C:** V, MC, S, D, AE, DC
**NO SMOKING** in the restaurant
**OFF-STREET PARKING:** yes
**CHILDREN:** welcome

**NUMBER OF WINES:** 90
**HOUSE WINE:** £12.50
**RESERVATIONS:** advisable
**OUTDOOR EATING:** yes, but only snacks and sandwiches
**DRESS CODE:** smart casual
**ACCOMMODATION:** 60 rooms (single £110, double fr £130)

# THE DINING ROOM
### Tel: (01737) 226650
### 59a High Street, Reigate, RH2 9AE

## First Courses

Baby lobster salad with broad beans, smoked tomatoes
and beetroot dressing
9.50
Grilled duck cakes, caramelised pineapple and
chilli-mango salsa
6.50
Seared scallops with a lightly curried chick pea puree
and coriander yoghurt
7.50
Courgette flowers stuffed with goats' ricotta and ratatouille
6.95
Chilli-salt crayfish with mixed peppers
coriander and turmeric oil
6.95

## Main Courses

Marinated and roasted fillet of beef, smoked tomatoes
potato and truffle oil salad
15.95
Loin of lamb, white bean mash, mint pesto and
aubergine crisps
14.95
Roasted seabass with basil risotto and red pepper essence
15.95
Quail sausage roll with turnip puree and spiced pear
13.95
Seared tuna steak with a warm potato salad and
salsa verde
14.95

### Side Orders
2.75

| | |
|---|---|
| Potato mash with olive oil | Vine Tomatoes, shallot dressing |
| Thai spiced noodles | Dressed mixed leaves |
| Buttered spinach | French fries |

Looking down from this first-floor restaurant on to the humdrum activity of Reigate High Street below, proprietor Paul Montalto's dream of creating 'a restaurant with the atmosphere of a private dining-club' becomes reality. The decor has a simple elegance, the bar is sophisticated without being ostentatious, the staff are friendly yet efficient, and from the moment you settle into one of the incredibly comfortable high-back wooden chairs you cannot help but relax and enjoy yourself.

The modern English cuisine prepared by Anthony Tobin (a familiar face on TV's *Ready, Steady, Cook*) is superb, and the à la carte featured on the facing page changes every eight weeks. This is supplemented by a good value set lunch menu (2/3 courses at £7.50/10.00) presenting a choice of two starters, two mains and the dessert special. There is also a set menu in the evening (2 courses £14.95) which may offer Spiced soup of red mullet with aioli and croûtons to start, and Charred tuna with celeriac mash and rocket salad to follow. Both these menus change weekly.

Directions: Easily found in the centre of Reigate High Street.

## USEFUL INFORMATION

**SERVING TIMES:**
Lunch 12pm-2pm (Mon-Fri)
Dinner 7pm-10pm (Mon-Sat)
**CLOSED:** Saturday lunch and all day Sunday
**SEATING CAPACITY:** 50
**C/C:** V, MC, S, D, AE
**OUTDOOR EATING:** no

**NUMBER OF WINES:** 39
**HOUSE WINE:** £8.50
**NO SMOKING** in the dining area
**OFF-STREET PARKING:** no
**RESERVATIONS:** advisable, but compulsory at weekends
**CHILDREN:** welcome
**DRESS CODE:** smart

# LA BARBE
Tel: (01737) 241966
71 Bell Street, Reigate, Surrey, RH2 7AN

## Starters

Velouté de Moules au Safran
*Creamy mussel & saffron soup*
Oeufs Pochés Florentine
*Poached eggs served on a bed of spinach & topped with a cheese sauce*
Quaille à la Moutarde sur Lit de Choux Rouge au Bacon
*Fresh boneless quail cooked in a mustard sauce, presented on a bed of red cabbage & bacon*
Escargots de Bourgogne
*Snails cooked in garlic butter*
Terrine de Poireaux Sauce Vierge Truffée
*Fresh leek terrine served with a truffle dressing*
Feuilleté de Ris de Veau aux Navets et Madère
*Puff pastry case filled with pan-fried sweetbreads, turnips & madeira sauce*
Salade de Champignons Sauvages en Marinade
*Mixed salad garnished with a fresh selection of wild mushrooms marinated in olive oil, garlic & fresh herbs*
Tartare de Saumon Frais sur lit de Salade à l'Huile de Noix
*Fresh salmon tartare accompanied by rocket & lamb lettuce salad, laced with walnut dressing*

## Dinner Menu
Two course meal - **£20.95**
Three course meal - **£24.95**

## Main Courses

Fricassée de Pintade Sauce Chasseur
*Guinea fowl, tomatoes, shallots, white wine & tarragon casserole*
Médaillons de Venaison Poêlés Marchand de Vin
*Pan-fried venison served with a shallot & red wine sauce*
Jarret de Porc Braisé au Cidre
*Pig knuckle braised in cider & served with apple slices cooked in butter*
Escalope de Veau à la Crème
*Escalope of veal cooked with mushrooms & fresh cream*
Roulé de Pâtes Fraîches à la Muscade et Pignons de Pin
*Rolled fresh pasta filled with spinach, tomatoes, pine kernels, garlic & cheese*
Poivron Farci à la Morue, Sauce Tomate
*Roasted red pepper stuffed with salted cod with a light tomato sauce*
Ragoût de Lentilles de la Mer
*Pan-fried monkfish & scallops served on a bed of lentils*
Poisson du Jour
*Fresh fish of the day from Billingsgate Market*

All dishes are served with a selection of seasonal vegetables and Gratin Dauphinois

Pastel shades, wicker chairs and the reassuring aroma of traditional French cooking welcome you to this unpretentious restaurant. Under the same ownership for fifteen years, La Barbe has a loyal following and a deserving reputation for its excellent cuisine.

The dinner menu shown opposite changes every eight weeks to allow for seasonal variations and to make the best use of local produce wherever possible. A slightly less extensive version is offered at lunch (2 or 3 courses at £16.45 and £18.95 respectively). There is always a good vegetarian range and special diets may be easily accommodated, although telephoning beforehand is strongly advised. Desserts are all home-made and feature dishes such as Fresh Banana and Almond Flake Tart, Traditional Iced Nougat, Crème Brûlée laced with Lime, and delicious home-made sorbets.

For those of you who only feel secure when communicating via modem, then why not try out their web site at www.la-barbe.demon.co.uk.

Directions: From Reigate High Street go down Bell Street with Safeway on your right. La Barbe is about 100 yards further along on the left.

### USEFUL INFORMATION

**SERVING TIMES:**
Lunch 12pm-2pm (Mon-Fri)
Dinner 7.15pm-9.45pm (Mon-Sat)
**CLOSED:** Saturday lunch and all day Sunday
**SEATING CAPACITY:** 65
**C/C:** V, MC, S, D, AE

**NUMBER OF WINES:** 66
**HOUSE WINE:** £11
**NO SMOKING** area available
**OFF-STREET PARKING:** no
**RESERVATIONS:** advisable
**OUTDOOR EATING:** no
**CHILDREN:** welcome

# RINGLESTONE INN
### Tel: (01622) 859900
Ringlestone, near Maidstone, Kent, ME17 1AX

**THE LARDER - Appetisers & Cold Snacks**

Ringlestone Pot  £3.45
A thick chicken, vegetable & bean soup with sherry & croûtons
Mussels Provençale  £4.95
Served chilled in a tangy tomato & sherry sauce with garlic & gherkins
Cold Smoked Trout  £6.85
Served on a bed of crunchy lettuce & cucumber with fresh lemon wedges

**RINGLESTONE PIES - The Ringlestone Speciality**

Turkey, Bacon & Walnut  £8.65
Simmered with onions, leeks & thyme in our walnut liqueur
Beef in Black Beer & Raisin Wine  £8.65
Marinated & simmered in black beer & raisin wine with prunes & oregano
Lamb & Apricot Wine  £8.65
Casseroled in apricot country wine with apricots, rosemary, peppers & leeks
Game Pie with Redcurrant Wine  £9.25
Made with venison, wild duck, rabbit & pheasant in redcurrant wine
Vegetable & Nut  £8.25
A pie for all seasons with nuts, herbs, fresh vegetables & birch wine
Fish in Elderflower Wine  £8.65
Salmon & prawn gently cooked with elderflower wine, leeks, tomatoes & cream

**THE STOVE - Main Course Dishes**

Fresh Pink Trout  £9.65
With all the bones removed then baked with butter, lemon, almonds & oatmeal
Grilled Plaice Fillets  £9.65
Topped with mango chutney & bananas (or just lemon butter)
Scotch Rump Steak  £10.75
With black pepper, grilled & served with mushroom & blackberry wine sauce
Pork Loin Steaks (two)  £9.65
Coated in barbecue spices & grilled with apples
Cidered Chicken Casserole  £6.95
Leg of chicken simmered with tomatoes, herbs, leeks, cider, peppers & garlic
Lamb, Coconut & Banana Curry  £6.95
Not too hot, served with yoghurt & chutney on a bed of rice

**THE SNACKS - One Course Hot Meals**

Kentish Pork Sausages  £5.35    Macaroni with Tuna & Clams  £6.45
Beef, Bacon & Spinach Lasagne  £6.45    Chilli Beef Goulash  £6.45

Set deep in the peace and tranquillity of the Kent countryside, The Ringlestone Inn has seen very little change since its construction in 1533. Original brick and flint walls and floors, oak beams, inglenooks and antique English furniture are the setting for this dining pub's imaginative home-made bar food.

The evening menu (a small selection appears opposite) is ever-changing and many of the dishes are flavoured with the country fruit wines for which the inn has become famous. Don't expect to find sun-dried tomatoes, ginger, coriander or lemon grass here.

The hot and cold lunchtime buffet offers a seasonal variety of traditional country recipes. During the summer months the idyllic country garden with its landscaped lawns, rockeries, ponds and waterfalls is a pleasure.

Directions: At the roundabout on the A20 take the left exit signposted to Hollingbourne. At the crossroads by the water tower above Hollingbourne, turn east towards Doddington, then straight ahead at the Black Post crossroads. The Ringlestone Inn is along this road on your right.

### USEFUL INFORMATION

**SERVING TIMES:**
Lunch 12pm-2pm (every day)
Dinner 7pm-9.30pm (every day)
**SEATING CAPACITY:** 70 inside, 130 in the garden and on the terrace
**C/C:** V, MC, S, D, AE, DC
**OUTDOOR EATING:** yes
**OFF-STREET PARKING:** yes

**NUMBER OF WINES:** 20
**HOUSE WINE:** £8.35
**RESERVATIONS:** advisable, but bookings are only taken for dinner
**CHILDREN:** welcome
**ACCOMMODATION:** 3 rooms (B&B single £85, double £95) and special offers are available

# MICHELS'
### Tel: (01483) 224777
High Street, Ripley, Surrey, GU23 6AQ

ASPARAGUS FLAN WITH GREEN ASPARAGUS TIPS
ON A CREAM OF FAVA BEANS AND RED PEPPER DIAMONDS  £8.00

GOAT'S CHEESE SOUFFLE WRAPPED IN A CRISP PANCAKE,
SERVED WITH WALNUT SAUCE AND SALAD LEAVES  £8.00

CURED SALMON STACKED WITH CRISP POTATO AND CELERIAC
BOUND WITH LEMON CREAM  £10.00

A WARM GATEAU OF DUCK LIVER FOIE GRAS
AND CHERRY TOMATO COULIS  £13.00

RAVIOLI OF CORNISH LOBSTER ON RAW MUSHROOMS
TOSSED IN MUSTARD DRESSING,
FRENCH BEAN SALAD AND SAUCE AMERICAINE  £15.00

\* \* \*

PAN FRIED COD STEAK WITH THYME AND BLACK PEPPER,
SET ON BRANDADE LIGHTLY FLAVOURED WITH GARLIC,
SURROUNDED BY COURGETTE FLOWERS AND MARINATED RED PEPPERS,
SERVED WITH WARM OLIVE OIL DRESSING  £19.00

BRAISED SLAB OF DOVER SOLE WITH FRIED GREEN ASPARAGUS
AND MORELS, FLAVOURED WITH CHERVIL AND CHICKEN JUICE  £22.00

PAN-FRIED CALVES LIVER WITH BUTTERED SORREL LEAVES
AND CRISP SWEET POTATO CURLS  £18.00

SLICES OF FARMED AND WILD PIGEON BREASTS,
A CABBAGE PARCEL OF THE LEG AND LIVER AND A PASTRY PAN
WITH MUSHROOMS, SERVED WITH MADEIRA SAUCE  £19.00

CONFIT SHANK OF SPRING LAMB WITH SPRING VEGETABLES,
IN LAMB JUICES SHARPENED WITH REDCURRANTS AND MINT  £19.00

MAGRET OF TRELOUGH DUCK, BAKED IN A HERB SEA-SALT CRUST,
WITH BEARNAISE SAUCE, FRIED POTATOES AND MUSHROOMS  £20.00

\* \* \*

*A plate of British farm cheeses will precede your choice of sweet*

SPICED CAKE ICE CREAM WITH WARM CARAMELIZED APPLE
AND FRESH APPLE JUICE  £7.50

RICE COOKED IN VANILLA BEANS' MILK,
TOPPED WITH RASPBERRIES AND VANILLA ICE CREAM  £7.50

TERRINE OF STRAWBERRIES AND RHUBARB
COOKED IN PORT, SERVED WITH YOGHURT ICE CREAM  £7.50

MILLEFEUILLE OF CHOCOLATE LEAVES AND CHOCOLATE MOUSSE
WITH POACHED RED CHERRIES  £7.50

Michels' is an elegant restaurant housed in the Georgian-fronted Clock House in the village of Ripley, approximately half an hour's drive from the centre of London. A splendid Victorian tiled floor (which, according to one illustrious guest, can also be seen in the House of Lords) welcomes you to the split-level dining room. The walls are hung with chef patron Erik Michel's wonderfully vibrant paintings, one of which appears on the contents page of this guide. Though he remains relatively undiscovered as a painter, his culinary artistry is well-renowned.

The menu is eclectic, with the dishes featured on the *carte* opposite evolving through the season. If you prefer, the 4-course Surprise Menu is an interesting option (£21 for lunch, £23 for dinner), backed up by a 4-course Gourmet Menu in the evenings (except Saturdays) which costs £30 per head and includes three glasses of specially selected wines.

Directions: Michels' is easily found in the centre of Ripley, which lies about 5 miles to the north-east of Guildford. Follow the signs to Ripley from the A3.

## USEFUL INFORMATION

**SERVING TIMES:**
Lunch from 12.30pm (Tues-Fri, & Sun)
Dinner from 7.30pm (Tues-Sat)
**CLOSED:** Sat lunch, Sun night and and all day Monday
**SEATING CAPACITY:** 45
**C/C:** V, MC, S, D, AE
**OUTDOOR EATING:** no

**NUMBER OF WINES:** 75
**HOUSE WINE:** £9.50
**RESERVATIONS:** advisable
**NO SMOKING** in the restaurant whilst those around you are eating
**OFF-STREET PARKING:** yes
**CHILDREN:** welcome (but only for Sunday lunch)

# LANDGATE BISTRO
Tel: (01797) 222829
5/6 Landgate, Rye, East Sussex, TN31 7LH

| | |
|---|---|
| Pea and mint soup | £3.40 |
| Leek and roquefort tart | £4.40 |
| Courgette terrine | £4.40 |
| Globe artichoke with tarragon hollandaise | £4.40 |
| Spicy chick-pea fritters with an avocado & cucumber salsa | £4.40 |
| Chicken quenelles with a cream and mushroom sauce | £4.40 |
| Salad of confit of duck with puy lentils | £5.40 |
| Salmon and smoked haddock fishcakes with parsley sauce | £5.40 |
| Local squid braised with white wine, tomatoes and garlic | £5.40 |

~~~~~~~

| | |
|---|---|
| Very fishy stew: a selection of local fish poached in stock and served with aioli, garlic bread and a salad | £10.70 |
| Poached fillet of turbot with a chive sauce | £10.70 |
| Steamed fillet of wild salmon with sorrel hollandaise | £11.70 |
| Monkfish and brill with an orange and vermouth sauce | £11.70 |
| Baked sea-bass with hollandaise sauce | £11.70 |

| | |
|---|---|
| Lambs' Kidneys with a grain mustard sauce | £8.90 |
| Lambs' sweetbreads with ginger and coriander | £8.90 |
| Calf's liver with sage and balsamic vinegar | £8.90 |
| Wild rabbit with white wine, thyme and garlic | £8.90 |
| Free-range chicken with white wine and tarragon | £8.90 |
| Gressingham duck with a sauce flavoured with fresh lime | £11.70 |
| Griddled chump of English lamb with butter-beans, bacon and basil | £11.70 |
| Noisettes of English lamb with a tomato and mint sauce | £11.70 |
| Fillet of beef in pastry with a béarnaise sauce | £11.70 |

New potatoes £1.00   Gratin potatoes £1.00   Mushrooms £1.00
Carrot and parsnip purée £1.00   Runner beans £1.00   Broccoli £1.00
Salad of green leaves £1.50   Garlic bread £1.00

Service is included in these prices

Landgate Bistro is an unpretentious restaurant which enjoys a quiet location in the historic town of Rye. Owned by Nick Parkin and chef Toni Ferguson-Lees since 1980, the bistro is now firmly established as one of the finest in the South East.

The emphasis here is on substance rather than style. The atmosphere is relaxed and informal; the menus are simply hand-written; the food, which is quite superb, is unfussily presented and to be savoured for its taste rather than admired for its appearance.

The à la carte menu, a sample of which is shown opposite, changes daily and this is supplemented from Tuesday to Thursday by a set price menu (3 courses + coffee £14.90 inc. service). House specialities include excellent local lamb and fish dishes. Desserts are all home-made and may feature dishes such as Jamaican Chocolate Cream (£3.90), Strawberry Shortcake (£3.90) and Nectarine Sorbet (£2.90).

Directions: From the High Street follow the signs to the original town wall still standing at Landgate. The bistro is a little further along on the left.

## USEFUL INFORMATION

**SERVING TIMES:**
Dinner 7pm-9.30pm (Tues-Sat)
**CLOSED:** for lunch every day and all day Sunday and Monday
**SEATING CAPACITY:** 30
**C/C:** V, MC, S, D, AE, DC

**NUMBER OF WINES:** 70
**HOUSE WINE:** £8.40
**OFF-STREET PARKING:** no
**RESERVATIONS:** advisable
**OUTDOOR EATING:** no
**CHILDREN:** welcome

# LA TERRASSE

Tel: (01303) 220444

Sandgate Hotel, The Esplanade, Sandgate, Folkstone, Kent, CT20 3DY

### Hors d'Oeuvre

*Foie Gras de Canard au torchon, gelée claire au Sauternes et ses grillées de Campagne £9.50*
Ballotine of duck foie gras with a clear Sauternes wine jelly & home-made toasted country bread

*Salade de Coquilles Saint Jacques poêlées et gazpacho £9.00*
Salad of pan-fried hand-dived scallops with gazpacho

*Fricassée de cuisses de grenouille, coulis de persil plat et gousses d'ail en chemise sur une embeurrée de pomme de terre £8.00*
Fricassée of frogs legs with a coulis of flat parsley & new season garlic

### Poissons

*Darne de Turbotin rôtie sur os aux Girolles, jus blond de volaille £17.00*
Roasted turbot on the bone with girolle mushrooms in a light poultry jus

*Filet de rouget poêlé, minute de légumes Provençales et tomate mi-confite et son fumet £14.50*
Pan-fried fillet of red mullet served with provençale vegetables & its own sauce

*Homard grillé au beurre de corail, tagliatelle de légumes £3.50 per 100 g*
Grilled lobster glazed with a coral butter served with vegetable tagliatelle & a tarragon sauce

### Viandes

*Noisette d'Agneau de "Romney Marsh" rôtie, jus simple à la fleur de thym et légumes grillés aux saveurs de Provence £17.00*
Roasted noisette of "Romney Marsh" lamb in its own juices scented with thyme & a tian of Provençale vegetables

*Côte filet de Veau rôtie au jus, girolles et fricassée de mange-tout (pour deux personnes) £35.00*
Roasted rib of veal with its own juice, girolles mushrooms & a fricassée of mange-tout

### Desserts

*Craquelin de Fraises Pressées, glace au fromage blanc £6.00*
Pressed strawberries between fine layers of delicate nougatine in its own coulis with a French fromage frais ice-cream

*Moelleux 'pur Caraïbe' Valhrona Chaud, crème d'amandes amères et glace à la Verveine £7.00*
A concentrated Valhrona 'pur Caraïbe' chocolate dessert with an almond cream and a Verveine ice-cream

Proprietors Samuel Gicqueau and Zara Jackson personally welcome guests to their home, Sandgate Hotel and restaurant La Terrasse, with warm English hospitality and unmistakably French flair. The hotel was built in the mid-19th century and its elegant lounge and charming dining room enjoy sea views through the high windows.

In Samy's restaurant, amid wrought iron fireplaces, silver candelabras and paintings of his Loire Valley homeland by Christian Gerard, you can savour his modern interpretations of traditional French cuisine and classical dishes.

All the staff are French and the service formal. The *carte* (a selection from which appears opposite) is seasonal, changing every three to four months. Fresh fish and lobster, caught on the shores of the hotel, are a speciality.

Directions: The Sandgate Hotel is situated approximately 2 miles to the west of Folkestone town centre on the A259 coastal road.

## USEFUL INFORMATION

**SERVING TIMES:**
Lunch 12.15pm-1.30pm (Tues-Sun)
Dinner 7.15pm-9.30pm (Tues-Sat)
**CLOSED:** Sun night & all day Mon
**SEATING CAPACITY:** 24
**C/C:** V, MC, S, D, AE, DC
**NO SMOKING** in the restaurant
**OFF-STREET PARKING:** yes

**NUMBER OF WINES:** 100
**HOUSE WINE:** £13.50
**RESERVATIONS:** essential
**OUTDOOR EATING:** a balcony with sea views for drinks only
**CHILDREN:** welcome
**ACCOMMODATION:** 15 rooms (B&B single £39, double £54-£67)

# THE RED LION
### Tel: (01483) 892202
### Shamley Green, near Guildford, Surrey, GU5 0UB

## BLACKBOARD MENU

Sirloin Steak Grill £11.75
Rump Steak & Guinness Pie £10.65
Pan-fried Breast of Chicken with a Cream of Leek & White Wine Sauce £10.65
Calves' Liver & Bacon £11.95
English Lamb Cutlets with a Rosemary & Redcurrant Glaze £11.45
Half a Crispy Roast Duck with a Black Cherry Sauce £11.65
Pork Fillet with an Oyster Mushroom Sauce £11.75
Lasagne al Forno served with Garlic Bread & a Greek Salad £7.45

Breast of Chicken with a Cream Cheese & Julienne of Vegetable Stuffing
& a Red Wine Pimento Sauce £10.65
Chicken Curry on a bed of Rice £7.45
Dijon Peppered Chicken £10.65
Fresh Farm Eggs with Home-cooked Ham & Chips £6.75
Crêpes filled with Chicken & Leeks £7.45

Fillet of Sea Bass with Pernod & Fennel Sauce £11.25
Lemon Sole Fillet with Parsley Butter £10.65
Fresh Sea Bass in a Parcel £10.75
Tagliatelle with Seafood or Cream of Fresh Mushrooms £7.45
Marinated Monkfish served with Oriental Stir Fry & Egg Noodles £9.65
Giant Prawns sautéed in Garlic Butter £11.25
Sole & Scallop Florentine with a Salad £10.65
Crêpes filled with fresh Seafood £7.45

Crêpes filled with Cream of Mushrooms £7.45
Grilled Mushrooms with a Garlic & Herb Stuffing topped with Brie £6.75
Peppers stuffed with Rice & served with Spicy Pesto Sauce £6.75

### PUDDINGS

Strawberry Cheesecake £3.50
Sticky Toffee Pudding £3.50
Bakewell Tart £3.50
Blueberry Pie £3.50
Chocolate Pecan Tart £3.50
Strawberry Rumonoff in a Chocolate Shell £3.50
Home-made Pineapple / Raspberry / Vanilla Ice Cream £3.50

The Red Lion is a traditional country pub that looks out over the village's pretty cricket green. The restaurant area is furnished in the style of a country cottage and many visitors comment that you feel as though you have been invited to a friend's home for a meal.

The menu is written up on a blackboard in the bar. Other than on Sunday lunchtimes (when the pub is too busy for à la carte dishes to be served in the gardens) there are no strict rules or regulations to adhere to: simply choose what you want to eat and sit anywhere you like.

Good home-made bar snacks are also available, such as Chicken, Grape and Mayonnaise Sandwiches (£3.50) and Ploughmans (from £4.75).

Directions: The Red Lion is situated opposite the cricket green in the village of Shamley Green, which lies about 3 miles to the south of Guildford on the B2128 Guildford to Cranleigh road.

### USEFUL INFORMATION

**SERVING TIMES:**
Lunch 12pm-3pm (every day)
Dinner 6.30pm-10pm (Mon-Sat)
7pm-9.30pm (Sun)
**SEATING CAPACITY:** 54 in the restaurant, 20 in the bar
**C/C:** V, MC, S, D, AE
**OUTDOOR EATING:** yes

**NUMBER OF WINES:** 30
**HOUSE WINE:** £8.95
**RESERVATIONS:** advisable, but essential at weekends
**OFF-STREET PARKING:** yes
**CHILDREN:** welcome
**ACCOMMODATION:** 4 rooms
(B&B single £40, double £45)

# KINGHAMS RESTAURANT
### Tel: (01483) 202168
Gomshall Lane, Shere, Surrey, GU5 9HB

*Fresh Melon and Citrus Fruit Compôte £3.95*
*Warm Salad of Roasted and Chargrilled Vegetables £4.95*
in olive oil and balsamic vinegar
*Atlantic King Prawns £6.50*
served with a warm garlic cream dip
*Country Pâté £3.95*
flavoured with our home-grown herbs
on a blackcurrant, port and orange sauce, served with melba toast
*Smoked Salmon Pillow £5.95*
filled with white crabmeat and avocado
*Mussels £4.95*
poached in white wine, cream, shallots and parsley
*Mediterranean Fish Soup £4.95*
freshly poached seafood accompanied by rouille, gruyère and croutons

*Chargrilled Prime Rib Steak £10.95*
served with a brandy and green peppercorn sauce or plain grilled
*Carved Breast of Leith Hill Farm Duck £12.95*
on puy lentils, braised with smoked bacon, shallots and thyme
on a rich red wine jus
*Pan-fried Veal Cutlets £10.95*
marinated in lemon and sage,
garnished with poached pears in ginger and an elderflower jus
*Medallions of Pork Fillet £10.95*
on a spiced coconut cream Thai sauce topped with peppered pineapple
*New Season Lamb Gigot Chop £10.95*
marinated in red wine, rosemary and garlic, with a mint pesto and herb jus
*Vegetarian Wild Mushroom Risotto £9.95*
served with freshly grated parmesan

*Grilled Lemon Sole £11.95*
scored and brushed with sun-dried tomato paste, lemon and parsley
*Monkfish Tail £11.95*
in a fennel crust on saffron cream sauce
*Chargrilled Tuna Loin £10.95*
served pink, topped with an avocado salsa and warm tomato dressing

Selection of fresh buttered vegetables and baby roast potatoes £2.50
Shere salad £2.00

"One cannot work well, feel well, love well, unless one has eaten well." So reads the menu at Kinghams Restaurant, where chef/proprietor Paul Baker presides over his style of modern English cooking (contrary to the sign outside which has not quite caught up with the times).

Inside the restaurant you feel as though you are in the owner's private country cottage and the friendly service from the staff adds to this wonderfully relaxed atmosphere. The à la carte menu on the facing page changes four or five times a year, although since there is quite a strong influence on fresh fish here, these dishes may be swapped around more frequently.

Local produce is used as much as possible and the two-course set price lunch (costing £10.95, also available Tuesday to Thursday evenings) provides excellent value for money.

Directions: The village of Shere is approximately 4 miles to the east of Guildford and signposted to the south of the main A25 Dorking-Guildford road.

## USEFUL INFORMATION

**SERVING TIMES:**
Lunch 12pm-2.30pm (Tues-Sun)
Dinner 7pm-9pm (Tues-Sat)
**CLOSED:** Sun night & all day Mon
**SEATING CAPACITY:** 47
**C/C:** V, MC, S, D, AE
**NO SMOKING** area available

**NUMBER OF WINES:** 45
**HOUSE WINE:** £9.50
**RESERVATIONS:** essential
**OFF-STREET PARKING:** yes
**CHILDREN:** welcome
**OUTDOOR EATING:** yes

# THE CHASER INN
### Tel: (01732) 810360
Stumble Hill, Shipbourne, near Tonbridge, Kent, TN11 9PE

*Dinner Menu*
*£22.50 per person*

Baked **Goats Cheese**, Garlic Croûtons with **Date & Apple** Chutney
\*\*
Tartlet of **Avocado, Bacon & Stilton** Cheese
\*\*
Gateau of **Smoked Salmon, Prawns & Herbs** with **Lime** Dressing
\*\*
A Smooth **Chicken Liver** Parfait with **Pear & Rosemary** Jelly

\*\*\*\*\*

Chef's Home-made Soup of the Day

\*\*\*\*\*

Fillet of **Rainbow Trout** on **Champ** with **Lime & Walnut** Dressing
\*\*
Supreme of **Chicken** glazed with **Honey**, Cracked Pepper & **Baby Spinach**
\*\*
Forest **Mushroom Risotto** with seared **Salmon**
\*\*
Medallions of **Beef** with Coarse **Grain Mustard & Watercress**
\*\*
**Leek, Tomato, Mushroom & Pimento** Strudel with Creamed **Herb** Sauce
\*\*
Confit of **Duck Leg** with Braised **Beetroot**

Served with Fresh Vegetables and Potatoes

\*\*\*

Choice of Home-made Sweets
\*\*
Cheese and Biscuits

\*\*\*

Coffee and Mints

Effusing the wealth and elegance of a bygone era, The Chaser, dating back to the 1880's when it was built in the grand, Colonial style with an impressive porticoed front, now stands imposingly on the brow of a hill in the picturesque Kentish village of Shipbourne.

Friendly staff and a warm atmosphere contribute to a well-established reputation for the quality and range of cuisine. An intimate and attractive restaurant with exposed beams and panelled walls offers set menus at dinner, an example of which is shown opposite, and lunch (3 courses £13.50). Both of these menus change monthly.

Alternatively you may choose to eat in the bar, where a seasonal menu features a nice mix of traditional meals like ploughman's (£4.50) and sandwiches (£3.75), as well as more imaginative dishes such as Marinated Brochette of Snapper, King Prawn with Saffron Risotto (£7.95) and Braised Knuckle of Lamb, Root Vegetables & Port Wine Gravy (£8.95). Helpings are very generous, so come hungry!

Directions: Head north from Tonbridge on the A227 and after about 3 miles you will see The Chaser on your left.

## USEFUL INFORMATION

**SERVING TIMES:**
Restaurant 12pm-2pm (Tues-Fri, + Sun)
7pm-9.30pm (Tues-Sat)
Bar: Lunch 12pm-2pm (every day)
Dinner 6.30pm-9.30pm (every day)
**CLOSED:** in the restaurant Sunday night, Sat lunch and all day Monday
**SEATING CAPACITY:** 36 in the restaurant, 50 in the bar
**C/C:** V, MC, S, D, AE

**NUMBER OF WINES:** 42
**HOUSE WINE:** £9.75
**OFF-STREET PARKING:** yes
**CHILDREN:** welcome
**RESERVATIONS:** advisable
**OUTDOOR EATING:** yes
**ACCOMMODATION:** 15 rooms (B&B £65 per double room)

# THE PEACOCK INN
### Tel: (01825) 762463
Shortbridge, Piltdown, East Sussex, TN22 3XA

#### A selection from the seasonal menu

| | |
|---|---|
| **Deep-fried Goats Cheese** | £4.75 |
| Coated with breadcrumbs and served with blackcurrant jelly | |
| **Smoked Chicken & Bacon Salad** | £3.95 |
| With a spicy vinaigrette dressing | |
| **Mediterranean King Prawns** | £6.95 |
| Served hot in garlic butter or cold with seafood & horseradish sauce | |
| **Murphy's Pie** | £6.95 |
| Prime beef with mushrooms, cooked in Murphy's Irish Stout, topped with flaky pastry & served with fresh vegetables or salad | |
| **Shortbridge Pie** | £6.50 |
| Tender pieces of chicken and leeks in a stilton sauce, topped with potatoes and served with fresh vegetables or salad | |
| **Seafood Pancake** | £6.25 |
| Salmon, cod & smoked haddock in a creamy white wine sauce wrapped in a pancake, topped with grated cheese & peeled prawns, grilled and served with fresh vegetables or salad | |
| **Breaded Scampi** | £6.75 |
| Served with salad garnish & french fries | |
| **Beef Stroganoff** | £7.50 |
| strips of fillet beef with mushrooms, brandy, tomato, paprika and fresh cream served with turmeric rice | |
| **Grilled Lamb Cutlets** | £8.95 |
| With sautéed mushrooms, tomato and mint jelly served with fresh vegetables or salad & choice of potatoes | |
| **Fillet Steak Old England** | £14.25 |
| Stuffed with stilton cheese wrapped in bacon and baked in the oven, served with fresh vegetables or salad & choice of potatoes | |
| **Vegetable & Cashew Nut Bake** | £5.95 |
| Cooked in a rich creamy sauce, topped with cheese and breadcrumbs, served with fresh vegetables or salad | |
| **Sweet & Sour Stir Fry Vegetables** | £5.75 |
| Cooked in a sweet & sour sauce, served with turmeric rice | |
| **Lemon Meringue Pie** | |
| **Blackcurrant Cheesecake** | |
| **Caramelised Oranges in Grand Marnier** | |
| **Lemon Sorbet with Vodka** | all £2.75 |

The Peacock is a beautiful 16th century inn, with exposed beams and open fires, enjoying a tranquil setting in East Sussex countryside only a few miles outside Uckfield.

Over the past ten years proprietor Matthew Arnold has built a reputation for serving great home-made food, sourced whenever possible from local suppliers. The seasonal menu, a sample of which appears opposite, features traditional pub meals alongside more imaginative and innovative dishes. It is supplemented by excellent daily specials such as Blinis with Smoked Salmon & Crème Fraîche (£4.95), Avocado, Bacon & Stilton Salad (£4.50), Cod topped with Tartar, Breadcrumbs and Cheese (£6.50), or Salmon and Coriander Fishcakes (£6.25).

The dessert menu changes several times a week but always includes a good selection of ice creams, sorbets and cheeses.

Directions: A few miles west of Uckfield, The Peacock Inn lies just south of the A272 and is signposted from the main road.

## USEFUL INFORMATION

**SERVING TIMES:**
Lunch 12pm-2.30pm (every day)
Dinner 6pm-10pm (Mon-Sat)
   7pm-9.30pm (Sunday)
**SEATING CAPACITY:** 45 in the restaurant, 28 in the bar
**C/C:** V, MC, D

**NUMBER OF WINES:** 30
**HOUSE WINE:** £8.50
**RESERVATIONS:** advisable, but not available in the bar
**OFF-STREET PARKING:** yes
**OUTDOOR EATING:** yes
**CHILDREN:** welcome

# RANKINS
### Tel: (01580) 713964
The Street, Sissinghurst, Kent, TN17 2JH

### Evening Menu
£22.00 - Two Courses    £26.00 - Three Courses

**First courses -**
Beetroot and Jurancon blue cheese salad
Jersey Royal salad topped with grilled red peppers, capers, shallots and parsley, extra virgin olive oil dressing
Cream of carrot soup with Indian spices
Baked Smokie pot with cheddar topping

**Main courses -**
Steamed cod, salmon and crab rosette with a dilled butter sauce
Pan-fried wood pigeon breasts served with rich mushroom sauce
Spicy bean stew with couscous and fried aubergine slices
Braised lamb fillets with a light port and orange sauce served with salsa verde of basil, parsley, olives and garlic

**Cheese -**
A finger of the cheese of the week taken as a fourth course  (£2.50)

**Puddings -**
Chocolate marquise with summer berry sauce
Coffee fudge pudding, coffee ice cream
Lemon tart, Jersey cream
Vanilla and chocolate ice creams
Jellied orange terrine with custard

Coffee, tea  (£2.00)
Liqueur coffees  (£3.50)

Rankins is housed in a typical timber-framed, weather-boarded building in the heart of the Weald of Kent. It is an unpretentious, low-key restaurant that has built itself an enviable reputation over the last eleven years.

Chef/proprietor Hugh Rankin basically cooks what he likes to eat. For example, he can't stand goat's cheese - so you won't find that as an ingredient. The menu is a real melting-pot of ideas and constantly evolving. The food is eclectic, offering dishes influenced not only by French and Italian cuisine but also drawing on Thai and Indian inspiration. Quality is never compromised. Puddings are robust ("they're never dinky") and the service informal and very friendly.

Sunday lunches (the restaurant's only lunchtime serving) are very popular. The fixed price à la carte generally offers a choice of four dishes at each course and is priced at £20.00 for 2 courses and £23.00 for 3 courses.

Directions: Rankins is situated on the main street in Sissinghurst, the A262 which links Biddenden to Goudhurst.

### USEFUL INFORMATION

**SERVING TIMES:**
Lunch 12.30pm-2pm (Sundays only)
Dinner 7.30pm-9pm (Wed-Sat)
**CLOSED:** for dinner Sun to Tues, and lunch every day except Sunday
**SEATING CAPACITY:** 26
**C/C:** V, MC
**OFF-STREET PARKING:** no

**NUMBER OF WINES:** 30
**HOUSE WINE:** £9.50
**RESERVATIONS:** advisable
**OUTDOOR EATING:** no
**CHILDREN:** welcome
**NO SMOKING** in the restaurant until after 10pm

# THE CHEQUERS
Tel: (01444) 400239
Slaugham, near Haywards Heath, Sussex, RH17 6AQ

## Befores

**FRESH MUSSELS (£1 extra)**
Served with garlic butter or white wine, garlic and cream

**FRESH ANCHOVIES**
Marinated in olive oil and vinegar, served with cream crackers

**COUNTRY MUSHROOMS**
Country mushrooms grilled to order and topped with cheese, tomato and horseradish, or garlic butter

**DEVILLED WHITEBAIT**
Pan-fried in butter and sprinkled with cayenne pepper

**HOME-MADE TARAMASALATA**
Very moreish and probably addictive. Served with hot toasted pitta bread and for a mere £1 extra fresh prawns as well

**BABY CALAMARI**
Nothing like the deep-fried rubber bands that you get in Spain. Tender and succulent, pan-fried in butter, with or without garlic

**CHICKEN KEBABS**
Marinated overnight and grilled to order, served with a wedge of lemon or spicy tomato sauce

**INDIAN TIGER PRAWNS (£3 extra)**
Pan-fried with garlic

**SUSSEX SMOKED SALMON (£1 extra)**
Fresh Scottish salmon smoked in Poynings

**PARMA HAM WITH MELON (£1 extra)**
Delicious!

**AVOCADO FILLED WITH WHITE CRAB MEAT & PRAWNS (£1 extra)**

## Fish, Meat and Poultry

**FISH KEBABS**
Fresh monkfish, salmon, prawns with mushrooms & peppers, grilled to order, served with a light pimiento sauce on a bed of rice (garlic on request)

**CHEF'S FISH MASALA CURRY**
The choicest fresh fish cooked incredibly well in a cream of masala sauce

**CHEF'S SALMON & FRESH PRAWN CAKES (£1 extra)**
Back by popular demand! Served with a delicious leek & tomato sauce

**FRESH SCALLOPS (£2 extra)**
Fresh and plump breadcrumbed and pan-fried with bacon

**SALMON EN CROUTE (£1 extra)**
Fresh salmon wrapped in puff pastry oven-baked and served with a delicious cream of prawn sauce

**LAMB KLEFTICA (£1 extra)**
Shoulder of lamb pot roasted for 5 hours with mixed herbs and oregano

**CHICKEN CHILLI FRY**
Breast of chicken pan-fried with fresh chillies, onion and peppers, served on a bed of rice. Hot!

**HALF A ROAST ENGLISH DUCK**
Served with a rich black cherry, fresh pineapple and sherry sauce

**CHEQUERS SCOTCH FILLET (£2)**
Fillet steak grilled to your liking served on a croûton with pâté and topped with a cream of black pepper sauce

**FRESH VEGETABLES OF THE DAY or SALAD INCLUDED**

Competing with Mrs Smith's fishfingers at no.23, and Mrs Roberts' fish pie at no.18, The Chequers was eventually voted 'Best Seafood Restaurant in Slaugham 1996'. Rumour has it that they actually finished third, but were awarded first prize on a successful appeal that they were the only restaurant.

Although sadly not frequented by the Roberts and Smith families anymore, The Chequers is very popular and enjoys a great reputation for its seafood. Proprietor Paul Graham makes regular trips to Billingsgate, and the extensive menu (a small selection from which is featured opposite) is consequently supplemented by daily specials such as Fresh fillets of halibut pan-fried and served with smoked ham and leek sauce, or Fresh goujons of sole served with home-made tartare sauce. Lunch and dinner are selected from the same menu (3 courses £20 and £22.50), and there is also a luncheon table d'hôte (1 or 2 courses at £11.25 and £15.25).

Directions: About 3 miles south of Crawley on the A23, follow the signs to Slaugham. The Chequers is easily found in the middle of the village.

### USEFUL INFORMATION

**SERVING TIMES:**
Lunch 12pm-1.30pm (every day)
Dinner 7pm-9.30pm (Mon-Sat)
**CLOSED:** Sunday evening
**SEATING CAPACITY:** 80
**C/C:** V, MC, AE
**NO SMOKING** in the restaurant before 9.30pm

**NUMBER OF WINES:** 130
**HOUSE WINE:** £8.75
**OFF-STREET PARKING:** yes
**RESERVATIONS:** advisable, but compulsory at weekends
**OUTDOOR EATING:** yes
**ACCOMMODATION:** 6 rooms (B&B single £55, double £75)

# THE BELL

Tel: (01233) 770283
Smarden Lane, Smarden, Kent, TN27 8PW

## TODAY'S BLACKBOARD SPECIALS

### Starters

Seafood Avocado  £3.50
Potted Shrimps  £3.20
Garlic Mussels  £2.95
Minestrone Soup  £2.25

### Main Dishes

Tuna Steak with Fresh Chillis & Garlic  £7.50
Chicken Wellington  £8.25
Large Cod in Bear Batter  £6.75
Half Lobster Thermidor  £12.50
Grilled Trout & Almonds  £7.25
Poached Salmon Hollandaise  £7.50
T Bone Steak  £12.50
Mixed Grill  £10.50
Cheesed Off Chicken  £6.75
Sausages with Mashed Potato & Onion Gravy  £4.75
Mackerel Salad Platter  £5.45
10oz Rump Steak with Black Peppercorn Sauce  £10.95
Home-made Shepherd's Pie with Chips & Peas  £4.75
Home-made Steak & Kidney Pie with Chips & Peas  £6.75
Vegetable Lasagne with Salad  £4.75

### Puddings £2.75

Amaretto Cheesecake Gâteau  £2.75
Chocolate Fudge Cake  £2.75
Treacle & Walnut Tart  £2.75
French Apple Flan  £2.75
Banoffee Ice Pie  £2.75
Strawberry & Rhubarb Pie  £2.75
Raspberry Sponge Pudding  £2.75

The Bell at Smarden is a traditional inn, built in 1536 during the reign of Henry VIII and set amidst the peaceful Kent countryside. The three bars, with their oak beams, candles and inglenook fireplaces, exude character and though The Bell still remains a country pub where the locals congregate for a drink or two, the straightforward pub food is all home-made and worthy of a visit.

The daily specials are written up on blackboards in the bars and you can expect a choice of good wholesome food from the main menu, with dishes such as sausages with mashed potato & onion gravy (£4.75), shepherd's pie (£4.75), steak & kidney pie (£6.25), Thai red chicken curry (£5.75), lamb balti (£5.75), or 10oz rump steak with black peppercorn sauce (£10.95).

Directions: The village of Smarden is approximately 8 miles to the west of Ashford and is signposted from the surrounding roads. In Smarden itself, take the tiny road next to the Chequers pub and follow this to a T-junction. Turn left at this junction and The Bell is along this road on your left.

### USEFUL INFORMATION

**SERVING TIMES:**
Lunch 12pm-2pm (Mon-Fri)
    12pm-2.30pm (Sat & Sun)
Dinner 6.30pm-10pm (Mon-Sat)
    7.30pm-10pm (Sun)
**SEATING CAPACITY:** 60
**C/C:** V, MC, S, D, AE
**NO SMOKING** area available
**OUTDOOR EATING:** yes

**NUMBER OF WINES:** 29
**HOUSE WINE:** £6.75
**RESERVATIONS:** advisable, but essential at weekends
**OFF-STREET PARKING:** yes
**CHILDREN:** welcome
**ACCOMMODATION:** 4 rooms
(B&B sgl £30, twin £37, dbl £42)

# COLE'S RESTAURANT
### Tel: (01403) 730456
Worthing Road, Southwater, West Sussex, RH13 7BS

### Starters

**PRAWN, APPLE AND CELERY COCKTAIL**, topped with a Marie Rose sauce £4.25

**SALMON BASKET**, of filo pastry filled with smoked salmon, asparagus and mushrooms with a chive yoghurt £5.95

**BAKED GOATS CHEESE**, with sesame seeds served on a bed of mixed leaves £4.75

**TERRINE OF SALMON AND CRAYFISH**, with melba toast and dill dressing £4.95

**A SALAD OF SMOKED HAM**, with pink grapefruit and avocado with a poppy seed dressing £5.25

### Fish ~ Meat ~ Vegetarian

**DOVER SOLE**, plain grilled served with tartare sauce or meunière £17.95

**PAN-FRIED SCALLOPS**, with saffron sauce £14.50

**PRIME SCOTTISH FILLET STEAK**, grilled to your liking, garnished with watercress and tomato £15.75

**HALF A ROAST DUCK**, boned and served with an orange and ginger sauce £14.75

**FILLET OF PORK**, stuffed with apricots and pine kernels, wrapped in filo pastry and baked £13.95

**SAUTEED CALVES LIVER**, with sweet and sour onions £11.95

**A SAVOURY LOAF**, of pecan nuts, herbs and cottage cheese £11.75

*All dishes include a selection of fresh seasonal vegetables and potatoes, or if preferred a green or mixed salad*

Seven years ago the Cole family opened the doors to their beautifully converted 17th century barn, which stands proudly next to its own lily pond, and started what is now a highly respected and popular restaurant. The dining area is elegant, yet inviting, and retains exposed beams and a large open fireplace.

Elizabeth Cole rules the kitchen and prepares a cuisine which she describes as 'fairly English with classical influences'. She insists on using fresh, local produce whenever possible and on giving her guests value for money, so the portions are generous.

The main à la carte, a selection from which is shown opposite, is offered at lunch and dinner. It changes seasonally but is regularly supplemented by daily specials. Delicious home-made desserts (£4.25 each) may include Mascarpone and Basil Parfait, Fruit Brûlée, Chocolate Truffle Torte, or Sticky Toffee Pudding.

A table d'hôte (2 or 3 courses at £12.95 and £15.00) is also offered at luncheon. Sunday lunch is the same price but includes a traditional roast dish.

Directions: Southwater is situated just south of Horsham. Follow the signposts to the village from the A24, and Cole's is at the north end of the main street.

**USEFUL INFORMATION**

**SERVING TIMES:**
Lunch 12pm-2pm (Tues-Sun)
Dinner 7pm-9.30pm (Tues-Sat)
**CLOSED:** all day Monday, and Sunday evening
**SEATING CAPACITY:** 36
**C/C:** V, MC, S, D, AE, DC

**NUMBER OF WINES:** 50
**HOUSE WINE:** £10.95
**OFF-STREET PARKING:** yes
**RESERVATIONS:** advisable
**DRESS CODE:** smart
**NO SMOKING** in the restaurant
**OUTDOOR EATING:** no

# THE PLOUGH
## Tel: (01795 890256)
Stalisfield Green, Faversham, Kent, ME13 0HY

*Starters*
**Melon with Raspberry Coulis £2.95**
*Fresh Melon served with Raspberry Sauce*

**King Prawns with Garlic Butter £5.95**
*Large Prawns grilled with Garlic Butter, garnished with Salad*

*Pasta Dishes (as a main course £5.50)*
**Cannelloni Ripieni £3.00**
*Pancake Rolls with a Savoury filling and White Sauce*

**Spaghetti Bolognese £3.00**
*Freshly cooked Spaghetti served with Meat Sauce*

*Main Course*
**Fillets of Sole Nerone £9.95**
*Poached fillets with White Wine served with Mushrooms, Artichokes and Cream Sauce*

**Pollo Alla Cacciatore £8.95**
*Chicken Breast cooked with Onions and Mushrooms in Red Wine and Tomato Sauce*

**Anitra All'Arangio £10.95**
*Oven roasted Breast of Duck served with a rich Orange and Grand Marnier Sauce*

**Fillet Steak Forestiera £12.95**
*Slices of prime cut, tender Beef cooked with Bacon, Mushrooms, Wine and Cream Sauce*

*Dessert*
**Italian Trifle £2.65**
*Delicious Sponge with Summer Fruits, Italian Liqueur Custard and Cream*

**Lemon Brûlée £2.65**
*Lemon Sorbet, Raspberry Cream topped with Nuts*

**Deep Flan Apple Pie £2.45**
*Fresh Apples encased in rich Pastry with Custard or Cream*

Having sold their popular Italian restaurant in Faversham, husband and wife team Carlo and and Carol Corrado have now moved their operation to the idyllic and peaceful setting of the Plough Inn, a 15th century free house surrounded by rolling countryside at Stalisfield Green.

The à la carte menu (a selection appears opposite) is served in the intimate restaurant, whilst standard bar snacks are available in the traditional country pub atmosphere of the bar area.

The set price specials board changes daily and normally offers a choice of two starters (*Grilled Sardines with Garlic*, for example) and two main courses (such as *Braised Wild Hare*), plus a dessert, for around £16.95.

Directions: Stalisfield Green is located midway between the M2 and M20, roughly equidistant from both Faversham and Ashford. The village is signposted from the A251, A252 and A20.

## USEFUL INFORMATION

**SERVING TIMES:**
Lunch 12pm-2.30pm (every day)
Dinner 7pm-9.30pm (every day)
**SEATING CAPACITY:** 22 in the restaurant, 50 in the bar
**C/C:** V, MC, S, D
**NO SMOKING** in the restaurant

**NUMBER OF WINES:** 20
**HOUSE WINE:** £7.45
**RESERVATIONS:** advisable at the weekend
**OFF-STREET PARKING:** yes
**CHILDREN:** welcome
**OUTDOOR EATING:** yes

# THE WHITE HART
Tel: (01798) 873321
Stopham Bridge, Pulborough, West Sussex, RH20 1DS

## STARTERS

Pan-fried mushrooms in a creamy port & stilton sauce £4.25
Hors d'oeuvres platter £4.50
Cheese Arbroath smokie £3.95
Cravacado - avocado baked with crab meat, cheese & Cayenne pepper £3.95
Mexican prawns - tiger prawns in a creamy sauce with peppers,
 Tequila & Tobasco sauce £5.95
Portuguese sardines - grilled with lemon & garlic butter £4.00
Oak smoked salmon platter £5.95
Our very special fish soup £2.95
Fan of chilled melon - served with crab & prawns & marie rose sauce £5.95
 or served douched with port & with fruit sorbet £4.50

## MAIN COURSES

Oven baked salmon & broccoli au gratin £9.95
Fresh whole Dover sole - served with a mixed herb butter £13.50
Fresh halibut steak - grilled & served with a creamy horseradish
 & tarragon sauce £11.50
Gourmet scampi & prawn fricassée - pan-fried with garlic & fresh herbs &
 finished with white wine & cream, served with a timbale of rice £10.95
Pan-fired fillet of tuna - in extra virgin olive oil with a balsamic vinegar
 & lemon dressing £10.95
Fillets of fresh sole 'Bonne Femme' £10.50
Fresh swordfish steak - served with a tomato & basil sauce £10.50
Fillets of redfish 'Cantonese' - steamed fish topped with ginger, sugar,
 spring onions, soy sauce & sizzled with hot sunflower oil £10.95
Monkfish & bacon brochette - skewers of monkfish & smoked bacon
 served upon a beurre blanc sauce £11.50
Half shoulder of lamb - roasted & served with a rosemary
 & redcurrant gravy £10.50
Supreme of chicken - chargrilled & served with a spiced apricot
 & tarragon sauce £8.50
Chargrilled rib-eye steak - served with your choice of either a garnish of
 mushrooms & tomatoes or with an au poivre sauce £10.95

*****

All of the above dishes are served with a selection of fresh market vegetables
or a side salad

# STOPHAM BRIDGE 183

The White Hart is a traditional country pub built of Sussex stone in the 14th century. It is situated in a pretty spot next to a bridge that crosses the River Arun. The bridge itself was built in 1306 and is now designated as an "ancient monument", forming part of the new Whey and Arun canal route.

The pub is very rustic, with exposed beams, and specialises in fresh fish, brought in daily by their supplier down the road in Shoreham. The small dining area was once used as a forge - the photograph of a horse being shod there goes some way to proving this point.

The menu featured opposite changes seasonally and is supplemented by daily specials such as Fillet of Turbot Veronique (£11.50) or Char-grilled Salmon with a Honey and Grain Mustard Vinaigrette (£10.50).

Directions: The White Hart is signposted just off the A283 Pulborough to Petworth road, approximately one mile to the west of Pulborough.

## USEFUL INFORMATION

**SERVING TIMES:**
Lunch 12pm-2.30pm (every day)
Dinner 6.30pm-9.30pm (Mon-Sat)
 6.30pm-9pm (Sun)
**SEATING CAPACITY:** 22 in the restaurant, 30 in the bar
**C/C:** V, MC, S, D, AE, DC

**NUMBER OF WINES:** 40
**HOUSE WINE:** £8.75
**RESERVATIONS:** advisable
**OFF-STREET PARKING:** yes
**OUTDOOR EATING:** yes
**NO SMOKING** area available
**CHILDREN:** welcome

# MANLEYS
Tel: (01903) 742331
Storrington, West Sussex, RH20 4BT

### LE DINER

### AMUSE-BOUCHE

********

### SALADE DE POIRE AU VIN ROUGE ET GORGONZOLA
Poached pear in red wine with a gorgonzola dressing

### CAILLE ROTIE ET FARCIE A LA MOUSSE DE FOIE GRAS
Boned quail, roasted and served with purée of foie gras on a potato galette

### FEUILLETE AUX CREVETTES ROYALES ET LEGUMES ROTIS
Marinated grilled king prawns with roasted vegetable in puff pastry

**************

### CONFIT DE CANARD AU CHOIX ROUGE ET ROSTI
Crispy confit of duck with rosti, red cabbage and raspberry glaze

### FRAICHEUR DE LA MAREE
Fish of the day

### MEDAILLONS DE CHEVREUIL A L'AIGRE-DOUX ET GRIOTTES
Local venison fillets with a sweet and sour sauce, wild cherries and potato croquette

### SUPREME DE VOLAILLE AUX CHAMPIGNONS DE BOIS A LA CREME
Roast breast of chicken with local mushrooms and cream sauce

**************

### BAISER DE MERINGUE A LA MAISON
Meringue filled with butterscotch ice cream topped with butterscotch sauce and pecan nuts

### PROFITEROLLES AUX CHOCOLAT
Choux pastry filled with grand marnier and hot chocolate sauce

### CREME BRULEE

### ASSIETTE DE FROMAGE

********

### CAFE ET FRIANDISES

£33.50

Named after the old headmaster of the public school which once stood here, Manleys is now one of the premier restaurants in the South East. The split-level dining area is immaculate and elegant, enjoying familiar characteristics of the Queen Anne period, exposed oak beams and a large inglenook fireplace.

This comfortable and refined ambiance prepares you for the gourmet experience which follows. Lovingly prepared by chef proprietor Karl Löderer for twenty years, the cuisine is a combination of classical French, Austrian and English.

The main à la carte (2 courses £32.50) changes seasonally and is complemented by monthly table d'hôte menus at luncheon (2 or 3 courses for £15.00 and £19.60 respectively), and dinner (3 courses £33.50), a sample of which is shown opposite. Sunday lunch is £23.50.

Desserts appear on their own menu which changes regularly, but may feature Thin layers of strudel pastry with marinated berries and cream (£6.50), better known, of course, as simply Beerenfruechte in Strudelteigblaettern!

Directions: Approaching Storrington from the east on the A283, Manleys is found on the left-hand side of the road on the outskirts of the town.

### USEFUL INFORMATION

**SERVING TIMES:**
Lunch 12.15pm-1.45pm (Tues-Sun)
Dinner 7.15pm-9.30pm (Wed-Sat)
**CLOSED:** all day Monday, and for dinner on Sunday and Tuesday
**SEATING CAPACITY:** 48
**C/C:** V, MC, S, D, AE
**DRESS CODE:** smart
**NO SMOKING** area available

**NUMBER OF WINES:** 140
**HOUSE WINE:** £14.80
**OFF-STREET PARKING:** yes
**CHILDREN:** welcome
**RESERVATIONS:** advisable
**OUTDOOR EATING:** no
**ACCOMMODATION:** 1 suite
(£95 incl. continental breakfast)

# THE OLD FORGE
Tel: (01903) 743402
Church Street, Storrington, West Sussex, RH20 4LA

## FIXED PRICE A LA CARTE MENU
£21.50 for 2 courses £27.50 for 3 courses

Mushroom and Coriander Pâté layered between Gaufrette Potatoes, with a Roast Plum Tomato Coulis

Gravadlax, Leek and Goat's Cheese Pastry with a selection of Salad Leaves

Foie Gras and Chicken Liver Parfait with Toasted Brioche, Grape and Green Apple Chutney

Stir-fried Chicken and Pancetta Salad

\* \* \* \* \* \* \* \* \* \*

Grilled Wing of Skate on Roasted Peppers moistened with Honey and Caper Vinaigrette

Pan-fried King Scallops with Saffron Rice and a Tomato and Coconut Milk Sauce

Roast Best End of Lamb sliced around Deep-fried Celeriac and served with Sercial Madeira Sauce

Peppered Pork Tenderloin with Garlic Spinach, served with a White Onion Cream

Fillet of Beef with Cured Ham and Bone Marrow set on a Red Wine Jus

\* \* \* \* \* \* \* \* \* \*

Praline and Banana Frangipane with Caramelised Banana Ice Cream

White Chocolate and Coconut Charlotte and a Red Fruit Coulis

Traditional Summer Pudding with Devon Clotted Cream

Bitter Chocolate Scroll with Almond Tuile and Charles Melton Shiraz Sauce

Still retaining the original lead-working forge and bellows, The Old Forge is a 16th century town-house restaurant run by Clive and Cathy Roberts.

A slight change in style from the last nine successful years is imminent, with the recent addition to the team of Jonas Tester. His classical French training brings an extra dimension to the kitchen, the subtlety of his cooking complementing the very positive flavours and robust sauces inspired by Clive. The menus will continue to feature modern British cooking, drawing on a large cross-section of international ingredients.

In addition to the fixed price à la carte featured on the facing page, there are also daily set price menus for both lunch (£15 for 3 courses) and dinner (£17 for 2 courses, £22 for 3 courses). An excellent way to introduce yourself to The Old Forge is to visit one Sunday lunchtime, when the prices are slightly cheaper (£13.50 for 2 courses) but the cooking no less inspiring.

Directions: The Old Forge is easily found in Church Street in the town centre.

## USEFUL INFORMATION

**SERVING TIMES:**
Lunch 12.30pm-1.30pm (Wed-Fri, Sun)
Dinner 7.15pm-9pm (Wed-Sat)
**CLOSED:** all day Monday & Tuesday, Saturday lunch & Sunday night
**SEATING CAPACITY:** 36
**C/C:** V, MC, S, D, AE, DC

**NUMBER OF WINES:** 50
**HOUSE WINE:** £9.75
**RESERVATIONS:** advisable
**OUTDOOR EATING:** no
**CHILDREN:** welcome
**OFF-STREET PARKING:** no
**NO SMOKING** in the restaurant

# THE WHITE HORSE INN
### Tel: (01798) 869221
Sutton, near Pulborough, West Sussex, RH20 1PS

## BLACKBOARD SPECIALS

**STARTERS OR LIGHT SNACKS**
Home-made Soup of the Day  £3.40
Fresh Scallop and Green Peppercorn Terrine  £5.60
Roasted Aubergine, Pepper, Asparagus and Courgette Salad  £5.20
Home-made Chicken, Apple and Walnut Terrine  £4.20
Fresh Calamari sautéed with Garlic, Onion, Tomato and Parsley  £5.20
Home-made Crab and Prawn Won Tons with a Chilli Sauce  £5.80
Warm Salad with King Scallops and Duck Breast  £6.80
Grilled Polenta with Roasted Peppers in Balsamic Vinegar  £4.80
Home-made Gravadlax with Mustard and Dill Sauce  £5.60

**MAIN COURSES**
Fresh English Cod and Chips  £5.90
Fried Liver, Bacon and Onions  £5.80
Caramelized Chicken Thighs with Ginger and Garlic  £7.40
Grilled Whole Plaice or Lemon Sole  £8.20
Chargrilled Tuna Steak with a fresh Mango Salsa  £9.80
Half a Roast Duck with Apple and Gooseberry Sauce  £10.80
12oz Chargrilled Rib-eye Steak  £11.20
Thai Prawn Curry with Jasmine Rice  £9.20
Whole Fresh Crab and Langoustine Platter  £11.80
Monkfish and Tomato Risotto, Asparagus and Red Pepper Sauce  £10.40
Locally-reared Roast Suckling Pig  £9.40
Lamb Steak with Honey and Fresh Rosemary  £8.60
Fresh Halibut with Sun-dried Tomatoes, Capers & Crème Fraîche  £9.20
Cold Poached Salmon Salad  £8.20

**DESSERTS  ALL HOME-MADE**
Sherry Trifle  £3.40
Chocolate Nut Crunch  £3.40
Meringues with Strawberries and Whipped Cream  £3.40
Treacle Tart  £3.40
Lemon and Lime Fool  £3.40
Crème Brûlée  £3.40
Tiramisu  £3.40
French Lemon Tart  £3.40
Chocolate Bread and Butter Pudding  £3.40
Rhubarb and Almond Crumble  £3.40

The White Horse is a charming Georgian country inn that dates back to 1746. Half-clad walls and wide planked flooring are in traditional old painted and scrubbed pine and the inn is split into two sections - the Village Bar with its roaring log fire, still a popular meeting place for local residents, and the Dining Room, with a definite bistro feel to it.

The kitchen has built up an enviable reputation for its varied country cooking with an emphasis on traditional dishes. The menu, written up on the blackboard, changes from day to day.

Lighter snacks are also available in the bar area, with their excellent speciality sandwiches, such as Tomato and Mozzarella with Fresh Basil in Ciabatta Bread (£3.00) or Home-made Gravadlax with Cream Cheese on a Toasted Bagel (£3.20), worthy of a mention.

Directions: The village of Sutton is located approximately 4 miles to the south of Petworth and is signposted from the A285 Petworth to Chichester road.

## USEFUL INFORMATION

**SERVING TIMES:**
Lunch 12pm-2pm (Mon-Fri)
    12pm-2.30pm (Sat & Sun)
Dinner 7pm-9.30pm (every day)
**SEATING CAPACITY:** 40
**C/C:** V, MC, S, D, AE, DC
**OFF-STREET PARKING:** yes

**NUMBER OF WINES:** 40
**HOUSE WINE:** £8.80
**RESERVATIONS:** advisable
**OUTDOOR EATING:** yes
**CHILDREN:** welcome
**ACCOMMODATION:** 6 rooms
(B&B single £48, double £58-£68)

# THE HORSE GUARDS INN
### Tel: (01798) 342332
Tillington, Petworth, West Sussex, GU28 9AF

**DINNER MENU**

*Starters*

Chilled Gazpacho Soup £3.75
Platter of Smoked Salmon £5.95
Greek Salad £4.25
Platter of Gravadlax with a Dill & Mustard Sauce £5.95
Fan of Chilled Melon with Strawberries & Cointreau £4.50
Salad of Figs, Toasted Walnuts & Parma Ham
with a Dolcelatte Dressing £4.75
Leaf Spinach and Bacon Salad with an Avocado & Lime Dressing £4.75
Grilled Goat's Cheese with Olive Oil, Sun-dried Tomatoes & Basil £5.25
Baked Flat Mushrooms with Mozzarella & Tarragon £4.59
Warm Crab and Pineapple Tart with a Tomato & Chive Salsa £4.75

*Main Courses*

Whole Grilled Dover Sole £16.95
Roast Halibut Supreme with a Spicy Crust
& a Red Pepper & Walnut Veloute £10.25
Griddled Swordfish Steak with Tomato, Lemon & Crispy Leeks £9.25
Saltimbocca - Pan-fried Veal Escalope with Sage & Parma Ham £12.50
Half a Roast Duck with a Honey & Orange Sauce £12.25
Grilled Sirloin Steak Garni £12.25
Medallions of Fillet Steak with Spring Onion & Chive Butter £14.75
Whole Roast Poussin with Lemon, Coriander & Capers £10.95
Calves' Liver Pan-fried with Bramley Apples
& flamed with Calvados £10.50
Pork Fillet Grilled & served with Plum & Ginger Wine Sauce £9.95
Macaroni & Asparagus with Roast Cherry Tomatoes
& Fresh Herb Butter topped with shaved Parmesan £5.95
Mushrooms, Walnuts & Leeks in a Stilton Sauce
topped with Filo Pastry £6.75

Originally built as three separate cottages, The Horse Guards Inn is a charming 17th century dining pub with a reputation for good food.

Apparently it is the only inn or pub in the country that bears the "Horse Guards" name. There are strong links to the regiment, who were billeted in the park in Petworth in the 1850's. For a number of years they patronised what was then known as The Star Inn. The pub was thus nicknamed The Horse Guards by the locals and the name caught on.

The Dinner Menu is supplemented by a daily specials blackboard which might include Fillet of Sea Bass with Garlic Butter and Langoustines (£14.95) or Roast Rack of Lamb with Honey and Rosemary (£12.95). At lunchtime you can choose from either the Lunch Menu or Bar Snacks Menu.

Directions: The Horse Guards Inn is situated in Upperton Road, which is signposted from the centre of Tillington, about 1 mile west of Petworth along the A272 Petworth-Midhurst road.

## USEFUL INFORMATION

**SERVING TIMES:**
Lunch 12pm-2pm (Mon-Sat)
    12.30pm-2.30pm (Sun)
Dinner 7pm-10pm (every day)
**SEATING CAPACITY:** 65
**C/C:** V, MC, S, D, AE
**OFF-STREET PARKING:** no

**NUMBER OF WINES:** 50
**HOUSE WINE:** £9.95
**RESERVATIONS:** advisable
**OUTDOOR EATING:** yes
**CHILDREN:** welcome (over 6 yrs)
**ACCOMMODATION:** 3 rooms
(B&B from £55 per room)

# LOS PARRALES

Tel: (01732) 359973
6-8 East Street, Tonbridge, Kent, TN9 1HG

### COLD TAPAS

| | |
|---|---|
| Tortilla Espanola | £2.50 |
| *Spanish omelette* | |
| Jamon Serrano Platter | £4.75 |
| *Spanish cured ham* | |
| Anchoas a la Vinagreta | £2.95 |
| *Anchovies with olive oil, garlic & parsley* | |
| Ensalada del Pozo | £2.95 |
| *White beans, tuna & potato salad* | |
| Pulpitos a la Gallega | £3.95 |
| *Marinated octopus, peppers & onions* | |
| Gazpacho | £2.95 |
| *Vegetable soup served cold* | |

### HOT TAPAS

| | |
|---|---|
| Albondigas | £3.95 |
| *Pork meatballs in basil, tomato & chilli sauce* | |
| Champinones al Romero | £2.95 |
| *Mushrooms with garlic & rosemary* | |
| Gambas al Ajillo | £4.95 |
| *Large prawns in garlic & chilli* | |
| Calamares Romana | £3.95 |
| *Deep fried squid rings in batter* | |
| Empanadillas | £3.95 |
| *Spinach, pine nut & cheese pastry parcels* | |
| Higados de Pato | £3.95 |
| *Sauté duck livers with sage* | |
| Chorizo al Vino | £2.95 |
| *Spanish sausage cooked in wine* | |
| Patatas Bravas | £2.95 |
| *Sauté potatoes in spicy tomato sauce* | |
| Gambas a la Plancha | £4.95 |
| *Grilled large prawns* | |
| Pinchitos | £3.95 |
| *Grilled lamb sticks marinated in cumin, coriander & ginger* | |
| Alas de Pollo piri piri | £3.50 |
| *Spicy chicken wings* | |
| Patas de Cangrejos | £3.95 |
| *Crablets* | |

### STARTERS

*from the tapas menu*

### MAIN COURSES

| | |
|---|---|
| Salmon | £8.50 |
| *Salmon with lime & ginger* | |
| Rape al Ajillo | £9.95 |
| *Monkfish with garlic & parsley* | |
| Pato a la Sevillana | £9.95 |
| *Duck with oranges, thyme & olives* | |
| Costillas de Cordero | £9.95 |
| *Lamb cutlets with rosemary served with white beans* | |
| Cordero con Albaricoques | £9.95 |
| *Leg of lamb, apricots & coriander served with rice & chick peas* | |
| Pollo Parrales | £8.95 |
| *Chicken breast with grapes & saffron* | |
| Conejo Paisana | £8.95 |
| *Rabbit with wild mushrooms & Jamon Serrano* | |
| Paella (minimum two persons) | £8.95 |
| *Cost per person* | |
| Vegetarian dish of the day | £7.50 |
| Filete de Ternera a la Pimienta | £11.95 |
| *Fillet steak with green peppercorn sauce* | |

*All main meals include vegetables, salad or rice*

### DESSERTS

| | |
|---|---|
| Home-made sweet selection | £2.95 |
| Sorbets & Ice Creams | £2.95 |
| Cheese | £3.50 |

With the greatest of respect to McDonalds and Wimpy, Tonbridge has long been regarded as a culinary desert, so fearing the worst I approached this relatively new Spanish restaurant with a certain amount of trepidation. I need not have worried.

The building itself is part-listed and old hanging hooks in the main dining area serve as reminders that it was once a slaughterhouse and butcher's shop. Los Paralles was named in honour of the eighty year old vine that grows above the bar, and owners Juan and Linda Sanchez have quickly established a reputation for serving delicious and authentic Spanish cuisine.

The main menu featured opposite changes about eight times a year but there are always at least six additional daily specials (3 tapas, 3 main). Everything here is home-made and Juan makes weekly trips to Billingsgate and Spitalfields markets to ensure that his produce is of the highest quality. Cheeses and wines are all appropriately Spanish!

Directions: East Street is found at the north end of Tonbridge High Street next to Lloyds Bank (East Street is a one-way street which may be approached by car from Bordyke).

## USEFUL INFORMATION

**SERVING TIMES:**
Lunch 12.15pm-2pm (Tues-Sat)
Dinner 7pm-10pm (Tues-Sat)
**CLOSED:** Sunday and Monday
**SEATING CAPACITY:** 40
**C/C:** V, MC, S, D

**NUMBER OF WINES:** 40
**HOUSE WINE:** £7.95
**RESERVATIONS:** advisable
**OUTDOOR EATING:** yes
**OFF-STREET PARKING:** no

# SANKEY'S

Tel: (01892) 511422
39 Mount Ephraim, Tunbridge Wells, Kent, TN4 8AA

## STARTERS AND LIGHT MEALS

6 Whitstable Oysters *full and plump* £5.00
Smoked Salmon *from Loch Fyne* £6.50
Mediterranean Prawns *pan-fried in garlic, sliced chilli and fresh lime juice* £8.75
Greenland Prawns *tossed in garlic butter and flamed with Cognac* £5.50
Selection of Smoked Fish *with horseradish sauce* £6.50
Soupe de Poissons *with home-made rouille, grated gruyère and croutons* £4.50
Moules Marinières *steamed in wine, shallots and garlic* £5.00
Grilled Goat's Cheese *on a bed of leaves, pesto and balsamic vinegar* £4.50

## CRUSTACEA

Cornish Cock Crab *steamed and dressed, served cold with mayonnaise* £14.50
Fresh Whole Lobster *approx. 1/ lb.* £25.00
Plateau de Fruits de Mer *freshly prepared and served chilled* £17.50

## MAIN COURSES

Normandy Fish Stew £15.00
*finished with Noilly Prat and cream*
Griddled Loin of Venison £15.75
*presented on a garlic mash with carrot and swede, port wine sauce*
Whole Grilled 16oz Sea Bass £16.50
*with braised fennel and a fresh tomato sauce*
Steamed Fillet of Brill £15.75
*placed on char-grilled vegetables and glazed with a Dijon and herb beurre blanc*
Sankey's Paella £10.50
*our seafood version served in the traditional pan with all the trimmings*
Tempura of Garden Vegetables £9.75
*deep-fried in a fresh batter served with a tossed spinach and shallot salad*
Classic Grilled Scottish Salmon £11.00
*with a fresh asparagus and Hollandaise sauce and a selection of fresh vegetables*
Scotch Fillet Steak £14.80
*grilled and garnished with a beef tomato and herb crust, button mushrooms, floured onion rings and French fries*

Mention seafood anywhere around this area and the conversation invariably includes the name of Guy Sankey. Having built up a little country pub to near cult status by providing the finest lobsters, crabs, oysters, scallops and fresh fish for miles around, Guy then moved his operation to this Dutch gabled, Victorian villa in Tunbridge Wells ten years ago. The success story continues, with Sankey's Seafood Restaurant and Cellar Wine Bar still flourishing.

The restaurant comprises four rooms each with its own character, all air-conditioned and cluttered with original paintings, prints and memorabilia. As availability is always variable, the *carte* (an example of which appears opposite) is printed daily, supplemented by a 2-course set price lunch for £7.50.

The same dishes are available in the Cellar Wine Bar, but here they also offer a simpler bistro style menu with daily specialities displayed on blackboards, such as Hake Steak with Rosemary & Olive Oil (£6.50), Thai-style Prawn Curry & Coconut Milk (£6.50) or Grilled Lamb Fillet with a Red Wine & Mushroom Sauce (£6.50).

Directions: Sankey's is 100 yards along from (and on the opposite side of the road to) the Kent & Sussex Hospital at the northern end of the town on Mount Ephraim (the A264).

**USEFUL INFORMATION**

**SERVING TIMES:**
Lunch 12pm-2pm (Mon-Fri)
Dinner 7pm-9.30pm (Mon-Sat)
**CLOSED:** Sat lunch & all day Sun
**SEATING CAPACITY:** 60 in the restaurant, 40 in the cellar wine bar
**C/C:** V, MC, S, D, AE, DC
**OFF-STREET PARKING:** no

**NUMBER OF WINES:** 80
**HOUSE WINE:** £10.00
**RESERVATIONS:** advisable, but essential at weekends
**CHILDREN:** welcome
**NO WHEELCHAIR ACCESS**
**OUTDOOR EATING:** yes
**NO SMOKING** area available

# THACKERAY'S HOUSE

Tel: (01892) 511921
85 London Road, Tunbridge Wells, Kent, TN1 1EA

### STARTERS

Pigeon breast and artichoke salad, celeriac remoulade £6.75
Lobster and mango salad, "nuoc cham" £9.95
Home cured bresaola £7.90
Goat's cheese salad, tapenade, sweet peppers and crispy fried artichoke £6.95
Mussel and shrimp risotto £6.75
Six warm Loch Fyne oysters with mirin and soy (or plain) £6.90
Watercress soup (hot or chilled) £5.75
Mini Bouillabaisse (prawn, red mullet, gurnard, scallop, mussel, squid) £7.90

### MAIN COURSES

Turbot fricassée with scallops and fresh peas £18.95
Organic Angus/Hereford beef sirloin, colcannon, sweet and sour onions £21.50
Organic lamb fillet, aubergine, cumin lentils and turmeric potatoes £16.25
Szechuan peppered Hereford duck breast with kumquats £17.90
Grilled John Dory fillet and king prawns, chilli salt squid, crab vinaigrette, rocket and fennel salad £17.50
Guinea fowl with fresh truffle, broad beans & goat's cheese gnocchi £16.90
Braised monkfish, lobster sauce £17.90
Roast sea bass fillet, saffron risotto & red pepper sauce £19.50
Main courses served with a vegetable garnish, extra vegetables at £1.75 each

### DESSERTS

Strawberries and vanilla ice cream £4.75
Apricot, walnut, ginger and toffee pudding £4.75
Chocolate Armagnac and griotte cherry loaf, coffee sauce £4.75
Charentais melon sorbet £4.75
Selection of British and Irish farmhouse cheeses £4.75

In a pretty 17th century house facing the common where William Makepeace Thackeray once lived, the combination of an elegant dining room on the ground floor (presided over by chef/patron Bruce Wass) and an informal bistro downstairs (with Peter Lucas in the kitchen) continues to thrive.

Eclectic, modern British cooking is the order of the day with Italian and Thai influences often in evidence on the menus, which change daily. In addition to *Thackeray's House*'s carte (featured on the facing page), the main dining room's fixed price menus offer a choice of two-course lunches for £12 or £19.50, a midweek dinner menu costing £19.50 for two courses and £24.50 for three courses, plus a five-course menu priced at £45.00 per head.

The price differential *Downstairs at Thackeray's* reflects the use of simpler ingredients. Their à la carte menu might include Queen Scallop, Crab and Tomato Linguine (£4.90) or Slow-cooked Duck with Puy Lentils (£8.90), whilst the two-course set-price lunch (at £7.50) represents excellent value.

Directions: Thackeray's is easily found at the top of the London Road in the centre of town, facing the common and next to the Conservative Association.

## USEFUL INFORMATION

**SERVING TIMES:**
Lunch 12.30pm-2.30pm (Tues-Sun)
Dinner 7pm-10pm (Tues-Sat)
**CLOSED:** Sun night & all day Mon (downstairs also closed Sun lunch)
**SEATING CAPACITY:** 50 upstairs, 36 downstairs
**C/C:** V, MC, S, D

**NUMBER OF WINES:** 370
**HOUSE WINE:** £12.75 upstairs, £11.75 downstairs
**CHILDREN:** welcome
**RESERVATIONS:** advisable
**OUTDOOR EATING:** downstairs
**OFF-STREET PARKING:** no

# ALEXANDER HOUSE
Tel: (01342) 714914
Turners Hill, West Sussex, RH10 4QD

*A Selection from the A La Carte*

Creamed Leek Soup with Mussels, Saffron
and Crème Fraîche £6.50

Ceviche of Salmon, Herb-fried Brioche and Coriander £10.50

Salad of Veal Kidneys, Home-dried Tomatoes, Basil and
Balsamic Vinegar £12.50

Bourride of Red Mullet, Crispy Leek and Sevruga Caviar £11.00

~~~~~~

Whole Grilled Scottish Lobster, Rosemary, Garlic and Lemon £32.00

Roasted Monkfish, Smoked Bacon, Buttered Leeks
and Sorrel Sauce £24.00

Chargrilled Line Caught Halibut, Chantrell Mushrooms,
Clams and Thyme Galette £26.00

Pan-fried Loin of Lamb, Roasted Sweetbreads, Tomato
and Basil Jus £26.00

Braised Squab Pigeon, Honey Sauce and Truffle £24.00

~~~~~~

Savarin of Raspberries, Frothy Vanilla Cream £8.50

Hot Mango Tart and Coconut Ice £8.50

Caramel Blancmange with Orange £8.50

Selection of English and Continental Cheeses £11.50

Coffee and Petits Fours £3.75

As is perhaps befitting of an estate once owned by the family of the famous poet Percy Bysshe Shelley, nature and art harmonise contentedly throughout this exclusive 17th century hotel, which enjoys 135 acres of its own private gardens and parkland.

The restaurant itself effuses an understated luxury and is renowned for its classic English and French cuisine and superb service. The main à la carte shown opposite is supplemented by daily table d'hôte menus at luncheon (2 or 3 courses at £14.75 and £16.75 respectively) and dinner (3 courses £26). A typical selection in the evening may include Seafood Soup with Dill Sour Cream to start, Chargrilled Tuna with Garlic Fine Beans, New Potatoes and Pesto Dressing to follow, and Orange Crème Caramel with Summer Red Fruits to finish. Coffee, which is included in the price, may be taken in the elegant lounge areas.

Directions: Turners Hill is a small village about 3 miles east of Junction 10 of the M23. At the crossroads in the village take the B2110 in the direction of East Grinstead, and continue until you see the hotel entrance on your left.

### USEFUL INFORMATION

**SERVING TIMES:**
Lunch 12.30pm-2pm (every day)
Dinner 7.30pm-9.30pm (every day)
**SEATING CAPACITY:** 60
**C/C:** V, MC, S, D, AE, DC
**OUTDOOR EATING:** yes
**NO SMOKING** in the restaurant

**NUMBER OF WINES:** 280
**HOUSE WINE:** £14.50
**OFF-STREET PARKING:** yes
**RESERVATIONS:** advisable
**DRESS CODE:** smart
**ACCOMMODATION:** 15 rooms
(single £99.50, double fr £135)

# HOOKE HALL
Tel: (01825) 761578
High Street, Uckfield, East Sussex, TN22 1EN

A Selection from the evening A La Carte

Insalata di pollo marinato al balsamico e vegetali £4.75
*balsamic marinated chicken salad with vegetables*
Tagliata d'anatra con insalata di sedano e caprino dressing balsamico £5.50
*thinly sliced duck breast with celery and goat cheese, balsamic dressing*
Insalata di fave soncino asparagi e filettini di sogliola £5.50
*broad bean, lamb's tongue, asparagus and sole salad*
Brioches di gamberoni e vegetali fritti £6.00
*fried king prawns brioches with fried vegetables*

### PRIMI PIATTI

Risotto alle verdure estive e basilico £4.50
*creamy risotto with vegetables and basil*
Tagliolini neri alla pancetta affumicata e porri £5.00
*black tagliolini with bacon and leeks*
Ravioli al salmone affumicato e crema di lenticchie £4.75
*home-smoked salmon ravioli with a lentil cream sauce*
Primi Piatti as a Main Course £8.50

### PESCI

Filetto di branzino al pomodoro avocado e maggiorana fresca £15.75
*sea bass fillet with tomato, avocado and fresh marjoram*
Medaglioni di coda di rospo al pomodoro marinato su rosti di patate £14.75
*monkfish medallions with marinated tomato on a potato rosti*
Involtini di sogliola e zucchine al vapore all'olio d'oliva pugliese £15.75
*steamed Dover sole and courgette rolls with puglia olive oil*

### CARNI

Fegato di vitello alla Veneziana con polenta £15.50
*calf liver with braised onions and polenta Venetian style*
Filetto di manzo al Montepulciano e midollo £15.50
*beef fillet with Montepulciano red wine and marrow sauce*
Nodino di vitello alla salvia e patate novelle £16.00
*veal loin steak with sage and new potatoes*

Contorni £2.50
*vegetables and salads*

If you have any doubts about the apparent anomaly of an Italian restaurant in an elegant Queen Anne town house, then try 'La Scaletta' at Hooke Hall. You will not be disappointed.

The hotel itself is beautifully decorated, ornate and traditional, with antiques and oak-panelling, yet with the personal touches of the delightful owners Alister and Juliet Percy helping to create an atmosphere that is at once luxurious and inviting.

The cuisine is predominantly North Italian, and a sample from the evening à la carte is shown opposite. At luncheon you may either choose from a slightly less extensive à la carte or a good value table d'hôte menu (which offers 2 courses at £9.50 and 3 courses at £12.50). Desserts may include Pistachio soufflé with dark chocolate shavings (£5.25), Mango parfait with a strawberry coulis (£4.75), as well as delicious home-made ice creams and sorbets. All menus change monthly.

Directions: Hooke Hall is easily found at the northern end of Uckfield High Street. The entrance to the restaurant is on the left.

### USEFUL INFORMATION

**SERVING TIMES:**
Lunch 12pm-2pm (Mon-Fri)
Dinner 7.30pm-9pm (Mon-Sat)
**CLOSED:** Saturday lunch and all day Sunday
**SEATING CAPACITY:** 34
**C/C:** V, MC, D, AE
**OFF-STREET PARKING:** no

**NUMBER OF WINES:** 30
**HOUSE WINE:** £10.75
**RESERVATIONS:** advisable
**OUTDOOR EATING:** no
**NO SMOKING** in the restaurant, but allowed in the study
**ACCOMMODATION:** 9 rooms (single from £45, double from £65)

# THE CHARDONNAY RESTAURANT

Tel: (01903) 892271
Old London Road, Washington, West Sussex, RH20 3BN

## *STARTERS*

*Warm potato crêpe with smoked salmon and crème fraîche*

*Half a fanned avocado with fresh prawns and a Marie Rose sauce*

*Home-made cheese and spinach gnocchi glazed with a cheese and cream sauce, garnished with fresh pesto*

*Gateau of flaked white crab meat, layered with avocado and tomato, garnished with fanned avocado and pink grapefruit segments*

*Grilled goats' cheese sprinkled with black pepper served on a tapenade toast, with warm puy lentils in a balsamic vinaigrette*

## *MAIN COURSES*

*Pan-fried Orkney scallops served with a lemon butter sauce, garnished with cabbage and bacon bound with cream*

*Half a roast guinea fowl with a prune and armagnac sauce*

*Roast best-end of new season lamb on an onion confit served with a raspberry vinegar jus*

*Sauté fillet of veal on a bed of spinach served with an aubergine, mushroom and tarragon sauce*

*Open lasagne with a nage butter sauce, served with fresh asparagus and oyster mushrooms*

## *DESSERTS*

*An island of baked meringue sprinkled with flaked almonds and covered with a crisp caramel shell, served on a pool of home-made vanilla sauce*

*A dark chocolate truffle tort, combining light Italian meringue, cream and couverture chocolate served with a chocolate sauce*

*A selection of home-made ice creams and sorbets*

Ignoring my mother's good advice about strange men and toilets, I allowed proprietor Carl Illes to give me a guided tour of his 'impressive loos'. Take it from me, the *Men's* is much nicer than the *Ladies'*. We get marble, they only get granite - something to do with the destructive power of nail varnish! Toilets aside, Carl and his wife Julie have much to be proud about. The Chardonnay is an elegant and popular restaurant, with a tasteful conservatory extension complementing the 18th century bar area.

As with the other members of the Illes mafia, Carl personally buys his produce from the London markets. The seasonal menu is extensive, allowing him ample opportunity to express his undoubted talent, and only a very small selection of dishes are featured opposite. Lunch and dinner may be 2 or 3 courses (£20.50/22.50 at lunch, and £21.50/23.50 at dinner).

There are some very nice touches here - just wait until your home-made petits fours are served with coffee. Also, the four flavours of bread are delicious, and each person gets a half loaf on a breadboard at their table. You may take home what you don't finish in a 'Chardonnay bag'!

Directions: From the Washington roundabout where the A24 crosses the A283, head north on the A24 for 200 yards. Turn left and then immediately left again. The Chardonnay is 100 yards further along on the left.

## USEFUL INFORMATION

**SERVING TIMES:**
Lunch 12pm-2pm (Tues-Sat)
Dinner 7pm-9pm (Tues-Thur)
    7pm-9.30pm (Fri-Sat)
**CLOSED:** Sunday and Monday
**SEATING CAPACITY:** 60
**C/C:** V, MC, D, AE
**NO SMOKING** area available

**NUMBER OF WINES:** 120
**HOUSE WINE:** £9.50
**OFF-STREET PARKING:** yes
**RESERVATIONS:** advisable, but compulsory at weekends
**OUTDOOR EATING:** no
**CHILDREN:** welcome

# WALLETT'S COURT
Tel: (01304) 852424
Westcliffe, St Margaret's at Cliffe, Dover, Kent, CT15 6EW

### A La Carte Menu

#### First Course

*Gazpacho Andalouse* - A chilled spicy summer soup of tomatoes, red peppers & cucumber with a hint of garlic, white wine & fresh herbs £6.00

*An Elixir of White Grapes and Cucumber with Limes* - A chilled appetiser of white grapes, limes and cucumber perfumed with coriander £6.00

*Smoked Breasts of Chicken with a Cumberland Sauce* - A platter of apple wood-smoked breasts of chicken served with a traditional Cumberland sauce of oranges & redcurrants in a port wine jelly £7.00

*A Salad of Quail* - A lollo rosso salad of sautéed breasts of quail accompanied by lightly boiled quails eggs £7.00

#### Main Course

*St Margaret's Bay Lobster Thermidor* - A classical dish of local lobster flamed in Cognac with a fine cream sauce of shallots & tarragon topped with cheese then baked £19.50

*Medallion Fillets of Kentish Wild Boar* - Chargrilled prime fillets of wild boar topped with herb butter then garnished with a compôte of bramley apples £18.00

*New Season's Romney Marsh Lamb* - A roasted rack of prime lamb sauced with its own fine gravy, served with a gâteau of spinach on a golden sautéed rosti £17.00

*Tournedos of Aberdeen Angus* - A tournedos of prime Scottish beef sautéed, to the rare side, sauced with a rich red wine jus then served with a confit of shallots £18.00

*Char-grilled Sea Bass with a Béarnaise Sauce* - Char-grilled fillets of locally caught prime sea bass served quite simply with a warm béarnaise sauce £17.00

All main courses are served with a plated selection of seasonal vegetables

#### Third Course

A choice of desserts or cheeses £6.00

#### To Finish

Fresh Filtered Coffee with hand-made Belgian chocolates £2.25

Wallett's Court is a country house hotel set in lovely open countryside within easy reach of the spectacular cliff scenery of Kent's Channel ports. The Grade II listed building has some fine and unusual features and, during its history, has been associated with figures such as Bishop Odo of Bayeux, Queen Eleanor of Castile, Edward Gibbon and William Pitt (who once owned the house).

These days Chris Oakley and his family preside over the hotel and its renowned restaurant, whose menu has been chosen with a Jacobean flavour to reflect the historic background of the main house. Fresh fish, robust sauces and lots of use of game are the hallmarks of the cooking here.

The *carte* featured opposite changes monthly and is supplemented by a £23.50 three-course set price menu.

Directions: Westcliffe is located approximately 4 miles to the north-east of Dover. From the A2 just outside Dover, take the A258 signposted from the roundabout to Deal. Then take the first right turning signposted to St Margaret's at Cliffe and Westcliffe and the hotel is 1 mile along the road on your right.

### USEFUL INFORMATION

**SERVING TIMES:**
Dinner 7pm-9pm (every day)
**CLOSED:** every lunchtime (private parties of 15 or more by arrangement)
**SEATING CAPACITY:** 35 in the dining room, 25 in the conservatory
**C/C:** V, MC, D, AE, DC
**NO SMOKING** in the restaurants
**OUTDOOR EATING:** no

**NUMBER OF WINES:** 85
**HOUSE WINE:** £14.00
**RESERVATIONS:** advisable
**OFF-STREET PARKING:** yes
**CHILDREN:** welcome
**NO WHEELCHAIR ACCESS**
**ACCOMMODATION:** 12 rooms (B&B sgl fr £40, double £65-£85)

# RENDEZVOUS

Tel: (01959) 561408
26 Market Square, Westerham, Kent, TN16 1AR

### Les Hors d'Oeuvres

*Panaché de champignons à l'aïl*
Pan-fried mushrooms with fresh garlic...3.95~6.95
*Poireaux vinaigrette, échalottes et croûtons*
Leeks vinaigrette, shallots and croûtons...4.25~5.95
*Poivrons rôtis et chèvre doux, laitues*
Roast peppers filled with goats cheese, on a mixed continental salad   4.50~6.50

### Les Salades Composées   4.95~6.95

*Salade Niçoise, saumon frais, pommes, haricots, tomates marinées et oeuf*
Fresh salmon, potato, french beans, marinated tomato and egg
*Suprême de poulet grillé, pommes, petite gème, courgette et tomate*
Grilled chicken breast, potato, little gem salad, courgettes and tomato

### Les Compositions Libres

*Omelette aux herbes fraîches, petite ou grande*...3.95~5.75
*Crêpe ménagère maison, sauce mornay*   4.95~6.95
*Pâtes fraîches*...4.95~7.25
Compose your own omelette, crepe or pasta dish, either *Jardinière*,
*Marinière*, or *Bayonnaise*, and with extra ingredients 90p each

### Les Viandes et Les Poissons

*Suprême de poulet grillé d'oignon, huile de thym*...9.95
Grilled chicken supreme served with mash, onion and thyme oil
*Pavé Niçoise, olives noires, tomates et basilic*...12.50
Scotch rump steak, black olives, tomato and basil, cooked only blue or rare
*Magret de canard, paprika, pâte et petits légumes pimentés*...13.50
Breast of duck cooked with paprika & served with fresh pasta & spicy vegetables
*Filet de saumon grillé, courgettes sautées, huile d'aneth*...9.95
Grilled salmon fillet served with sautéed courgettes & a dash of dill oil
*Filet de Cabillaud rôti, mariné au thym, pistache et beurre de persil aïllé*...9.95
Cod fillet marinated in thyme, pistachio, parsley and garlic butter
*Filet de Lotte rôti, lasagne de carotte, citron*...12.50
Monkfish fillet, carrots lasagne, lemon
*St Jacques sautées, basilic, pâte aux crevettes*...12.50
Scallops cooked with basil and served with fresh pasta and prawns

Visit the Rendezvous on a sunny day and you really could be in France. Tables are casually scattered on the pavement under a bright, billowy canvas, service is prompt and friendly, and there is a laid-back atmosphere that just demands you slow down, relax and enjoy the food.

Proprietor Laurent Y. St.Jean prides himself on using only the freshest ingredients and the results are exceptional. Portions are generous and, like the decor, a nice mix of the simple and the unusual. The extensive à la carte, a small selection from which appears opposite, changes about six times a year. There is always a good range of soups (from £3.30) and uncomplicated accompaniments such as home-made fries and fresh daily vegetables (£2.50).

At lunchtime a set menu offers astonishing value (2/3 courses during the week £5.95/7.95) and may feature Feuilleté de Poisson to start, with Quiche de Légumes and Tarte Normande to follow. Quite simply, delicious!

Directions: Easily found on the A25 in the middle of Westerham.

## USEFUL INFORMATION

**SERVING TIMES:**
Breakfast 8.30am-12pm (every day)
Lunch 12pm-3pm (every day)
All day menu 12pm-12am (every day)
**SEATING CAPACITY:** 45
**C/C:** V, MC, S, D, AE, DC
**NO SMOKING** area available

**NUMBER OF WINES:** 22
**HOUSE WINE:** £9.95
**OFF-STREET PARKING:** yes
**OUTDOOR EATING:** yes
**RESERVATIONS:** advisable
**DRESS CODE:** smart casual
**CHILDREN:** welcome

# WHITSTABLE OYSTER FISHERY CO.

Tel: (01227) 276856
The Horsebridge, Whitstable, Kent, CT5 1BU

## SAMPLE MENU

½ Dozen Scottish Oysters £6.00
Local Crab £6.00
Brown Shrimp Salad £5.00
Deep-fried Baby Plaice £4.50
Crab Claw Salad £5.00
Moules Marinières £5.00
Char-grilled Sardines stuffed with Garlic & Herbs £4.00
Scallops with a Basil Dressing £6.00
Morecambe Bay Potted Shrimps on Toast £6.00
Pan-fried Squid with Garlic & Fresh Herbs £6.00
Smoked Eel with Horseradish £7.50
Three Langoustines with Salad & Mayonnaise £6.50

\* \* \* \* \*

Deep-fried Cod in Beer Batter with Tartare Sauce & Chips £9.50
Char-grilled Mackerel with Red Gooseberry Sauce £8.50
Poached Skate Wing with Black Butter & Capers £9.00
Poached Turbot with Lobster Sauce £15.00
Roast Sea Bass with Garlic & Rosemary £15.00
Pan-fried Monkfish with Leeks & Cream £12.50
Grilled Whole Plaice £9.50
Lobster Mornay £12.50
Cornish Cock Crab £12.50
Half Lobster Salad £9.50
Whole Lobster Salad £17.50

Chips £1.50   New Potatoes £1.50   Spinach £2.00
Tomato Salad with Feta & Basil £3.00   Mixed Leaf Salad £2.00

\* \* \* \* \*

Crème Brûlée £3.95     Strawberry Parfait £3.95
Chocolate Mousse £3.95     Lemon Syllabub £3.95
Gooseberry Fool £3.95     Crème Caramel £3.95
Hot Chocolate Pudding £3.95     Honeycombe Ice-cream £3.95
Stem Ginger Ice-cream £3.95     Jersey Cream Ice-cream £3.95

The fish restaurant at the Whitstable Oyster Fishery Company is housed in an old oyster warehouse on the seafront in the centre of town. Bizarre but brilliant, they still cleanse their own oysters in the underground refrigerated room, whilst upstairs a cinema plays the latest Hollywood blockbusters.

The two inside dining areas seat around 150 people between them and are usually packed. During the Summer the patio is definitely the place to be, with tables looking out over the beach to the sea 30 yards away. The service is friendly and the atmosphere, as befits eating in a warehouse, very laid back.

The menu consists entirely of the very freshest fish and seafood, cooked simply but deliciously, so if you don't like fish, don't bother coming. The dishes are written up on the blackboard in the corner and are scrubbed off at regular intervals as the supplies of fish disappear.

Oysters are always on the menu and Whitstable Natives are in season from September to April. So why is the town's oyster festival held in July?

Directions: Whitstable Oyster Fishery Company is situated on the town's seafront at the end of the main shopping street.

## USEFUL INFORMATION

**SERVING TIMES:**
Lunch 12pm-2pm (Tues-Fri)
    12pm-2.30pm (Sat)
    12pm-3.30pm (Sun)
Dinner 7pm-9pm (Tues-Fri)
    6.30pm-10pm (Sat)
**CLOSED:** Sun night & all day Mon (open Mondays in June, July & Aug)
**SEATING CAPACITY:** 75 in the restaurant, 80 in the beach room
**C/C:** V, MC, S, D, AE, DC

**NUMBER OF WINES:** 16
**HOUSE WINE:** £9.95
**RESERVATIONS:** essential, especially at weekends
**CHILDREN:** welcome
**OUTDOOR EATING:** yes
**OFF-STREET PARKING:** no, but there is a public car park nearby
**ACCOMMODATION:** 7 huts along the beach, which range from £55 to £100 (room only)

# THE THREE CROWNS
Tel: (01403) 700207
Wisborough Green, near Billingshurst, West Sussex, RH14 0DX

## TODAY'S SPECIALS

*Starters*

Home-made cauliflower & lentil soup £2.25
Green-lipped mussels with ginger wine & capsicum £4.25
Chef's breaded stilton mushrooms £4.25
Deep-fried brie with cranberry sauce £4.25

*Home-made Pies*

Steak, kidney & mushroom pie with short crust pastry £5.95
Chicken & leek pie with short crust pastry £5.95
Game pie with suet crust pastry £6.85

*Main Courses*

Chicken & mushroom casserole, quarter chicken
slowly cooked in a creamy sauce with mushrooms £6.25
Pork steak with apple, rosemary & garlic £6.45
Mediterranean style cod £6.25
Escola Florentine - a delicious meaty fish from the South China Seas,
served on a bed of spinach & coated in a light cheese sauce £6.45
Queen scallops with smoked bacon & mushrooms,
served on a bed of rice £6.45
Prime Scotch T-bone steak served with mushrooms, tomatoes,
peas, onion rings £10.25
Prime Scotch 8oz fillet steak au poivre £10.75
Fillet steak with whisky sauce £10.75

*All specials are served with
a selection of fresh vegetables and a choice of potatoes*

Originally three cottages, this charming 15th century country inn lives up to its epithet 'a lovely pub in a beautiful village'. Owned and run by proprietors Brian and Sandie Yeo for ten years, The Three Crowns enjoys an excellent reputation for the quality of its food, whilst happily maintaining its more traditional roots as a village local.

An extensive main menu includes a healthy array of substantial dishes such as Grilled Dover Sole (£12.85) and Chicken Champignon (£6.95), as well as more traditional pub grub like Ham, Egg & Chips (£4.95), filled jacket potatoes (from £4.25), freshly made sandwiches (from £2.30) and the ever popular ploughmans (from £4.65). Daily specials appear on a large blackboard, and a selection of possible dishes are shown opposite.

Directions: Easily found in the centre of Wisborough Green, about 2 miles west of Billinghurst on the A272.

### USEFUL INFORMATION

**SERVING TIMES:**
Lunch 12pm-2pm (every day)
Dinner 6pm-9pm (every day)
**SEATING CAPACITY:** 30 in the restaurant, 30 in the bar
**C/C:** V, MC, S, D

**NUMBER OF WINES:** 16
**HOUSE WINE:** £6.85
**OFF-STREET PARKING:** yes
**CHILDREN:** welcome
**RESERVATIONS:** advisable
**OUTDOOR EATING:** yes

# THE PARSONAGE
### Tel: (01903) 820140
6-10 High Street, Tarring Village, Worthing, West Sussex, BN14 7NN

### *A LA CARTE MENU*

#### FIRST COURSE

**Salad of King Scallops Nouvelle £7.85**
Gently fried in the pan, set around a nest of salad leaves in a blue cheese vinaigrette, sprinkled with crispy bacon
**Feuilleté of Mushrooms £5.95**
Sautéed oyster, shiitake & champignons moistened with a wild mushroom sauce presented in a puff pastry pillow
**Crown of Galia Melon Ou Porto £6.50**
Filled with fresh raspberries & laced with port wine

**Fresh Asparagus Spears £5.95**
Served with a lemon butter sauce
**Half Dozen Deep Fried Thai Style Crevettes £6.25**
Spiced with soy sauce & ginger, wrapped in Oriental pastry, served with garlic mayonnaise
**Tiger Tails & Mango Salad £6.25**
Pacific prawns garnished with a gathering of salad leaves in a mango & basil vinaigrette

#### MAIN COURSE

**Grilled Dover Sole £15.95**
Garnished with herb butter & lemon
**Baked Selsey Crab Mornay £14.95**
Fresh, locally caught crab baked in the oven & topped with glazed cheddar cheese sauce
**Sea Bass Steak Estragon £14.50**
Simply grilled with milled black pepper, tarragon leaves, served with a salad garnish & new potatoes
**Medley of Seafood Español**
King scallops, scampi tails, Atlantic halibut & fresh salmon simmered in a Spanish saffron sauce around a nest of leaf spinach

**Fillet of Prime Scotch Beef £14.95**
Served with a herb crust on a mushroom & madeira sauce
**Ragout of Poultry & Asparagus £14.95**
Succulent white meat sautéed with white wine, red peppers & fresh asparagus spears, served in a light puff pastry pillow
**Char-grilled Lamb Cutlets £14.95**
With stilton, glazed field mushrooms, watercress & a red wine sauce
**Pan-fried Slices of Calves' Liver Anglaise £14.95**
With bacon, tomato & onions

#### DESSERT

A selection of freshly made desserts are available from £3.75

The Parsonage Restaurant occupies three of the early 15th century cottages along Parsonage Row in the village of West Tarring, one of the many manors in Sussex owned by the Archbishops of Canterbury in Anglo-Saxon times.

The restaurant is divided into three intimate rooms with period furnishings and offers modern British cuisine served traditionally (be prepared for substantial helpings). The à la carte menu featured opposite changes seasonally, although one or two of the dishes will differ from month to month. Fixed price luncheon and dinner menus are also available (£11.95 for one course, two courses £16.95, three courses £19.50).

For a quick bite to eat (at lunchtimes only) you can try the Bar & Garden Menu which might include Grilled Sea Bass with Herb Butter and New Potatoes (£6.95), Chicken Liver, Apricot and Walnut Terrine (£3.95) or Musketeer of Salmon Mode du Chef (£6.25).

Directions: Heading south towards Worthing on the A24, turn right at a mini-roundabout into Glebe Road. A few hundred yards along, turn right into Tarring High Street at the George & Dragon pub. The Parsonage is a few yards further along on the opposite side of the road to the pub.

## USEFUL INFORMATION

**SERVING TIMES:**
Lunch 12pm-1.45pm (Mon-Fri)
Dinner 7pm-9pm (Mon-Fri)
7pm-9.45pm (Sat)
**CLOSED:** Sat lunch & all day Sunday
**SEATING CAPACITY:** 36
**C/C:** V, MC, S, D, AE, DC
**OFF-STREET PARKING:** no

**NUMBER OF WINES:** 50
**HOUSE WINE:** £9.95
**RESERVATIONS:** advisable, but essential at weekends
**OUTDOOR EATING:** yes
**CHILDREN:** welcome
**NO WHEELCHAIR ACCESS**

# TRENCHERS

Tel: (01903) 820287
118-120 Portland Road, Worthing, West Sussex, BN11 1QA

### A selection from the A La Carte

*Rösti de crabe avec salade de roquette, vinaigrette d'homard
et de poivrons rouges*
CRAB AND POTATO CAKES WITH ROQUETTE SALAD DRESSED
WITH LOBSTER AND RED PEPPER OILS £10

*Salade tiède de suprême de volaille marinée avec épices d'orient
et cuit au lait de noix de coco*
THAI MARINATED BREAST OF CHICKEN COOKED IN COCONUT MILK
AND SERVED ON CORIANDER SCENTED SALAD LEAVES £8

*Feuillantine de coquilles St. Jacques et de crevettes, sauce aigre doux d'ananas*
FRIED SCALLOPS AND TIGER PRAWNS WITH WAFER THIN DEEP-FRIED FILO
AND SWEET & SOUR PINEAPPLE CREAM £10

*Friture de vivaneau au linguettini noir fraîche et tempura de legumes de saison*
FRIED FILLETS OF RED SNAPPER WITH BLACK LINGUETTINI PASTA
AND SEASONAL TEMPURA VEGETABLES £18

*Nage du Printemps au turbotin avec poireaux jeunes et pointes d'asperges*
A SPRING STOCK OF BABY TURBOT WITH YOUNG LEEKS
AND ASPARAGUS £20

*Diptygue de canard*
ROAST BREAST OF DUCK WITH CONFIT OF DUCK LEG SERVED WITH
CARAMELISED APPLES, HONEY AND ROSEMARY JUS £20

*Côtes de boeuf 'ancienne' rôti au goût de chêne*
RIB OF SCOTTISH BEEF ROASTED IN THE OLD FASHIONED WAY ON A PLANK
OF ENGLISH OAK WITH RED WINE AND SHALLOTS £42 for two people

*Petit fondant chaud au chocolat amer, glace de pistaches*
WARM BITTER CHOCOLATE FONDANT WITH PISTACHIO ICE CREAM £9

*Ile de noix de coco 'tropiques'*
COCONUT PARFAIT TROPICAL ISLANDS £9

*Feuillantine de banane caramelisée avec parfait de banane, sauce au caramel*
DELICATE LEAVES OF FILO PASTRY WITH CARAMELISED BANANA,
ICED BANANA PARFAIT AND BUTTERSCOTCH SAUCE £7

Ten years ago this pretty seaside town witnessed the birth of a new style restaurant and brasserie in one of its oldest but beautifully renovated houses. Worthing woke up to bright primary colours, innovative menus and the fact that food can be exciting. Self-taught chef Greg Pam is well known locally for the consistent quality of his modern cuisine, which blends classical principles and the imaginative use of fresh produce (enjoyable one day cookery classes are available for those keen to know more!).

Both the restaurant and the brasserie exude a warm and friendly ambience in which you may enjoy superbly fresh and elegantly presented food. The restaurant offers a seasonal à la carte with fixed price alternatives at both lunch (3 courses £15) and dinner (4 courses £21.50). In the brasserie a constantly evolving blackboard menu includes soups, pâtés, warm salads, gratins, wine-scented casseroles and seafood dishes as well as a popular daily four-course menu (£15 including half a bottle of wine).

The Sunday lunch à la carte (2 courses from £13 to £19) always has a traditional roast rib of beef (£13).

Directions: A few minutes walk from the town centre, Trenchers is opposite the parish church at the top of Portland Road which runs between Richmond Road and Montague Street, the main shopping area of Worthing.

## USEFUL INFORMATION

**SERVING TIMES:**
Lunch 12pm-2.30pm (every day)
Dinner 6.30pm-10pm (Mon-Sat)
**CLOSED:** Sunday evening
**SEATING CAPACITY:** 45 in the restaurant, 50 in the brasserie
**C/C:** V, MC, S, D
**CHILDREN:** welcome

**NUMBER OF WINES:** 142
**HOUSE WINE:** £9
**OFF-STREET PARKING:** no
**RESERVATIONS:** advisable
**NO SMOKING** in the restaurant dining room, but allowed in the lounge and the brasserie
**OUTDOOR EATING:** yes

# THE WIFE OF BATH
### Tel: (01233) 812540
4 Upper Bridge Street, Wye, Ashford, Kent, TN25 5AW

## Dinner Menu
£22.75 for 3 courses inc VAT

### First Courses

Watercress & green pea soup

Millefeuille of smoked salmon & potato with chervil cream

A tartlet of roasted peppers & grilled goats' cheese

Tuna "Carpaccio" (thin slices of marinated raw tuna)

A salad of Parma ham with plum tomatoes & spiced croûtons

Chicken & pickled walnut terrine served
with an onion marmalade

### Main Courses

Fish of the day

Roasted rack of spring lamb with sweet garlic & rosemary

Pan-fried breast of duck with local cherries & thyme

Paupiettes of lemon sole
stuffed with a prawn & lime mousseline

A curried spinach & potato strudel with a chilli & garlic sauce

Fillet of beef
grilled with aubergines & field mushrooms in pesto (£2.00 supp)

### Puddings

A daily choice of home-made ice creams,
puddings & cheese

Built in 1760, The Wife of Bath is now a restaurant with rooms situated in Wye's historic main street which leads down to the trout-filled River Stour. Rather like the lady herself, this establishment has a delightfully relaxed and friendly attitude.

The menus feature modern English cuisine created from the finest local produce - venison from the Brabourne Estate, asparagus and soft fruits from Wye farms and seafood fresh from the fishing boats at Hythe. From wholegrain bread to ice creams and sorbets, everything is prepared in their own kitchens under the expert eye of chef Robert Hymers.

In addition to the fixed price à la carte on the facing page (the only choice in the evenings), there is a full à la carte available at lunch, together with an excellent table d'hôte priced at just £8.95 for two courses.

Directions: The village of Wye is situated approximately 4 miles to the northeast of Ashford, signposted from the main A28 Ashford to Canterbury road. From the A28, follow Bridge Street across the river and keep straight ahead. The Wife of Bath is found on the right hand side of the road.

### USEFUL INFORMATION

**SERVING TIMES:**
Lunch 12pm-2.30pm (Tues-Sat)
Dinner 7pm-10pm (Tues-Sat)
**CLOSED:** all day Sun & Mon
**SEATING CAPACITY:** 45
**C/C:** V, MC, S, D, DC
**OFF-STREET PARKING:** yes

**NUMBER OF WINES:** 70
**HOUSE WINE:** £9.95
**RESERVATIONS:** advisable
**OUTDOOR EATING:** no
**ACCOMMODATION:** 6 rooms
(B&B fr £45 per room, including Continental breakfast)

# THE WALNUT TREE
Tel: (01622) 814266
Yalding Hill, Yalding, Kent, ME18 6JB

### Starters

**An Hors d'Oeuvre of Fresh Tropical Fruit £4.25**
Served with a drizzle of Green Chartreuse

**Smoked Halibut £4.50**
Slices of finely smoked halibut served on a bed of leaves
& covered with lemon juice & black pepper

**Wild Boar Pâté £3.95**
Complimented with a strawberry coulis & served on warm toast

**Paupiettes of Smoked Salmon & Cream Cheese ££5.50**
The finest smoked salmon rolled with cream cheese & draped over a selection of
leaves, finished with black pepper & a lemon juice dressing

### Main Courses

**Warm Crispy Peking Duck Salad £9.50**
Served with a fresh fruit & leaf salad & a cucumber raita

**Fillet Steak Avignon £12.75**
Prime scotch fillet, stuffed with Stilton, wrapped in bacon,
oven baked & finished with rich Burgundy sauce

**Pork Stincotto £11.95**
Shank of pork roasted in its own juices & finished in a sauce of cream,
apple & herbs served with fresh vegetables & potatoes of the day

**Fresh Coulibiac of Salmon £10.75**
Flaked poached salmon, chives, prawns & smoked salmon bound together &
encased in puff pastry. Served with a red pimento & chilli sauce,
fresh vegetables & potatoes of the day

**Roasted Vegetables & Farfalle Pasta au Gratin £8.25**
Fresh vegetables combined with a farfalle pasta & cooked with garlic
in a mornay sauce, served with wild rice

### Desserts

**Crème Brûlée £3.75**
**Chocolate Cherry Trifle £3.25**
**Fresh Strawberry Tartlets £3.75**
**Cherry & Apple Pie £3.25**
**Cheese & Biscuits £4.50**

Originally built as a Kentish yeoman's house in 1492, The Walnut Tree is now a traditional country inn, furnished in period style with exposed beams and inglenook fireplaces. It is situated in the picturesque Medieval village of Yalding, lost amongst the hop fields and apple orchards of Kent.

The candlelit restaurant (a sample of the à la carte menu appears opposite) is complemented by the excellent home-made bar food in the pub, where dishes might include Olde English Sausages with Bubble'n'Squeak (£4.95), Beef, Mushroom & Guinness Pie with Potatoes & Fresh Vegetables (£6.25), Fresh Darne of Salmon, Oven-poached with Lemon Juice, Black Pepper & Fresh Herbs (£8.25) or Whole Seabass with a Spring Onion & Ginger Sauce (£10.95).

Directions: The Walnut Tree is situated in the pretty village of Yalding, which lies approximately 5 miles to the south-west of Maidstone on the B2010.

### USEFUL INFORMATION

**SERVING TIMES:**
Lunch 12pm-2.30pm (every day)
Dinner 6.30pm-9.30pm (every day)
**SEATING CAPACITY:** 50 in the restaurant, 20 in the bar
**C/C:** V, MC, S, D, AE, DC
**NO SMOKING** in the restaurant
**OUTDOOR EATING:** yes

**NUMBER OF WINES:** 30
**HOUSE WINE:** £7.25
**RESERVATIONS:** advisable
**OFF-STREET PARKING:** yes
**CHILDREN:** welcome
**ACCOMMODATION:** 2 rooms (B&B £22.50 per person per night)

# ALPHABETICAL INDEX OF MAIN ENTRIES

## A

Albion Tavern, Faversham 80
Alexander House, Turners Hill 198
Amberley Castle, Amberley 8
Anchor, Barcombe 12
Angel Hotel, Midhurst 130

## B

Badgers, Petworth 146
Bailiffscourt, Climping 40
Bassetts, Frant 88
Bell, Outwood 142
Bell Inn, Smarden 176
Bistrot Saint-Pierre, Haywards Heath 102
Bull Inn, Newick 138

## C

Cafe de Paris, Guildford 94
Camellia Restaurant, Lower Beeding 124
Castle Inn, Chiddingstone 34
Chardonnay, Washington 202
Chaser, Shipbourne 168
Chequers Hotel, Slaugham 174
Chestnut Tree, Boreham Street 18
Cisswood House, Lower Beeding 120
Cole's, Southwater 178
Comme Ça, Chichester 28
Compasses, Gomshall 92
Crabtree, Lower Beeding 122
Cricketers, Duncton 56
Crown Inn, Chiddingfold 32

## D

Dering Arms, Pluckley 148
Dining Room, Reigate 152
Dove, Dargate 50
Downland Hotel, Eastbourne 62
Duck Inn, Pett Bottom 144
Duke William, Ickham 108

## E

Eastwell Manor, Ashford 10
Elsted Inn, Elsted Marsh 74

## F

Fleur de Sel, Haslemere 100

## G

Gables, Billingshurst 16
George and Dragon, Burpham 24
George and Dragon, Dragon's Green 54
Gravetye Manor, East Grinstead 64
Griffin Inn, Fletching 86
Griffins Head, Chillenden 38
Gun Inn, Gun Hill 96

## H

Haxted Mill, Edenbridge 68
Honours Mill, Edenbridge 70
Hooke Hall, Uckfield 200
Horse Guards Inn, Tillington 190
Horsted Place, Little Horsted 118
Hungry Monk, Jevington 110

## I

Inn on the Lake, Godalming 90

## J

Jeremy's, Lower Beeding 122

## K

Kentish Rifleman, Dunks Green 58
Kinghams, Shere 166
King William IV, Littlebourne, 116
King William IV, Mickleham 128

## L

La Barbe, Reigate 154
Landgate Bistro, Rye 160
Langshott Manor, Horley 106
La Scaletta, Uckfield 200
La Terrasse, Sandgate 162
Lime Tree Hotel, Lenham 112
Los Parrales, Tonbridge 192

# ALPHABETICAL INDEX OF MAIN ENTRIES

## M

Manleys, Storrington 184
Maxine's, Midhurst 132
Michels', Ripley 158
Middle House Hotel, Mayfield 126
Moonrakers, Alfriston 6

## N

Newick Park, Newick 140
Nutfield Priory, Redhill 150

## O

Ockenden Manor, Cuckfield 48
Old Forge, Storrington 186
Old Manor House, Midhurst 134
Old Vine, Cousley Wood 46
One Paston Place, Brighton 22
Orangery, Battle 14

## P

Parsonage, Worthing 212
Partners and Sons, Dorking 52
Peacock Inn, Shortbridge 170
Platters, Chichester 30
Plough Inn, Stalisfield Green 180
PowderMills Hotel, Battle 14

## R

Rankins, Sissinghurst 172
Read's, Faversham 82
Red Lion Inn, Fernhurst 84
Red Lion Inn, Shamley Green 164

Rendezvous, Westerham 206
Ringlestone Inn, Ringlestone 156
Ristorante Tuo e Mio, Canterbury 26

## S

Sandgate Hotel, Sandgate 162
Sankey's, Tunbridge Wells 194
Sevens, Farnham 78
South Lodge Hotel, Lower Beeding 124
Spread Eagle Hotel, Midhurst 136
Stane Street Hollow, Codmore Hill 42
Sundial, Herstmonceux 104
Sun Inn, Dunsfold 60

## T

Tanyard Hotel, Boughton Monchelsea 20
Thackeray's House, Tunbridge Wells 196
Thackrey's, Lewes 114
Three Crowns, Wisborough Green 210
Tottington Manor, Edburton 66
Trenchers, Worthing 214
Tuo e Mio, Canterbury 26

## W

Wallett's Court Hotel, Westcliffe 204
Walnut Tree, Yalding 218
White Hart, Stopham Bridge 182
White Horse, Chilgrove 36
White Horse, Hascombe 98
White Horse, Sutton 188
Whitstable Oyster Fishery Co, Whitstable 208
Wife of Bath, Wye 216
Windmill Inn, Ewhurst 76
Withies Inn, Compton 44
Woolpack, Elstead 72

# MAP OF THE AREA